World Hunger and the World Economy

And Other Essays in Development Economics

Keith Griffin

President
Magdalen College, Oxford

First published 1987

Published by
THE MACMILLAN PRESS LTD
Houndmills, Basingstoke, Hampshire RG21 2XS
and London
Companies and representatives
throughout the world

Printed in Hong Kong

British Library Cataloguing in Publication Data
Griffin, Keith
World hunger and the world economy: and
other essays in development economics.
1. Developing countries — Economic
conditions
I. Title
330.9172'4 HC59.7
ISBN 0–333–41993–6
ISBN 0–333–41994–4 Pbk

To
Wang Geng Jin
friend, teacher and colleague

Contents

List of Tables

List of Figures

Monetary Fund, protectionism in the advanced economies, new rules governing international trade and, of course, Third World debt.

David Worswick kindly commented on an early draft of 'The Debt Crisis and the Poor'. His observations were very helpful although he does not necessarily agree with my conclusions.

Lastly, I would like to thank my secretary, Mrs Iris Patrick, who prepared the essays when they were first published as well as the final typescript of this volume. Her skill, patience and speed are greatly appreciated.

K. B. Griffin

Magdalen College, Oxford
January 1986

Preface

Hunger, poverty and inequality, and the national and international policies that create and then perpetuate these conditions, have been recurring themes in my work. The ten essays in this volume were written in the first half of this decade and most of them were first presented as lectures, conference papers or seminars to audiences in Britain, the United States, Italy, Holland and Mexico. This volume can be regarded as a sequel to *International Inequality and National Poverty* published nearly ten years ago.

The lead essay, 'World Hunger and the World Economy', reflects two currents of thought: Amartya Sen's innovative book on *Poverty and Famines*, in which he argues that starvation cannot generally be interpreted as a simple consequence of a decline in the availability of food; and my own *Political Economy of Agrarian Change*, in which I argued that technological changes which increase food output will not necessarily reduce hunger in the absence of appropriate institutions and policies. The essay in this present volume can be seen as an attempt to counter the view, widely held and forcefully advocated by the International Food Policy Research Institute in Washington, that accelerated growth of food production will suffice to eliminate malnutrition and acute poverty in the Third World. The essay gained much from comments and careful editing by W. Ladd Hollist and F. LaMond Tullis.

The essay 'Rural Poverty in Asia' is a direct descendant of research initiated at the International Labour Office in Geneva and published in a book jointly edited with Azizur Rahman Khan entitled *Poverty and Landlessness in Rural Asia*. In the edited book we concentrated on presenting the facts about rural poverty in Asia and showed that in many parts of that vast region the incidence of poverty had not declined even, in some cases, where sustained growth in average incomes had occurred. In the essay, slightly revised and reprinted here, the emphasis is on trying to understand how poverty can increase despite growth of production and on elucidating the policies necessary to combat poverty. Eddy Lee, then Director of the ILO's Asian Regional Team for Employment Promotion (ARTEP), supported the work and provided valuable comments. James Boyce also made useful suggestions for revision. Some of the material in this chapter was used in the joint paper with John Gurley on 'Radical

Analyses of Imperialism, the Third World and the Transition to Socialism: A Survey Article', *Journal of Economic Literature*, September 1985.

Communal, cooperative or collective tenure systems are widely regarded in the West as failures. It seems to me, however, that this judgement is questionable and indeed that communal tenure systems can make a positive contribution to rural development. The general argument is presented in Chapter 3 in an essay that benefited much from the comments of Andrea Boltho, Ajit K. Ghose, Ken Post, Louis Putterman and Frances Stewart.

The next three chapters are devoted to various aspects of the economic reforms introduced in China starting in 1978. Chapters 4 and 6 follow directly from a book I edited, *Institutional Reform and Economic Development in the Chinese Countryside*. 'The Chinese Economy After Mao' (Chapter 4) contains an overview of the reform process, and once again I am indebted to Ladd Hollist and LaMond Tullis for their sympathetic editing. 'Possibilities for Development in Arid Regions: The Case of Xinjiang' (Chapter 6) is the story of the economic reforms in one region – the huge desert area in north-western China. It is a heartening story which I hope will be of interest not only to specialists on China but also to those concerned with rural development in the arid regions of Africa. The work in Xinjiang was sponsored and financed by Eddy Lee of ARTEP; arrangements for investigations in the field were made by an old friend, Wang Geng Jin, to whom this book is dedicated.

Chapter 5 deals with 'Industrial Reforms in China'. I am grateful to Andrea Boltho, Wlodzimierz Brus, John Enos, Sir Henry Fisher, Eddy Lee, Cyril Lin and Michael Kaser for helpful comments. Financial assistance was provided by the British Academy, the Hayter Travel Fund of Oxford University and by ARTEP.

In 1982 I was asked by the Ethiopian government and the ILO to lead a large mission and prepare a wide-ranging report on development problems and policies in Ethiopia. The report, unfortunately, was not published, but the essay in this volume, 'The Economic Crisis in Ethiopia', contains a distillation of my views of that unhappy country. LaMond Tullis and Ladd Hollist, yet again, made several helpful editorial suggestions. The solution to Ethiopia's problems depends not on a change in the weather but on successfully launching a programme for rural development. The essay in this book, written jointly with Roger Hay, 'Problems of Agricultural Development in

Socialist Ethiopia', includes an analysis of the problems and
gested strategy for overcoming them.

I have long had 'Doubts About Aid' and if anything my sce
has increased with the passage of time. Chapter 9 in this volur
latest, rather informal, statement of my views. The argu
illustrated with data from twelve countries that were del
selected with a bias toward very poor countries in Africa
region widely believed to be most in need of foreign aid.
was written at the request of Michael Lipton and gained
criticism, although in fairness to him it must be said that h
agree with the thrust of the argument.

The debt crisis in Africa and Latin America is a consequ
insufficient foreign aid but of the prolonged world recessio
interest rates in Europe and the United States, the overv
the dollar and the sharp deterioration that has occurred
of trade of many Third World countries. In 'The Debt C
Poor' it is argued that unless the management of the wo
improves, the debtor nations will have little choice but
their debts in one form or another. The decision by
payments on its debt to 10 per cent of its export
precedent, and one that I welcome.

Many developing countries are experiencing a massi
of funds to the industrialised countries. This perver
sources from poor countries to rich cannot continu
without major economic, political and social repercu
America and sub-Saharan Africa. In Latin America, f
disposable financing (the net inflow of capital min
profits and interest on overseas debt) was –US$18.4
–US$30.1 billion in 1983 and –US$26.7 billion i
duling the commercial debts at high real rates of int
postpone and then aggravate the crisis. The Wester
to write off a significant proportion of their Third
indeed several have begun to do already. Ideally,
should form a 'debtors' cartel'; failing that, a maj
should assume the role of a 'default leader'; failin
countries will have to do as Peru has done and tak
such as declaring a moratorium on capital and in
The hope is that eventually the crisis will be res
World forcing the creditor countries to initiate
tiations over a range of issues: the reorganisation

1 World Hunger and the World Economy

Let us begin with two propositions. First, there is no world food problem, but there is a problem of hunger in the world. Food and hunger are, of course, related and it is tempting to argue that an increase in food output will lead to a reduction in hunger, malnutrition and starvation; but alas the connection is not so straightforward or simple. Indeed many cases can be found in which hunger increased, or failed to diminish, despite a rise in food supplies per head.

Second, even if there were a direct connection between the availability of food and the incidence of hunger, it does not follow that each region or country or continent should aim to be self-sufficient in basic foodstuffs. Presumably, nobody would suggest that the city-states of Hong Kong and Singapore would be better off or better fed if they produced fewer manufactured goods and more rice; or that Saudi Arabia and Botswana should switch from oil and mineral extraction to farming; or even, perhaps, that Cuba should reduce its production of sugar and concentrate on growing more cereals and beans. What matters in countries such as these, as far as the average is concerned, is the resource endowment people enjoy, the opportunities that exist for profitable international trade and the overall rate of growth of domestic product per head.

On the whole, economic growth has been encouraging, even in the recent years of oil price explosions and global recession. During the period 1970 to 1982 Gross Domestic Product (GDP) per capita increased 3.2 per cent a year in China and India (the two largest Third World countries), 0.8 per cent in what the World Bank describes as the 32 'other low-income economies' and 3.0 per cent in the 60 'middle-income economies'.[1] Of course some countries did much better than others, but only in the 23 'low-income economies' of sub-Saharan Africa was there a general tendency for per capita GDP to fall. During the period 1970 to 1983 the rate of decline was about 1.1 per cent a year and in consequence production per head today is little different from that of a quarter century ago.[2] The situation in these 23 countries evidently is very serious, but from a global perspective it may be some consolation to know that the low-income

Table 1.1 Average Annual Percentage Rate of Growth of Agricultural Product per Head

	1960–70	*1970–82*	*1960–82*
Low-income economies	−0.1	0.4	0.2
India	−0.4	−0.5	−0.5
China	−0.7	1.4	0.4
Others	0.2	−0.3	−0.1
Middle-income economies	0.9	0.6	0.7
High-income oil exporters	n.a.	0.6	n.a.
Industrial market economies	0.3	1.1	0.7

Source: IBRD, *World Development Report 1984*, New York: Oxford University Press, 1984.

economies of sub-Saharan Africa account for less than one tenth of the population of all low-income countries combined. Seen from this angle the scale of the problem, in terms of the number of people affected, is thus relatively small.

Turning from growth of total product to growth in the agricultural sector, the picture is broadly the same. That is, there has been a sustained increase in world output of agricultural products since 1960 and most of the major groups of countries and geographical areas of the world have participated in this increase. Only in India and the 'other low-income economies' has agricultural production per head failed to rise (see Table 1.1). Elsewhere there has been expansion, with the 'middle-income countries', followed by China, leading the way. It is slightly worrying, however, that in a number of Third World countries the performance of the agricultural sector in the 1970s and early 1980s appears to have been worse than in the 1960s. Growth of agricultural output per head slowed down in the 'middle-income countries', in India and in the 'other low-income economies', whereas it accelerated sharply in China, the United States and several of the other industrial market economy countries.

There is no evidence whatever that food is becoming increasingly scarce in the world. On the contrary, the data indicate that for the world as a whole the amount of food produced continues to rise and it is safe to assume that never in history has the physical supply of food per capita been greater than in the last 10 or 20 years. If mankind continues to suffer from hunger – and we are now witnessing the worst famines in 40 years – the explanation cannot be in terms of a global inadequacy of food.

Table 1.2 Average Annual Percentage Rate of Growth of Food Output Per Head

	1960–70	*1970–80*
China	n.a.	1.4*
Low-income economies (excluding China)	0.2	−0.3
India	n.a.	0.8*
Middle-income economies	0.7	0.9
All developing countries (excluding China)	0.4	0.4
Industrial market economies	1.3	1.1
Nonmarket industrial economies	2.2	0.9
Total World (excluding China)	0.8	0.5

*1971–80

Sources: IBRD, *World Development Report 1982*, New York: Oxford University Press, 1982, Table 5.1, p. 41; FAO, *Socio-economic Indicators Relating to the Agricultural Sector and Rural Development*, Rome: 1984, Table 16, p. 51.

Moreover the rise in food production is not confined to the advanced industrial economies, capitalist and socialist. We hear much about the high calorie diets in the Soviet Union and Eastern Europe[3] and about the 'food mountains' in the West, but few people seem to realise that food has become relatively abundant in many parts of the Third World too. In China, food output per head increased about 1.4 per cent a year in the decade of the 1970s and in the rest of the world the increase was about 0.4 per cent a year (see Table 1.2). In India there was a sharp fall in non-food agricultural production and consequently, as we have seen, there was a poor performance in the agricultural sector as a whole; but food production per head has expanded rapidly since 1970 at 0.8 per cent a year. Those who believe that the solution to hunger is to put 'food first' should be cheered by India's example,[4] but the sad truth is that the average nutritional status of the Indian population has not improved since the late 1960s.[5] The so-called green revolution in India, 'while it has indeed dramatically improved yields in particular crops (e.g. wheat) in particular regions (e.g. the north-west), has not led to any acceleration in the overall rate of growth in agriculture'[6] nor, it might be added, to any reduction in hunger. Yet today, paradoxically, India is an exporter of food grains.

In the middle-income economies, too, food output per head has grown rapidly since 1970, viz. 0.9 per cent a year and, as in India, food production has expanded much more swiftly than the rest of the agricultural sector. Only in the low-income economies other than China and India, and above all in sub-Saharan Africa, has per capita food production declined. Even there, however, the decline is associated not with a bias against food production for domestic consumption and in favour of cash crop production for export, but with a generally poor economic performance as reflected in negative growth per head of GDP, investment, exports, manufacturing and agriculture.[7]

This brief survey of some of the readily available facts suggests that hunger is not caused primarily by inadequate production of food, nor can it be cured except in the long run merely by increasing production further. There are exceptions, of course, and one can emphasise the situation in sub-Saharan Africa; but the number of people living in poor countries in which food production per head has declined accounts for only a small fraction of the world's population.[8] And the number of people in those countries who are hungry is a smaller fraction still. It seems clear, therefore, that a commodity-oriented analysis of hunger will not take us very far. Instead we need to focus on people and on the factors that determine the amount of food they consume. The volume of food production may be part of the answer, but in most circumstances it is unlikely to constitute the principal explanation.

A number of attempts have been made to calculate the extent of malnutrition. One of the best studies was prepared by the World Bank, in which the authors estimated calorie deficits by income groups for the whole of Latin America, Asia, the Middle East and Africa. They concluded that in 1965 approximately 840 million people, or 56 per cent of the population of the regions studied, had diets deficient by 250 or more calories a day.[9] The Food and Agriculture Organisation (FAO) undertook a study using a similar methodology except that the analysis was conducted at the country level rather than at the level of large regions. This refinement resulted in an estimate for 1972–4 of 455 million people suffering from insufficient protein – energy supply, or about 25 per cent of the Third World's population.[10]

Studies such as these can be and have been criticised,[11] and the criticisms may be justified in that there is a tendency both to exaggerate nutritional requirements and to understate the extent to which poor people manage by one way or another to acquire enough to eat. But there can be little doubt that there are today several hundreds of millions of people who must make do on poor and monotonous diets, who suffer various forms of malnutrition to a greater or lesser degree and who, in a distressingly large number of cases, are dying from starvation and associated diseases. The exact number of people suffering from hunger is unimportant, it is enough to know that the number is huge.

Anyone who has thought about the matter knows that hunger is not distributed evenly or randomly throughout a society; it is largely (but not exclusively) a rural phenomenon and within the rural areas is concentrated among the poor. That is, hunger tends to be associated with particular classes and occupational groups: landless agricultural labourers, small tenant cultivators, deficit farmers with too little land to be self-sufficient and who consequently must supplement their income with part-time off-farm jobs, pastoralists living on or beyond the fringes of the arable land, and fishermen and petty artisans supplying traditional goods and services in traditional ways.

THE FUNDAMENTAL CAUSE OF HUNGER

The fundamental cause of hunger, then, is the poverty of specific groups of people, not a general shortage of food. In simple terms, what distinguishes the poor from others is that they do not have sufficient purchasing power or effective demand to enable them to acquire enough to eat. More generally, the heart of the problem is the relationship of particular groups of people to food, not food itself. This relationship is governed by what Amartya Sen calls 'entitlement systems', that is, the set of relations embodied in a society's laws, customs and conventions that determines the ability of people to command food.[12]

One is 'entitled' to food through the application of one's own labour, through trade, through production, through the return on one's assets or through transfer or gift. Unfortunately, the bundle of 'entitlements' of many people, either chronically or episodically, is not large enough to permit adequate nutrition. This can be so for a variety of reasons. For example, the productivity of one's own labour may be permanently low because of primitive technology and inadequate investment, or productivity may fall precipitously for a period of time because of, say, epidemic disease. Employment opportunities in a particular locality may be scarce and they could decline further as a result of the introduction of labour-saving equipment. Alternatively, the daily wage rate could be too low for adequate subsistence and at certain times of the year or in periods of crisis the real wage could fall further as a result of a decline in the demand for labour or a rise in the price of food. Similarly, the command over food of a small farmer producing cash crops will depend on the sales price of his output. This in turn could be determined by the purchasing policy of state marketing boards, a government's exchange rate policy, the level of world prices or short-term fluctuations in a country's international terms of trade, and other factors.

The ownership of land, livestock and other productive assets, as well as jewellery and other forms of savings, are part of the 'entitlement system'. Indeed the extent to which a household can transform assets into food often determines whether or not starvation occurs. One of the most common features of famine conditions is distress sales of assets by already poor households. Small landowning cultivators in periods of drought, for instance, starve partly because their reduced output leads to a direct decline in food consumption, partly because their reduced output leads to a decline in cash income and hence to lower market purchasing power, and partly because distress sales lead to a fall in the price of land and consequently in the rate at which their assets can be transformed into food. An analogous situation faces the pastoralists. A drought causes a reduction in the number of livestock. More important, however, it forces herdsmen to sell their animals and this, in turn, leads to a sharp fall in the price of cattle and hence in the value of the herdsman's assets. 'The pastoralist, hit by drought, [is] decimated by the market mechanism.'[13] His assets decline in quantity and in unit value; his ability to command grain in the market vanishes, and he starves.

This approach to the analysis of world hunger naturally directs one's attention to the distribution of income and wealth; to organisational mechanisms which supplement income in determining entitlements to food, e.g. rationing systems; and to institutional arrangements concerned with property rights which govern access to productive assets, the most important of which are land and water rights.

There is considerable evidence from a number of countries, not conclusive but sufficiently well documented that it must be taken seriously, that the incidence of poverty among certain groups, above all in the rural areas, has failed to decline significantly even where growth in per capita production has occurred.[14] In such countries hunger has persisted despite greater average prosperity. This does not refer to those countries in sub-Saharan Africa and elsewhere

where per capita growth has been negative, but to the more typical Third World countries that have enjoyed an unprecedented rise in average income per head. Asia contains several examples, and one of these is India.

As Michael Lipton says, 'what is truly amazing . . . is that, by general agreement, despite India's long period of steady and unprecedented real growth . . . of output-per-person, there has been no *substantial* fall in the proportions of persons in absolute poverty, upon any plausible and constant definition of those terms; nor in the extent to which, on average, those persons fall short of the poverty line.'[15] A recent series of ten studies sponsored by the International Labour Organisation reaches a similar conclusion for much of South and South-east Asia. After reviewing research on Bihar, the Punjab, Kerala and West Bengal in India and on Pakistan, Nepal, Bangladesh, Thailand, Sri Lanka and the island of Java in Indonesia, the organisers of the project conclude:

> there has been no major shift in extent and nature of poverty in rural Asia between the early 1960s and the mid or late 1970s. . . . in no case has there been a dramatic breakthrough in the reduction of rural poverty. In several cases there [has] been a reduction in poverty levels between the early and late 1970s but this only resulted in bringing back poverty to the levels prevailing in the early 1960s. In only two cases – Thailand and the Punjab – has there been a reduction in poverty compared to the 1960s but even here levels of poverty remain high and, especially in the Punjab, the margin of reduction was not great.[16]

A similar story could be told in parts of Latin America and the Middle East. In Egypt, for instance, the number of rural poor increased by nearly two million between 1958/9 and 1978, and the proportion of the rural population below the poverty line increased over the period from 22.5 to 25 per cent.[17] This was associated with, and partially caused by, a rise in the incidence of landlessness from 40 per cent of agricultural households in 1961 to 45 per cent in 1972.[18] Again, in Morocco, real household consumption of the poorest 20 per cent of the population fell sharply in the 1960s in both rural and urban areas,[19] and it is highly likely that this process continues to the present day, at least in the rural areas, if only because of the sharp negative trend in agricultural production per head that began around 1970.

The persistence of inequality, poverty and hunger is due not so much to the absence of growth as to the characteristics of the growth that has occurred. That is, in many Third World countries, perhaps a majority, growth has been accompanied, first, by rising landlessness;[20] second, by greater reliance of the poor on casual, non-permanent employment; and third, by increased unemployment or a reduction in the number of days worked per person per year.[21] In other words, a significant number of small landowning peasants and tenants has been converted into a wage-earning class of casual agricultural labourers. This implies, fourth, that the asset base of the rural poor has suffered considerable erosion, in the sense that a declining proportion of the poor has assured access to productive assets and, for those who continue to have access, the quantity and hence the average value of their assets is falling.[22]

Fifth, to make matters worse, the real daily wage rate of this growing number of wage earners appears either to have remained stagnant (as in India as a whole[23]) or to have fallen (as in Bangladesh, Nepal and the Philippines[24]); cases of higher real wages (as in Thailand or, in some periods, Pakistan) appear to be exceptions to the general rule. As a result of these various processes, sixth, landless households have tended to experience a fall in their real yearly incomes. A careful study of India by Pranab Bardhan, for example, shows that the annual wage income of agricultural labour households fell by 16 per cent in real terms between 1964/5 and 1974/5. Moreover, of the 15 states studied, in only one (Uttar Pradesh) did real incomes rise; in the other 14 they fell between 1 per cent (in Karnataka) and 44 per cent (in Orissa).[25]

Finally, it should be remembered that the poor and the hungry are often the victims of political, social and economic discrimination. In some countries discrimination is based on caste (India), in others on language (Sri Lanka) or race (as in Andean America), in still others on tribal origin (as in parts of Africa) or on religion (as in the supression of Muslims in the Philippines). The effect of discrimination in the labour market is to restrict occupational mobility, to augment the supply of those forced to seek low-wage employment and, particularly when, as is often the case, it is combined with a high degree of land concentration, to give large landowners and other employers oligopsonistic power in determining wage rates.[26] When discrimination is superimposed on rigid social and class stratification and a low average productivity of labour, widespread hunger is almost certain to result.

Moreover, output growth in such a system may actually increase rather than reduce poverty and hunger. This could occur if a landlord-biased growth process results in the introduction of labour-displacing machinery such as tractors and combines;[27] or if technical change is accompanied by the eviction of tenants and a rise in landlessness; or if small peasants are driven out of cultivation because the powerful irrigation pumps owned or controlled by large landowners lower the water table so much that the traditional irrigation techniques used by small farmers cease to be effective;[28] or if large landowners persuade the government to raise the official support price of foodgrains and thereby impoverish wage earners and small deficit farmers who purchase grain in the market;[29] or if village artisans are displaced by heavily protected, mass-produced urban-manufactured goods, etc.[30] These are not mere theoretical possibilities; all of these things have happened repeatedly in many countries. Indeed, a careful statistical study in West Bengal has shown that the probability of an agricultural labour household falling below the poverty line, and hence risking hunger, is significantly greater if the household happens to be located in a district where agricultural production has grown at a faster rate![31]

Just as hunger can persist and even increase in a country in which growth is taking place, so too can famine and starvation occur even when there has been no decline in the availability of food. In fact, a startling finding of Amartya Sen's research is that in a number of major famines – the great Bengal famine of 1943, the Bangladesh famine of 1974 and the Ethiopian famines of 1972–4 – there was no significant fall in the supply of foodgrains.[32] Acute hunger was caused not by a sharp drop in production but by a rapid change in the distribution of income.[33] Moreover, even in those cases where hunger was caused by a fall in output, as in the Kampuchean famine of 1979,[34] one will not get very far in analysing the extent and incidence of starvation by focusing on time series of production. The cause of hunger, as Sen reminds us, is a shortage of income rather than an overall shortage of food,[35] and some households have a much greater shortage of income than others.

INTERNATIONAL LINKAGES

In a world of sovereign nation-states the government of each country must assume the larger part of the responsibility for ensuring that everyone under its administrative authority has enough to eat. This responsibility is an inescapable consequence of the way the world is presently organised. Indeed, if a government is consistently unable to guarantee its own people enough to eat, then it is doubtful that the minimum condition for statehood exists. Perhaps the world should be organised differently, perhaps we need powerful supra-national organisations that can overrule national governments, but for the time being at least we shall have to accept the world as it is and not pretend otherwise.

This does not imply that hunger is exclusively a national phenomenon or solely a national responsibility. Clearly there are international forces at work that affect the geography of hunger. These forces should not be, and have not been, ignored. Certainly the economists have written a great deal about the major economic issues and policy questions – the pattern of international trade, direct investment by transnational corporations and other flows of private capital, concessionary loans and grants (including food aid), international stockpiles of grains and commodity price stabilisation schemes. It is not proposed to review these lengthy discussions here, but rather to treat of three relatively neglected topics: the role of Western ideas and ideology, the transfer of Western technology and the nature of the state in the Third World.

Before turning to these three neglected topics, it is worth mentioning, a bit dogmatically perhaps, my personal views on two of the international linkages I intend to pass over – foreign aid and direct investment. Foreign aid, whether loans or grants, whether in cash or in kind such as food, has done little or nothing on average to accelerate the long-run rate of growth of Third World countries. It has done even less to reduce inequality in the distribution of income within the recipient countries and consequently has had no discernible impact on reducing the incidence of hunger and malnutrition.[36] In the short run, during famine conditions, emergency relief aid obviously has a role to play. That role could be played more effectively, moreover, if international stockpiles of grain were available and under the direct control of the relief agencies. Stockpiles of grain under the control of the European Community and the US government are less easily mobilised quickly in an emergency because their use is subject to political calculation and cumbersome bureaucratic delays.

If aid is largely ineffective in reducing world hunger, it is likely that direct investment by transnational corporations will be even less relevant. Indeed, if government policy is biased against the poor and the hungry, it is inconceivable that foreign investors could counteract that bias; more likely, they would reinforce it. On the other hand, if the government were pursuing a 'basic needs' strategy of development, it is likely that the opportunities for profitable investment in the country by transnational corporations would diminish.[37] The reason for this is that the superiority of transnational over local firms lies in their marketing skills for sophisticated products, the provision of mass-produced Western-designed consumer durables and the development of advanced capital-intensive technology. These are services that are not likely to be required in large volume in countries where the alleviation of hunger is top priority.

Let us, then, return to the three issues that have been singled out for discussion.

I Ideas and ideology

There are, of course, many Western ideas, and there is more than one Western ideology. Marxism, for example, is a product of the West, not of the East. The dominant ideology in the West, however, is capitalism and it is this ideology of free enterprise, free trade and free movement of capital[38] that has shaped the international order and that has been recommended whenever possible to the countries of the Third World. If it is true, as is often claimed, that democratic socialism is about equality, then it is equally true that modern capitalism is about production. That is, the dominant view, the view most widely held in the West, is that faster growth rather than improved distribution of the fruits of growth is the answer to many problems, including the problem of world hunger.

Scepticism has already been expressed about the effectiveness of accelerated growth of food production as a general solution to problems of hunger, malnutrition and starvation. In pushing this solution, relentlessly and with little qualification, Western ideas have been less than helpful. Indeed they have often been harmful in that they have diverted attention away from more important issues. Specifically, a corollary of the emphasis on growth is Western hostility to government interventions to improve either the distribution of income or the distribution of food alone, i.e. to increase the 'entitlements' of the hungry directly through food rationing schemes and similar programmes. Yet we know that the public distribution of food, even in exceedingly poor countries, can have an enormous impact on reducing hunger, as the experiences of food rationing in Sri Lanka, Egypt, China, Cuba and the state of Kerala in India demonstrate.[39] Indeed, had Ethiopia established a nationwide food rationing system, as it was advised to do in 1982,[40] many of the current horrors occurring in that country almost certainly could have been avoided.

Joined with the ideology of free markets is that of private enterprise. The paradigm in Western thought, when it comes to the agricultural sector, is the family farm, although in practice Western thought has been able to accommodate itself to a wide variety of tenure arrangements: tenant cultivation, large mechanised farms, foreign-owned plantations and small peasant holdings. All of these, to some extent at least, are acceptable, but what is not generally acceptable in Western eyes, whether liberal or conservative, is communal, cooperative or collective tenure systems.

Yet nearly one third of the world's population lives in countries where collective agriculture in one form or another is the characteristic mode of production. These countries include not only the Soviet Union and much of Eastern Europe but also several Third World countries such as China, North Korea, Mongolia and Cuba. The record of the latter group of countries as regards the reduction of hunger compares very favourably with other Third World countries where individual, non-communal tenure systems predominate. The key example, because of its immense size, is China. The broad facts about China's experience no longer are in dispute. Thus it is known that the attempt in 1958, at the beginning of the Great Leap Forward, to form very large communes and apply communist principles of production and distribution was an utter failure and this undoubtedly helped to precipitate the disastrous famine from 1959 to 1961.[41] After the Great Leap Forward, however, the communes were successfully reorganised: adequate production incentives were created[42] and mechanisms to ensure a highly equitable distribution of foodgrains were installed. Today, thanks in part to a new set of reforms introduced after 1978, probably less than 3 per cent of China's population suffers from chronic under-nutrition.[43] The contrast, say, with India, Pakistan and Bangladesh – other large and poor countries in South Asia – could hardly be more vivid.

It is not coincidental that countries with well developed communal tenure systems have tended to perform better than average. In fact, there are good reasons to believe that communal tenure systems have an advantage by: (i) ensuring that labour is fully employed, (ii) achieving a more equal distribution of income, (iii) sustaining a high rate of capital accumulation, (iv) providing a framework for industrialising the countryside and (v) promoting grass-roots participation in the organisation and delivery at the local level of a wide range of social services, including educational, family planning and health facilities.[44] This does not imply that communal tenure systems can flourish under all conditions – far from it – but it is a mistake for us in the West to regard them as an anathema rather than as one possible way to reduce hunger and rural poverty.

All of us, of course, are a product of our own societies: our historical memory, our cultural heritage and our individual educational background. Western society, and particularly North American society, is very different from the societies of most Third World countries. Where Americans enjoyed an open frontier and cultivated individualism, self-reliance and competition, most of the Third World experienced colonialism, restricted social and economic mobility, and few opportunities for material betterment. Capitalism was liberating in Europe and North America; in the rest of the world it was imperialistic and enslaving, or at least was perceived by the indigenous people to be so. Collective action thus became not only acceptable in many parts of the Third World, but during the struggles for national independence it often was regarded as essential. Similarly, once independence was achieved, a reaction against the economic system of the former colonial masters was common. The colonial governments preached the virtues of the market, of free enterprise and of non-intervention by public authorities. The newly independent governments, in contrast, viewed the state as an engine of growth and development and feared that free trade, uninhibited competition with Western enterprises and the unrestricted operation of market forces would result in a neo-colonialism that was little better than the old colonialism. The newly independent countries, while seldom socialist or communist in orientation, tended to reject a full-blooded capitalist solution but instead became receptive to ideas and ideologies that included a place for government ownership of some of the means of production, for intervention in market processes and for some cooperative and collective institutions.

II Transfer of technology

Ideas alone, however, do not change the world; technology also is a powerful force. Indeed it is a peculiarly Western conceit that there are technological solutions to political and social problems. If there is an ideological conflict with the Soviet Union, the solution is to send a man to the moon. If there is a threat to world peace, the solution is to invent more accurate and more destructive armaments. If the population is thought to be growing too rapidly, the solution is to produce a better contraceptive. And if the problem is hunger, then the solution is to discover higher-yielding varieties of wheat and rice. This overweening faith in the power of science has put the technician, the engineer and the scientist in the place once occupied by the Creator himself.

Alas, technological change cannot obviate the need for social and institutional change. Partly because of the absence of adequate change, the import of Western agricultural technology into inegalitarian and socially divided Third World countries often has accentuated inequality and occasionally has further impoverished the weakest sections of the rural population. For example, the introduction of mechanical farming methods in Arsi province, Ethiopia, under a Swedish aid programme resulted in the eviction of more than 5000 tenant households between 1967 and 1975.[45] The introduction of mechanised wells and pumps in Niger and Mali, under a French scheme, and at a time when agricultural policies were causing pasturage to shrink, led to overgrazing by livestock and contributed to the ecological collapse of the Sahel in the early 1970s and with it the destruction of the Tuareg people.[46]

Even the 'green revolution' has proved to be less green than was once hoped and it certainly has not made revolution of a different hue less likely.[47] Perhaps the most avidly promoted Western (or American) agricultural technology in the Third World is large multipurpose dams. In fact, the very first loan ever made by the World Bank to a Third World country, to Chile in 1948, was for a dam and there is no sign that the Bank or any other aid agency has lost its enthusiasm for large-scale water management projects. There are plenty of signs, however, that large dams have produced very low economic returns, have damaged forestry and fisheries, have caused widespread salination of the soil and have inflicted much hardship on ordinary men and women.[48] This transfer of technology from the Tennessee Valley to other river basins in the world – be they in the Maghrib, the Nile Valley, the Middle East or the Indo-Pakistan sub-continent – has done remarkably little to alleviate global hunger.

Western aid, Western projects and Western technology embodied in aid-financed projects are part of the problem of hunger, not part of the solution. Even the World Bank has begun to accept that the economic mess in which much of sub-Saharan Africa finds itself is due in part to the policies of foreign aid donors. 'In many African countries', according to the Bank, 'the pattern of development spending has become increasingly determined by the aggregation of aid programs.'[49] Yet the donors, sadly, have placed little emphasis on agriculture, rural development or programmes designed to raise the living standards of the poor. On the contrary, as the Bank says, 'Financing big infrastructure projects has represented a large part of past donor programs.'[50] Yet these big projects with their advanced technology have produced neither growth nor an equitable distribution of income; they have produced a disaster. Again, in the Bank's own words, 'The heart of Africa's economic crisis is the low rate of return on its capital investment. Much of this failure comes from investment programs that have been extensively financed from external sources.'[51] Thus it is that the continent that has relied most heavily on Western aid and technology is also the continent where famine is widespread and malnutrition is increasing at an alarming rate.

Improvement in Africa requires much more than a shift from infrastructure projects to rural development. Indeed, case studies of agricultural projects and policies in seven countries, three in East Africa (Kenya, Tanzania and the Sudan) and four in West Africa (Ghana, Niger, Nigeria and Senegal), show clearly that irrigation projects and settlement schemes usually have failed to meet their production goals, and that, more generally, policies and projects have tended to increase inequality and have had little impact on reducing rural poverty and hunger.[52] Possibly the most spectacular current attempt to apply advanced technology to rural development is the FAO scheme to eradicate the tsetse fly over seven million square kilometres of land in Africa from the Sahel to Botswana and Mozambique.[53]

The intention is to eradicate trypanosomiasis from the region and thereby permit the land to be cleared of forest and converted to grazing for 120 million head of cattle. The 1.5 million tonnes of low-grade beef that could be produced each year presumably would be exported to Europe and North America. The project, however, is woefully misguided and certain to fail. First, dangerous chemical pesticides are used. Many of these are banned in the West because they are a threat to humans, wild animals and fish. Second, these dangerous chemicals are applied through aerial spraying. The dosage is hard to control and the area intended to be sprayed is often hard to identify from the air and, consequently, chemicals are frequently dumped in the wrong place. Third, such crude methods of applying the chemicals mean that it is unlikely that the project will succeed in eradicating the tsetse fly. Moreover, fourth, if the tsetse fly were eradicated and its habitat transformed into pastures for cattle, it probably would produce little economic benefit in the short run and considerable harm in the long run. The reason for this is that the tsetse fly occupies much marginal land on the fringe of the desert and semi-arid areas of Africa. If the tree and bush cover of these lands is removed to permit cattle ranching, the likely effect will be increased soil erosion, a further spreading of the desert, impoverishment of the local population and famine of the type now common in the Sahel.

III The nature of the state

Part of the reason for the meagre success of imported technology has to do with the technology transferred, but another important part has to do with the nature of the state in the Third World. It is taken for granted, here, that the state is not a neutral institution, that governments reflect particular class and group interests and that government policies are designed on balance to promote the interests of those who control the state. Sophisticated analysts often argue that the state is 'relatively autonomous' of the dominant economic class[54] and even the unsophisticated have pointed out that when threatened from abroad the state may adopt a nationalist rather than a class orientation. Still others note that in the period immediately after independence, political leaders who participated in the freedom movement seemed to enjoy more latitude for action than politicians in more ordinary times.[55] All of these points are true, but for most purposes one will not go far wrong in assuming that the state acts on behalf of the dominant economic interests in society.

What *are* the dominant economic interests? In some parts of the Third World, including parts of Asia, political power has accrued to those who control the productive sectors of the economy, namely, large landowners and industrialists. In the Philippines, for instance, it is the plantation owners and the industrialists; in India, the industrialists and large wheat farmers in the north; in Pakistan, the industrialists again. In most of Latin America, these same groups are well entrenched, the class structure is well defined and the political system (but not necessarily an individual government) is relatively stable, until of course it is overthrown by a revolution, as in Cuba or Nicaragua. In Mexico, power is concentrated in the hands of the industrialists and the large landowners in the irrigated regions of the north; in Guatemala, power is shared between those who own large coffee plantations and the cattle and cotton growers along the Pacific coast; in Colombia, power traditionally alternates between the manufacturing centre in Medellín and the upper classes of Bogotá. In some Third World countries, the class hierarchy is in flux as various groups struggle against one another to fill the power vacuum created by the departing colonialists; while in other cases, notably in Africa, a military and bureaucratic elite has taken power.

There is a link between the class structure of the state and government economic policy. In the great majority of countries, public policy – be it investment allocation, monetary and tax policies, exchange rate and foreign trade policies or social programmes – is biased towards the urban areas,[56] towards industry, towards large farmers, towards upper income groups – in short, towards everyone except the poor and the hungry. The Western powers – through such things as economic aid programmes, diplomatic initiatives and military assistance – tend strongly to support the very governments whose policies are responsible for perpetuating poverty and hunger in their countries, and to oppose reformist, radical and revolutionary regimes which hold out hope of a better life to the poor. Thus in Chile, the West opposed the Allende government but supports the Pinochet dictatorship; in Nicaragua, it installed and then supported the Somoza dictatorship and now alleges the Sandinista government is undemocratic; in China, it supported Chiang Kai-shek and refused even to recognise the People's Republic; in Vietnam, it supported reaction and tried to bomb Ho Chi Minh's government back to the stone age. And so it goes, on and on, seemingly without end, in Guatemala and El Salvador,[57] in Morocco and the Sudan, in Pakistan and in the Philippines. In far too many cases where the state oppresses the impoverished and the malnourished, the status quo is strengthened by the active intervention of the West.

SUMMARY

Hunger exists in spite of encouraging global improvements in economic growth rates, and in spite of a sustained increase in world output of agricultural products since 1960. As hunger is not caused primarily by inadequate production of food, it cannot be cured, except in the very long run, merely by increasing the production of food. Thus a commodity-oriented analysis of hunger will not take us very far. Instead, we need to focus on people and on the factors that determine the amount of food they consume.

The fundamental cause of hunger is the poverty of specific groups of people, not a general shortage of food. In simple terms, what distinguishes the poor from others is that they do not have sufficient purchasing power or effective demand to enable them to acquire enough to eat. The problem is the relationship of particular groups of people to food, not food itself.

Relationships that establish 'food entitlements' are governed by a society's laws, customs, and conventions, and by the domestic and international economic policies that grow from them. This approach to the analysis of world hunger naturally directs attention to the distribution of income and wealth and to institutional arrangements concerned with property rights that govern access to productive assets.

The incidence of poverty among certain groups, above all in the rural areas, has failed to decline significantly even where growth in per capita production has occurred. Hunger persists despite greater average prosperity. The persistence of inequality, poverty, and hunger is due not so much to the absence of growth as to the characteristics of the growth that has occurred – rising landlessness; greater reliance on casual, non-permanent employment; increased unemployment; reduction in the asset base of the rural poor; stagnation or reduction in the real daily wage rate; a fall in yearly household income; and political, economic, and social discrimination. When these economic and social conditions prevail, growth in total economic output may actually increase rather than reduce poverty and hunger.

Important international linkages are also at work. Much has been written about patterns of international trade, direct investments by transnational corporations and other flows of private capital, concessionary loans and grants (including food aid), international stockpiles of grains and commodity price stabilisation schemes, and others. This essay has examined the contribution of Western ideas and ideology, Western technology, and the nature of the Third World state to the continuation of pockets of hunger in the world today.

The dominant capitalist ideology of free enterprise, free trade, and free movement of capital has shaped the international order and has been recommended whenever possible to Third World countries.

However, Western society, and particularly North American society, is very different from societies of most Third World countries. Where capitalism for Americans meant individualism, self-reliance, and competition, for most of the Third World, where hunger is prevalent, it meant colonialism, restricted social and economic mobility, and few opportunities for material betterment. Not surprisingly, such countries have been open to ideas and ideologies that included a place for government ownership of some of the means of production, for intervention in market processes, and for some cooperative and collective institutions. What is needed is a pragmatic view of all these institutions and practices. Where individualism, self-reliance, and competition can contribute to a reduction of hunger and poverty, let them prevail. Where they cannot, let them be tempered, and if temperance entails government intervention and the fostering of cooperative enterprises, let their possibilities be explored devoid of ideological dogmatism.

Technology, as well as ideas, changes the world. But technology cannot obviate the need for social and institutional change that is prevalently needed in most Third World countries if poverty and hunger are to be reduced significantly. Capital-intensive farming, 'green revolutions', massive water-management projects – none have contributed to an equitable distribution of income or to an appreciable reduction in global hunger. Appropriate technology is situation-specific and can hardly ever be a direct plant from a Western country.

Finally, we turn to the Third World state. Part of the reason for lack of success with imported technology, and also the maintenance of social and political institutions inimical to the reduction of poverty and hunger, can be laid to the dominant interests that control Third World states. States controlled by large landowners and industrialists infrequently develop economic policies that help reduce hunger. Investment allocation, monetary and tax policies, exchange rate and foreign trade policies, or social programmes, all have been biased toward urban areas, toward industry, toward large farmers, toward upper income groups – toward everyone except the poor and the hungry. Sadly, Western powers, through such activities as economic aid programmes, diplomatic initiatives, and military assistance, tend strongly to support the very governments whose policies are responsible for perpetuating poverty and hunger in their countries.

Thus it is that in the international sphere ideas, technology, and political power often reinforce local social structures within the Third World. These structures generate a distribution of income which makes it impossible for large numbers of poor people to acquire food, whether through purchase or self-provisioning, almost regardless of the total amount of food available. At present we in the West more often lean in the wrong direction than in the right. In simple terms, we are biased towards landlords and their allies rather than towards the peasantry and other ordinary working people. We can do relatively little directly to eliminate world hunger, but it would help if we would cease to provide massive amounts of military assistance and if we would thereby give the poor in the Third World a little more room for manoeuvre to advance their own cause.

Notes

1. See, IBRD, *World Development Report 1984*, New York: Oxford University Press, 1984. Annex: World Development Indicators, Tables 2 and 19. 'Low-income economies' are defined as those with a GNP per capita of less than $410 in 1982 and the 'middle-income economies' as those with more than $410 (rising to $6840 in Trinidad and Tobago).
2. IBRD, *Toward Sustained Development in Sub-Saharan Africa*, Washington, DC: 1984, Table 1.1, p. 10. The rate of growth of GNP per capita during 1960–82 was negative in eight of the 23 countries, viz. Chad, Somalia, Niger, Guinea-Bissau, Zaire, Uganda, Madagascar and Ghana (ibid., Table 1, p. 57).
3. According to FAO, in 1980 calorie supply in Eastern Europe and the Soviet Union was 132.8 per cent of requirements and 138.6 per cent in the USA. FAO, *Socio-economic Indicators Relating to the Agricultural Sector and Rural Development*, Rome: 1984, Table 27, pp. 84–6.
4. Frances Moore Lappe and Joseph Collins, *Food First*: *Beyond the Myth of Scarcity*, Boston: Houghton Mifflin, 1977. It should be stressed, however, that the authors of this book advocate much more than merely giving priority to food production in the Third World.
5. Per capita calorie supply in India was 87.3 per cent of requirements in 1967–70 and 86.2 per cent in 1980 (FAO, *Socio-economic Indicators*).
6. Pranab Bardhan, *The Political Economy of Development in India*, Oxford: Basil Blackwell, 1984, p. 11.
7. In the low-income economies of sub-Saharan Africa the per capita rates of growth in 1970–82 were as follows: GDP, −1.0 per cent; investment, −0.2 per cent; exports, −5.3 per cent; manufacturing, −2.3 per cent; agriculture, −2.1 per cent; food, −1.8 per cent. IBRD, *Toward Sustained Development*.

   Much of the objection to cash crop production for export may arise from the fact, not that it reduces the availability of food, but that it is sometimes closely associated with particularly inequitable land ownership patterns, e.g. large plantations or extensive ranches and farms owned by multinational corporations. The resulting poverty and hunger is a consequence of the distribution of assets, not of the composition of output.

8. According to FAO, *Socio-economic Indicators*, during the period 1971–80 there were 73 countries out of a total of 161 in which per capita food production either fell or failed to rise. These countries varied in size from St Lucia (with a population of 100 000) to Japan (118 million) and accounted for about 16 per cent of the total population of the world. If one excludes the rich countries (Hong Kong, Israel, Japan, Saudi Arabia, Belgium, Iceland, Poland and Portugal), then only 12 per cent of the world's population lived in poor countries characterised by falling per capita food production.
9. Shlomo Reutlinger and Marcello Selowsky, *Malnutrition and Poverty: Magnitude and Policy Options*, World Bank Staff Occasional Papers, No. 23, Baltimore and London: Johns Hopkins University Press, 1976, Ch. 2.
10. FAO, *The Fourth World Food Survey*, Statistics Series 11, Rome: 1977, p. 53. More recently the FAO has estimated the number of rural poor in 1980 to be 69.3 million. This can be regarded as an approximation of the number of malnourished in the countryside since poverty is defined with reference to minimum dietary requirements. See FAO, *Development Strategies for the Rural Poor*, Economic and Social Development Paper No. 44, Rome: 1984, Table 26, p. 84.
11. See Thomas T. Poleman, 'Quantifying the Nutrition Situation in Developing Countries', *Food Research Insititute Studies*, vol. XVIII, no. 1, 1981.
12. Amartya Sen, *Poverty and Famines: An Essay On Entitlement and Deprivation*, Oxford University Press, 1981.
13. Ibid., p. 112. The quotation refers specifically to the Ethiopian famine of 1972–4.
14. See, for example, International Labour Organisation, *Poverty and Landlessness in Rural Asia*, Geneva: 1977; Keith Griffin, *International Inequality and National Poverty*, London: Macmillan, 1978.
15. Michael Lipton, 'Conditions of Poverty Groups and Impact on Indian Economic Development and Cultural Change: The Role of Labour', *Development and Change*, vol. 15, no. 4, October 1984, p. 475; emphasis in the original.
16. Azizur Rahman Khan and Eddy Lee (eds), *Poverty in Rural Asia*, Bangkok: ILO (ARTEP), 1984, p. 17.
17. M. Riad El-Ghonemy, *Economic Growth, Income Distribution and Rural Poverty in the Middle East*, Rome: September 1984, Table 11, p. 32. Also see Samir Radwan, *Agrarian Reform and Rural Poverty: Egypt, 1952–75*, Geneva: ILO, 1977, Table 4.3, p. 46.
18. Ibid., Table 2.3, p. 23. Real wages in rural Egypt did not exceed the peak of 1966 until 1975, after which they continued to rise rapidly. The increase is almost certainly due to (i) migration abroad to Libya and the Gulf and (ii) migration to construction activities in booming urban areas, the boom itself having been fuelled by overseas remittances. See, Alan Richards, *Egypt's Agricultural Development, 1800–1980: Technical and Social Change*, Boulder, Colorado: Westview Press, 1982, Ch. 6.
19. Keith Griffin, *Land Concentration and Rural Poverty*, 2nd edn, London: Macmillan, 1981, p. 75.
20. In India, the proportion of agricultural labourers in the male rural

labour force rose from 15.7 per cent in 1961 to 25.2 per cent in 1971: Lipton, 'Conditions of Poverty Groups', p. 488.

21. For evidence from Kerala, West Bengal, the Punjab and Bihar in India see Khan and Lee (eds), *Poverty in Rural Asia*.
22. Ibid., p. 10.
23. Michael Lipton, 'Conditions of Poverty Groups', p. 483. Pranab Bardhan has shown that 'average daily earnings in agricultural operations by men belonging to agricultural labour households . . . *declined* by 12 per cent' between 1964/5 and 1974/5 for the whole of rural India: Pranab Bardhan, *Land, Labor and Rural Poverty: Essays in Development Economics*, Delhi: Oxford University Press, 1984, p. 189; emphasis in the original.
24. On Bangladesh and Nepal see Khan and Lee (eds), *Poverty In Rural Asia*; on the Philippines see ILO, *Poverty and Landlessness in Rural Asia*.
25. Bardhan, *Land, Labor and Rural Poverty*, Table 14.1 p. 190.
26. See Keith Griffin, *The Political Economy of Agrarian Change*, 2nd edn, London: Macmillan, 1979, Ch. 2; and Griffin, *Land Concentration and Rural Poverty*, Ch. 5.
27. See Griffin, *The Political Economy of Agrarian Change*.
28. See B. H. Farmer (ed.), *Green Revolution?*, London: Macmilan, 1977, Ch. 26.
29. See John W. Mellor, 'Food Price Policy and Income Redistribution in Low-Income Countries', *Economic Development and Cultural Change*, vol. 27, no. 1, October 1978; and Keith Griffin and Jeffrey James, *The Transition to Egalitarian Development*, London: Macmillan, 1981, Ch. 2 and Ch. 3.
30. For a more complete list of possibilities see Bardhan, *Land, Labor and Rural Poverty*, pp. 188–9.
31. Ibid., pp. 192–5. Ashwani Saith has shown that in India as a whole for 1960/1 to 1970/1, 'the proportion of the rural population living in poverty was increasing over this decade at an alarming rate of approximately 1.5 percentage points a year': Ashwani Saith, 'Production, Prices and Poverty in Rural India', *Journal of Development Studies*, vol. 17, no. 2, January 1981, p. 201. Finally, using a study of 13 states in India from 1959/60 to 1970/1, Dominique van de Walle finds that in five of them (Maharashtra, West Bengal, Assam, Andhra Pradesh and Punjab/Haryana) there is a significantly positive relationship between agricultural output and poverty, i.e. the higher the agricultural output, the higher is the number of persons in rural areas living in poverty. In three states (Gujarat, Karnataka and Uttar Pradesh) the relationship is significantly inverse, and in the remaining five states the relationship is insignificant: Dominique van de Walle, 'Population Growth and Poverty: Another Look at the Indian Time Series Data', *Journal of Development Studies*, vol. 21, no. 3, April 1985.
32. Sen, *Poverty and Famines*.
33. For a theoretical explanation see Griffin, *International Inequality and National Poverty*, Ch. 8.
34. William Shawcross, *The Quality of Mercy: Cambodia, Holocaust and Modern Conscience*, London: Deutsch, 1984.

35. Amartya Sen, *Resources, Values and Development*, Oxford: Basil Blackwell, 1984, p. 519.
36. See Griffin, *International Inequality and National Poverty*, Ch. 3.
37. Ibid., Ch. 2.
38. Note that the free movement of labour internationally is not part of Western capitalist ideology. See ibid., Ch. 4.
39. See, for example, Griffin and James, *The Transition to Egalitarian Development*; Harold Alderman and Joachim von Braun, *The Effects of the Egyptian Food Ration and Subsidy System on Income Distribution and Consumption*, IFPRI Research Report 45, Washington: July 1984; P. S. George, *Public Distribution of Foodgrains in Kerala – Income Distribution Implications and Effectiveness*, IFPRI Research Report 7, Washington: March 1979; James D. Gavan and Indrani Sri Chandrasekera, *The Impact of Public Foodgrain Distribution on Food Consumption and Welfare in Sri Lanka*, IFPRI Research Report 13, Washington: December 1979.
40. This was one of the recommendations of an economic mission to Ethiopia led by the author. The report is entitled *Socialism From the Grass Roots: Accumulation, Employment and Equity in Ethiopia*, Addis Ababa: ILO (JASPA), September 1982. It has not been released to the public.
41. The impact of the famine on the Chinese people can be seen in the following figures:

	Birth rate	*Death rate*	*Natural growth rate*
	(persons per thousand population)		
1958	29.22	11.98	17.24
1959	24.78	14.59	10.19
1960	20.86	25.43	−4.57
1961	18.02	14.24	3.78
1962	37.01	10.02	26.99

Source: States Statistical Bureau, *Statistical Yearbook of China 1983*, Hong Kong: Economic Information and Agency, 1983, p. 105.

42. See Keith Griffin, 'Efficiency, Equality and Accumulation in Rural China: Notes on the Chinese System of Incentives', *World Development*, vol. 6, May 1976.
43. Keith Griffin (ed.), *Institutional Reform and Economic Development in the Chinese Countryside*, London: Macmillan, 1984, Ch. 1.
44. Keith Griffin, 'Communal Land Tenure Systems and Their Role in Rural Development', in Sanjaya Lall and Frances Stewart (eds), *Theory and Reality in Development: Essays in Honour of Paul Streeten*, London: Macmillan, 1986, reprinted in the present work as Chapter 3.
45. Oxfam, *Behind the Weather: Lessons to be Learned: Drought and Famine in Ethiopia*, Oxford: Oxfam Public Affairs Unit, 1984, pp. 4–5.
46. Thurston Clarke, *The Last Caravan*, New York: Putnam, 1978.
47. Griffin, *The Political Economy of Agrarian Change*.

48. See, for example, E. Goldsmith and N. Hildyard, *The Social and Environmental Effects of Large Dams*, vol. 1, *Overview*, Wadebridge Ecological Centre, 1984. Also see the Special Report in *The Ecologist*, vol. 14, no. 5/6, 1984.
49. IBRD, *Toward Sustained Development*, p. 4.
50. Ibid., p. 5.
51. Ibid., p. 41.
52. Judith Heyer, Pepe Roberts and Gavin Williams (eds), *Rural Development in Tropical Africa*, London: Macmillan, 1981.
53. See Marcus Linear, 'The Tsetse War', *The Ecologist*, vol. 15, no. 1/2, 1985.
54. N. Poulantzas, *Political Power and Social Classes*, London: New Left Books, 1973.
55. Bardhan, *The Political Economy of Development in India*, Ch. 5.
56. Michael Lipton, *Why Poor People Stay Poor: Urban Bias in World Development*, London: Temple Smith, 1977.
57. See, for example, Raymond Bonner, *Weakness and Deceit: US Policy and El Salvador*, London: Hamish Hamilton, 1984.

2 Rural Poverty in Asia: Analysis and Policy Alternatives

Rural poverty cannot be studied in isolation. It has an historical origin and setting which simultaneously connect the present to the past and establish boundaries to what is possible in future. The history of rural poverty is, of course, part of the history of underdevelopment and the origin of the types of rural poverty observable today forms part of what Andre Gunder Frank calls 'the development of underdevelopment'.[1] Accordingly we begin this chapter with a brief discussion of underdevelopment in an historical context.

We shall argue that underdevelopment in general, and the rural poverty that is its most obvious manifestation, arose from the way the Third World was incorporated into an international economic and political system dominated initially by Europe and later by America. This Western hegemony, however, encountered continuous resistance and after decades, even centuries, of struggle the old colonial and imperial regimes have virtually disappeared from the face of the globe. In their place has emerged a system of nation states. The scores of countries which comprise the new nation-state system enjoy at least nominal independence and often a considerable measure of sovereignty over their internal affairs. Thus rural poverty in the contemporary world must be seen as largely a national phenomenon: it is national governments which have inherited the responsibility for reducing poverty and which design and implement policies for doing so.

The state, however, is a social institution, not a neutral piece of apparatus. Societies or polities, we argue, are composed of classes or distinct groups which are frequently in competition and conflict with one another. It is therefore appropriate to consider the class structure that has developed in the Third World and to locate rural poverty within specific groups of a social hierarchy. This is done in the second section of this chapter.

In a stratified society the groups that are poor are unlikely to be the groups that control the government and the state. On the contrary, economic and political power usually go together and hence in most countries it is those who are relatively well off economically who tend to determine government policy and exercise political authority. This being so, an important issue is raised, namely, whether it is realistic to expect that existing governments will adopt domestic economic policies which directly or indirectly benefit the poor, and above all the rural poor. This is the question that is examined in the third section of the chapter.

In the final section, we assume that those in power wish to alleviate rural poverty. The measures they are willing or able to introduce, however, will be determined in part by their room for manoeuvre, i.e. by the shifting balance of political forces, national and international, at play in the society. At any given moment in time some policies may be feasible and other 'politically impossible', but no one, least of all an outsider, can say in advance which is which. General advice, therefore, is unlikely to be immediately applicable and perhaps the best that can be done is to set out the types of policies that are available to governments and their likely impact. At any rate, this is what we have done.

UNDERDEVELOPMENT IN AN HISTORICAL CONTEXT

It has long been argued by nationalists in the Third World and by social scientists in the West that underdevelopment is not an original state of nature but a product of historical forces. 'Europe did not "discover" the underdeveloped countries; on the contrary she created them.'[2] The impact of imperialism took various forms, differing from one place and one time to another, and it is an unfinished task of modern scholarship to write the history of the colonised people, as opposed to the history of the colonising powers.[3] Britain in India and Africa, France in Indochina and Africa, Holland in Indonesia, Belgium in the Congo, Spain in Latin America, Portugal in Africa and Brazil, pursued different policies and had different consequences and, moreover, these policies and consequences changed over time; but there is little doubt that in most parts of the world the ordinary people – farmers and fishermen, artisans and small traders – gained little and lost much from being conquered. The civilising mission of Europe was a myth invented to soothe the consciences of the conquerors, not the wounds of the conquered.

In many regions of the world the expansion of Europe resulted in a sharp decline in population, partly as a result of the importation of alien diseases, partly as a result of war and partly as a consequence of the destruction of the pre-existing social structure.[4] Notable examples of where this occured are the Andean region of South America, Mexico and Central America, Australia and the South Pacific.[5] In Africa, from Guinea to Angola, the capture and trade in slaves did much to depopulate vast regions[6] and to transform the economy from one based on settled agriculture back to long-fallow agriculture and nomadism. During the colonial period forced labour was used in many areas, notably in the Belgian, Portugese and French colonies, while elsewhere the combination of head taxes and the alienation of African lands resulted in the creation of a large and impoverished labour force that had no alternative but to work on European-owned plantations, farms and mines.[7] Africa is widely regarded in the West as the most 'traditional' of the underdeveloped regions, yet there is nothing that is truly traditional about rural Africa, if by traditional one means pre-imperial and pre-colonial. Land use and land tenure systems, population densities, the organisation of labour and the patterns of migration, even many of the crops that are grown: all these things were profoundly affected by European penetration into the continent.

China represents a rather different case because the country was never wholly colonised. Instead China was incorporated into a nefarious trading arrangement against her will and forced to import opium in exchange for useful products. The consequence was widespread drug addiction, the transfer abroad of part of her economic surplus which could have been used for capital accumulation and growth, partial colonisation and conquest, the payment of indemnities and the granting of special privileges to foreigners, the weakening of her indigenous social structure, and in the three decades before the revolution of 1949, a sharp decline in the standard of living of the mass of the population, including, of course, the mass of the rural population.[8] Underdevelopment in China cannot be attributed solely to imperialism; it is more likely that internal and external forces interacted in a process of mutual causation, but it would be implausible, to say the least, to claim that the impact of the West (and later Japan) on China was wholly or even on balance beneficial.

The apologists for European, American and Japanese imperialism point to three sources of economic benefit to Third World countries. First, it is argued that colonialism destroyed feudal or pre-capitalist economic systems and encouraged the creation of a capitalist labour market. Presumably this is thought to have been of benefit to the rural population since the majority of the labour force lived in rural areas. Second, the imposition of free trade in commodities, even if on a restricted basis, permitted the principle of comparative advantage to operate. Since the apologists assumed that the Third World had a comparative advantage in agricultural and mineral products, this too should have increased the well-being of the rural population. Third, uninhibited international capital flows, largely in the form of direct investment in plantations, mines and public utilities, allowed investment and growth to occur in capital-scarce underdeveloped countries which otherwise would have remained stagnant. Thus imperialism was good for the conquered peoples: it led to a higher level of output because of improved allocative efficiency and a higher rate of growth of output because of a faster rate of capital accumulation.

The facts, alas, are not consistent with the apologists' expectations. Let us consider the period 1870–1913.[9] This was the heyday of the old order, for it was a period of relatively free trade and rapid industrialisation in the West which coincided with the formation of a unified world market and the maximum extension of the colonial system. After 1913 the old order went into 35 years of decline. First came the First World War; this was followed by falling terms of trade for primary commodities in the 1920s, then by the great depression of the 1930s and finally by the Second World War. This was a period of disaster for the tropics. In the late nineteenth century, however, the old order had a chance to show what it could do for the Third World.

From 1883 to 1913 the trend rate of growth of industrial output in the 'core' countries of the UK, France, Germany and the USA was about 3.65 per cent per annum. Unfortunately, as Arthur Lewis shows, despite this growth 'the core was not really importing that much' from the tropics. Foreign investment, on the other hand, increased much faster, at 4.25 per cent a year from 1886/90 to 1909/13, but most of this investment was located in the temperate rather than in the tropical countries of the 'periphery'. There were, however, massive exports of labour from India and China, but these migrants were channelled to other tropical countries, not to the high wage economies of the 'core' or to the temperate zone of the 'periphery'. Thus the empirical evidence assembled by Lewis lends no support to the orthodox thesis, even in the period most favourable to their thesis.

It is possible, however, to go further and attempt to refute each of the three points raised by the apologists for imperialism. It can be argued, first, that labour markets in the Third World during the colonial period were characterised by coercion, monopsony and various systems of labour control that were designed to reduce the level of remuneration of local people, ensure an adequate supply of labour to expatriate-controlled enterprises, and prevent both occupational and unregulated geographical mobility. Formal slavery was the exception rather than the rule, but the systems of labour control that were devised were equally harsh and far removed from the free labour markets of laissez-faire economics. In Kenya, for example, a cheap, regular African labour supply was obtained by sharply reducing the amount of land available to Africans and thereby creating overcrowded reserves; by imposing hut, poll and other taxes; by threatening to conscript Africans into the army if they were not working for wages; by using tribal headmen to recruit labour; by introducing an all-inclusive internal pass system in combination with policies to encourage immigration from neighbouring territories; and by using forced labour where all else failed.[10] Many features of these colonial labour markets persist today and constitute one aspect of the neo-colonialism or internal colonialism that afflicts so much of the Third World.[11]

Second, leaving aside 'free trade' in slaves, addictive drugs and guns, it is far from clear that the forcible insertion of the Third World into a trading system dominated by Western Europe and the United States operated to the advantage of Third World countries or, more to the point, to the advantage of the majority of the population in Third World countries. Even as orthodox an economist as John Hicks acknowledges that 'it would . . . . be absurd to pretend that those who are dispossessed by colonies of settlement are likely, even in the very long run, to be benefited' and more generally, he argues that the forcible imposition of free trade may well lead to 'mistakes that will be costly, often very costly'.[12]

The precise effects on the Third World of the spread of an integrated international market are the subject of much debate, but one interesting hypothesis is that the imposition of 'free trade' and the resulting growth of exports of primary products from the underdeveloped countries occurred 'at the expense of industrialisation of these countries and also at the expense of other crops or products primarily meant for domestic consumption'.[13] The case of de-industrialisation in India and Bangladesh is quite well established[14] and it is possible that something similar but perhaps of lesser magnitude occurred in China and other parts of the Third World. Most observers now agree that colonial authorities 'were typically hostile to domestic industrialisation'.[15] Clearly more research needs to be done on this topic, but enough is known to cast doubt on the proposition that freer trade brought immediate and substantial gains to all parties. Indeed the opposite proposition is at least as plausible, namely, that in the Third World the results of trade-induced changes in the commodity composition of output were unemployment, a decline in the supply of some foodgrains and only marginal gains for most of the population. This entire process of industrial contraction and unemployment, a shift from food to cash crops, and a decline in living standards of the urban and rural poor is summed up by Amiya Bagchi in the phrase 'export-led exploitation'.[16]

Export-led exploitation is the view of imperialism as seen from the periphery. Viewed from the centre, the purpose of modern imperialism in the eyes of many reflects the desire of large capitalist enterprises and their governments to secure essential imports on favourable terms (e.g. oil); to obtain protected markets for exports (including exports of arms); and to obtain uninhibited access to Third World countries for investment.[17] This quest for economic security and advantage leads inevitably to attempts to control foreign economies through direct intervention (including covert and overt military intervention) or indirectly by obtaining control over local political authority. Economic power and political power usually go hand in hand.

Third, a number of writers have begun to argue that far from gaining from international capital flows, the growth of Third World countries was severely damaged because a large part of their economic surplus was transferred abroad, where it was used to increase the consumption of the richer classes and raise the general level of investment abroad. This does not deny the obvious fact that some investment flowed to the Third World and thereby helped to increase their economic surplus, but the net flow of resources, it is claimed, was from the underdeveloped countries to the developed and not the other way round. Orthodox economists may accept that there were instances of plunder, pillage, unfair bargaining, unequal treaties, etc., but these are regarded as special cases[18] and perverse, whereas the radical view is that perverse flows of resources were and are the norm.

Modern research has unearthed a number of examples in which capital flowed from the periphery to the centre. Thus Spain's exploitation of Latin America's mineral wealth was reflected in an export surplus in Spanish America and higher consumption on the Iberian peninsula. Britain's possession of most of the West Indies resulted in a capital transfer to the mother country equivalent to 8–10 per cent of Britain's entire income in the closing years of the eighteenth century, 'and probably a larger percentage in the period preceding the American War of Independence'.[19] The Indonesian export surplus in 1876–80 was more than 6 per cent of Indonesia's income, and the presumed financial counterpart was profits transferred back to Holland by the Dutch East Indies Company which helped considerably to raise living standards in the mother country. The exploitation of Bengal by the British East India Company is of course notorious. Famine reduced the population by over a third during 1769–71 yet, from the mid-eighteenth until well into the nineteenth century, 5–6 per cent of Bengal's income was siphoned off as unrequited exports and locally financed expenditure on wars of conquest incurred by the East India Company.[20]

These figures acquire added significance when set beside Arthur Lewis's much quoted statement that 'the central problem in the theory of economic development is to understand the process by which a community which was previously saving and investing 4 or 5 per cent of its national income or less, converts itself into an economy where voluntary saving is running at about 12 to 15 per cent.'[21] In retrospect it now appears that Third World countries had no difficulty reaching and exceeding a savings rate of 15 per cent once they became independent and acquired greater control over their economies. The central problem of underdevelopment was that during the era of imperialism a high proportion of the economic surplus potentially available for domestic investment was transferred abroad in the form of unrequited exports or was used locally to pay for the cost of colonial administration, the maintenance of large standing armies and police forces and the high standard of luxury consumption of the expatriate ruling class.

Uninhibited capital flows on balance did little or nothing to raise investment and growth in the pre-independence period in those countries which account for most of the people in the Third World, e.g. in undivided India and Burma, in China, Indonesia, Indochina, Nigeria and Zaire. On the contrary, the net movement of financial flows was from the Third World to the advanced capitalist countries, and thus resource transfers constituted one of the mechanisms of underdevelopment. Even today, some analysts argue, contrary to both neo-classical and orthodox Marxist views, the natural tendency within the world economic system is for savings to flow from capital-scarce poor countries to capital-abundant rich countries, because the real rate of interest and the return on investment (especially in industries based on new technology) are higher in rich countries than in poor.[22] If further research supports this view, it follows that a relaxation of capital controls by Third World countries would in most cases reduce their relative rate of growth, shift the functional distribution of income in favour of profits and consequently lead to greater inequality in the distribution of income among households. The poor of the Third World, and perhaps above all the rural poor, are bound to lose in a world in which capital is free to move internationally but mass migration of labour is prohibited.

DOMESTIC CLASS STRUCTURE AND THE STATE

The great mass of the rural population is scarcely conscious of the international forces which impinge upon the Third World. Indeed most peasants probably know little about how their own society is organised and are unaware of the connections between social organisation, political structure and government policy. On the other hand the peasantry understand perfectly well the complexities of the economy and the society of the locality in which they live and work.

Neo-classical economists tend to ignore these complexities, simplifying their analysis by concentrating on the behaviour of atomistic individuals in a classless universe. Economists of a more radical persuasion, however, often assume that society is divided into identifiable groups or classes which have different and frequently competing interests. This clash of interests occurs not only in the marketplace, as when rural trade unions and plantation managers confront one another, but above all in the political arena, where the outcome of the struggle to control the state and government policies determines the distribution of income, the level of accumulation and the rate of growth of production.

Those writing in the Marxist tradition usually identify classes by their relationship to the means of production:[23] owners of capital assets who derive most of their income from profits are classified as capitalists; those who live off rents from land are classified as landowners; those who do not own productive assets and whose income is derived from wages or, more generally, from payments for their own labour, are regarded as the proletariat or working class. Further refinement can be obtained by separating the city from the countryside, although asset diversification by property owners and permanent or seasonal migration by workers makes it difficult to make a definitive assignment of specific persons to particular classes. None the less, within the urban areas aditional groups sometimes are identified, most commonly the self-employed and casual workers in the 'informal' sector and the salaried bureaucrats in the public administration. In the rural areas, in addition to the large landowners, it is customary to single out peasants (possibly distinguishing between those who employ labourers and produce a marketable surplus and those who do not) and landless agricultural workers.

The classification of the population into groups or classes evidently varies from one writer to another depending on the country or situation being analysed and the questions being posed. The notion of social stratification, however, is a feature common to almost all radical writing, whether Marxist or not. Class analysis has proved to be a powerful tool to understanding everything from political macrodynamics to economic micro-issues. This should not be too surprising since economists are alone in trying to understand human phenomena exclusively in terms of the behaviour of isolated individuals; no historian, sociologist, political scientist or anthropologist would systematically ignore all social formations larger than the nuclear household.

The richness of class analysis can be illustrated by citing a few studies in which it has been used to illuminate a wide range of issues. Barrington Moore, in what has become a classic, has used it to study the origins of the modern political systems in China, Japan and India.[24] Some economists working in Latin America have sought to explain sustained rapid inflation in terms of a struggle among groups to increase their share of the national income, or at least to prevent their share from declining as a result of strongly pressed demands by others.[25] In India, Ashok Mitra has used class analysis to examine the terms of trade between agriculture and industry.[26]

In a remarkable study Alain de Janvry has used class analysis to explain the genesis of land reforms in Latin America and to assess their economic consequences.[27] He argues that in most Latin American countries today the industrial bourgeoisie has formed an alliance with the 'junker landed elites'. The junkers provide the agricultural exports and industrial raw materials necessary to sustain import substituting industrialisation. The urban capitalists, in turn, protect the profits of the junkers by restricting imports of competing products, imposing low taxes and investing heavily in technical change in agriculture while ensuring that surplus rural labour helps to keep wages low. The rural labour force, whether employed on junker estates or as peasants in the traditional sector, is more proletarian than agriculturalist and consequently, for the majority of the rural working population, the availability of employment and the wage rate are more important in determining economic welfare than output per hectare on their small plots.

Shifting from long-term structural issues to short-term phenomena, Amartya Sen has written an equally illuminating book on the causes and incidence of famine.[28] In an original and lucid manner Sen presents an analysis of the causes of hunger that centres not on commodities but on the people who lack sustenance. He takes us away from the usual fixation on the supply of foodgrains and looks instead at why some groups of people do not have enough to eat. Sen's analysis is organised around the notion of 'entitlement systems', that is, the set of relations that determines the ability of people to command food. One is 'entitled' to food through the application of one's own labour, through trade, through production or through transfer or gift.

Famines occur when the entitlements of many people decline to such an extent that large numbers of people starve to death. This can happen for a variety of reasons. For example, employment opportunities can decline as a result of the introduction of labour-saving equipment; the daily wage rate can fall as a result of a decline in the demand for labour; a small farmer's command over food will suffer if there is a decline in the market price of the cash crop he produces or if the market value of his assets collapses. Famine can also occur if the price of food rises faster than other prices and money incomes in general. Food prices, in turn, will tend to rise if either supply decreases or demand increases.

In studies of West Bengal, Ethiopia, the Sahel and Bangladesh, Sen shows that the usual picture of famines is not correct. Seldom are they caused by a generalised shortage of food and never do they lead to mass hunger, indiscriminately spread among the population, affecting the poor and not-so-poor alike. Instead, the causes of famines are localised, arising as often on the demand as on the supply side, and the effects of famines are concentrated on particular social classes. Indeed the great merit of Sen's approach is that it leads one to look at the different situations faced by different groups or classes in society. For example, the famine of 1943 in Bengal actually occurred during a boom. There was no serious shortage of foodgrains. Instead there was a large expansion of war-related public expenditure in Calcutta which led to a sharp rise in the demand for food and in the price of food. In the countryside agricultural labourers experienced a precipitous fall in wages in terms of rice. Similarly, the relative price of fish fell, hurting fishermen. The demand for the services of artisans and specialised workers such as barbers also fell, and consequently the rate of exchange of their labour for food became adverse. Peasants and sharecroppers were not seriously affected, but the distress among labourers, fishermen and other inhabitants of the rural areas was such that about three million people died of starvation and disease.

The literature cited above, although some is of recent origin, has begun to be absorbed into the profession. Much debate now centres on the phenomenon of 'interlinked factor markets' and the related phenomenon of market 'isolation'. The former refers to a situation in which a single transaction specifies the prices and quantities of several factors of production. This can occur, for instance, when a landowner simultaneously rents land to his tenant, provides him with credit and hires the tenant or members of his family part-time for wages. In such a situation factor prices are not necessarily market clearing prices, nor do they reflect the balance of supply and demand in the normal sense. Indeed the price paid for a factor of production varies widely even within a restricted geographical area: this is what is meant by market isolation.

Neo-classical economists have attempted to explain interlinked factor markets and market isolation as responses to market imperfections, a desire to spread risk or reduce uncertainty, and the imperfect availability of information. That is, these phenomena are seen as having arisen in order to make markets function more efficiently than would otherwise have been possible.[29] The more interesting studies of these phenomena, however, place them firmly within a class context and regard changes in contractual arrangements as responses to changes in economic, legal, technological and political circumstances which affect the bargaining power of the contracting parties. A typical case would be a conflict of interest between a landlord and his sharecropping tenant,[30] but the method of analysis is quite general and can be used, for instance, to explain the response of landowners to 'usury' laws or to legislation prohibiting share tenancy, or to the introduction of new technology, or to the need to have guaranteed supplies of labour at particular times of the year. The emphasis, then, is not on the efficiency of the market in allocating resources, but on the ability of those who control resources other than labour and who own most of the productive assets to take full advantage of their economic power.

Even for those who are reluctant to employ a conflict model of society in analysing the major issues of development, class analysis has helped to call attention to the fact that the poor are not a single class but a heterogeneous collection of people, one group differing from another in terms of geographical location, demographic characteristics, occupation, etc. The interests of these various groups in poverty do not necessarily coincide and in many cases policy measures which help some of the poor actually harm others.[31] For example, an increase in the price of grain is likely to benefit those small peasants who produce a marketable surplus, and this group may be numerous as well as poor. On the other hand, the same price increase will harm those who must purchase grain in the market, including such groups of the poor as urban unskilled workers, landless agricultural labourers and small peasant farmers who do not grow enough grain to meet all the needs of their household. This last category may include small, poor peasants who specialise in cash crops as well as peasant producers of grain who supplement their supplies from the market by hiring themselves out as part-time wage labourers. This all seems rather obvious and neither radical nor novel until one recalls that much of the standard writing in development economics focuses on macro-economic growth rates, or on the priority to be given to agriculture as compared to industry, or on the balance between the cities and the countryside. That is, the focus is on aggregate production, or the commodity composition of output, or the geographical location of economic activity. Classes, as such, either are ignored or are assigned a subsidiary role.

The great virtue of the more radical literature is that it puts class conflict in the centre of the stage while recognising that the poor do not constitute a single class but, on the contrary, are composed of a number of classes or groups which may be affected in very different ways by particular government policies and programmes. The rich, of course, are also heterogeneous and divided. They may be divided by language or religion; they may be organised into competing regional blocs; they may have differing economic interests based on agriculture, manufacturing or trade and commerce. They may be divided along clan, tribal or family lines. Despite these divisions into squabbling factions, in most countries for most of the time the commonality of interests of the rich *vis-à-vis* the poor is sufficiently well perceived for them not to undermine their control of the state by internecine struggle. That is, the politics of factions – normal and formal politics – is rarely taken to an extreme and ultimately is subservient to the class interest of self-preservation. Control generally circulates within an elite – and in some countries the velocity of circulation is much faster than in others – but power is seldom shared with the poor. The fragmentation, heterogeneity and lack of organisation of the latter ensure their subservience, especially when the governing classes are able to maintain a close alliance with the military.

The state, then, is an instrument in the hands of the governing class. It may of course be used by the governing class as an instrument for all-round development, but in general it appears not to have been so used. More often it has been used to favour particular ethnic groups (as with the Sinhalese in Sri Lanka or the Malays in Malaysia), or the urban population at the expense of the rural (as in Ghana), or a caste of military officers (as in Pakistan), or an authoritarian monarchy (as in Morocco), or the dominant position of a group of large landowners (as in Nepal and Guatemala) or the interests of large industrialists (as in Brazil). The pursuit of class ambitions may lead to economic growth, but in many Third World countries it has also led to growing inequality and sometimes to further impoverishment of significant sections of the population. This, in turn, is associated with the intense and perhaps rising social and political unrest throughout the Third World, in Kenya and Chad, in Chile and El Salvador, in the Philippines and Bangladesh.

The problems of poverty, especially rural poverty, and of social unrest underline the necessity for purposeful government intervention. But given the class basis of the state, a question arises about the possibility of effective action. It is this question that we consider next.

THE STATE AND DOMESTIC POLICY

All economists agree that domestic policies are one of the basic causes of poverty in the Third World, in both urban and rural areas. Orthodox economists, however, assume that the state is essentially a benevolent institution which attempts to maximise a 'social welfare function'. If welfare is not in fact maximised this must be because policy mistakes have been committed, and it is the job of the economist to point out these mistakes to government so that they can be corrected. The most commonly used tool in this type of policy analysis is applied welfare economics.

Radical economists, on the other hand, have a different point of departure. They assume the state is non-neutral, that governments reflect particular class and group interests and that government policies are designed on balance to promote the interests of those who control the state. In some Third World countries, e.g. in Latin America, the groups who control the state are well entrenched, the class structure is well defined and the political system (but not necessarily an individual government) is relatively stable, until of course it is overthrown by a revolution, as in Cuba. In other countries the class hierarchy is in flux, as various groups struggle against one another to fill the power vacuum created by the departing colonialists. In some cases, notably in Africa, a military and bureaucratic elite has taken power, whereas in other cases, including parts of Asia, political power has accrued to those who dominate the productive sectors of the economy, viz. large landowners and industrialists.

Casual observation suggests that the less stable the class hierarchy, the more likely it is that government policy will favour the short-term interests of its supporters, including the army. If a group is likely to be in power for only a short period, it is natural that it will want to make hay while the sun shines. Be that as it may, what the orthodox economist regards as a mistake, the radical economist is likely to regard as a deliberate attempt to improve the position of particular interests. Using class analysis, the radical economist is less inclined to prescribe policies to governments than to try to explain why the policies in question were first introduced and to discover who has benefited from them.

The difference in approach is well illustrated by project analysis. The orthodox economist, surveying the 'distorted' prices prevalent in the Third World, advocates the use of 'shadow' prices in selecting investment projects, the shadow prices to be determined by estimating 'social' costs and benefits.[32] The radical economist responds with several points. First, if actual prices do not reflect social costs and benefits, then the logical thing to do is to change the actual market prices (since these affect all projects) rather than try to correct market prices by using shadow prices (since these affect only a minority of projects). Second, if, in spite of the above, governments choose to use social cost–benefit analysis, rather than to correct actual 'distortions', this is likely to be because in fact governments know that social cost–benefit analysis is likely to be ineffective and this is precisely what is desired. Third, governments wish neither to alter actual prices nor introduce an effective system of shadow prices because they know that if they were to do so the class distribution of benefits and burdens would be altered in a way that is unfavourable to the classes in power.[33] For example, in many countries exchange rates are overvalued; the consequent excess demand for foreign exchange to purchase imports typically has been contained by introducing import permits and other trade controls. The combination of an overvalued exchange rate and import controls then enables the government to bestow favours upon its supporters in the form of import licences, favours which result in large income gains in the form of scarcity rents. Similarly, the price of finance capital often is less than its opportunity cost and real interest rates sometimes are negative. Credit therefore must be rationed, and anyone who succeeds in obtaining the rationed credit is assured large profits. It is well known that when credit is allocated by administrative devices those who succeed in obtaining it tend to be the large and well established enterprises, not small and new borrowers. That is, the system is biased in favour of the rich and discriminates against the poor. Indeed the latter, if they get any credit at all, must rely on moneylenders and the 'informal' credit market.

It is for these reasons that the orthodox prescription of social cost–benefit analysis is fundamentally misconceived: it is unwanted by the rich and powerful classes who do well out of a 'distorted' system and it is unhelpful to the poor and powerless classes who are the victims of that system.

Similar problems arise in the realm of social expenditure. Health expenditure in the Third World has been concentrated (i) in the major cities, (ii) in large capital intensive hospitals and (iii) on curative medicine. Yet the majority of the population, i.e. the poor, live in the countryside, need simple clinics and a network of paramedical personnel and, above all, would benefit enormously if emphasis were placed on preventive rather than individual curative medicine, including the provision of clean water supplies and adequate sewage disposal, the eradication of malnutrition and the control of epidemic diseases.[34] This is widely acknowledged and in fact the WHO and UNICEF have managed to secure agreement from governments to promote 'primary health care' (PHC).[35] Why, then, are medical resources allocated in the way they are? Either governments are incredibly stupid (which is the implicit answer of the orthodox economist) or else they are not maximising social welfare in any meaningful sense but instead are maximising the benefits of the urban rich, including of course the urban-based medical profession. As Malcolm Segall makes quite explicit,

> The reshaping of the health sector in the direction of PHC inevitably encounters opposition from the main beneficiaries of the existing situation. On the consumer side these comprise . . . the urban rich. . . . On the producer side are the health care professionals, especially the doctors, and private capital in the form of the pharmaceutical and medical equipment industries, and those private hospitals and health insurance companies that are profit-making. This is a formidable enough alliance.[36]

The same sort of problem occurs in education. In most Third World countries a disproportionate amount of the resources available is allocated to university education at the expense of primary and secondary education. Moreover, the net private benefits of tertiary education often exceed by a wide margin the net 'social' benefits. The reason for this is that the private benefits reflect (i) large government subsidies per student in tertiary education and (ii) very great education-related wage differentials, often inherited from the colonial regime. To the orthodox economist it would seem sensible to reduce the wage differentials, reduce the subsidy to tertiary education and increase public sector support for primary and secondary education; but the problem is that none of these things is likely to happen because the present 'misallocation' of resources strengthens the elites who dominate most Third World countries.[37] That is, from the point of view of those who control the government there is no misallocation of resources.

The logic of this approach can be applied to questions of macro-economic development strategy. Applied welfare economics suggests that Third World countries ought to follow a policy of modified free trade.[38] Class analysis suggests that countries follow the policies they do, not because of a misunderstanding of the logic of the principle of comparative advantage but because of the interests of those who control the state. The pro-industry, anti-agriculture and anti-free-trade policies followed by Pakistan and Bangladesh, for example, reflect the fact that in both countries the ruling class consists of a coalition of industrialists, urban bureaucrats and the military. In Argentina the twists and turns of policy are the outcome of a struggle between a rising industrial class and an older, primary-products exporting, large landowning class now in relative decline. If the strategy of import substituting industrialisation were to disappear, it is unlikely that it would be replaced by free trade and laissez faire. More likely would be even greater efforts to form an alliance of Third World nationalist and populist forces and greater pressure to institute a New International Economic Order. Conventional economic analysis completely misses this political dimension of economic policy. Indeed some liberal economists are reduced to claiming that the enthusiasm of the Third World 'for some of the New International Economic Order items seems scarcely explicable, except in terms of bad advice'.[39]

A distinguishing feature of orthodox economics is its preoccupation with allocative efficiency. At one level, as we have seen, this is reflected in a concern with 'getting prices right' or if not, then at least using shadow prices. At another level, it is reflected in choosing the 'correct' sectoral priorities. The debate between agriculture versus industry comes in here. Insofar as radical economists have a coherent position, they tend to emphasise the importance of economies of scale and increasing returns and hence to favour industrialisation. Orthodox economists, sceptical of the benefits of protectionism and conscious of the difficulties of raising public finance for direct, selective subsidies for manufacturing, tend to come down in support of agriculture. On the whole, however, they are reluctant to disturb property relations and hence do not favour land reform.

Turning to foreign trade, the issue is often posed as a conflict between giving priority to promoting exports and encouraging import substituting industrialisation. This is obviously the other side of the coin examined in the preceding paragraph. Orthodox economists emphasise the 'distorting' effects on efficiency of overvalued exchange rates, tariffs and direct controls on foreign trade and hence tend to give priority to exports. Radical economists, in contrast, are less impressed by the efficiency produced by the free play of imperfect market forces and are less inhibited about price intervention. Thus to this extent it can be said that they are more inclined to favour import substituting industrialisation. It should be clear, however, that there is nothing particularly radical about an overvalued exchange rate and, moreover, such an exchange rate, by encouraging imports and discouraging exports, appears to be inconsistent with achieving either priority.

The true division between orthodox and radical economists centres on distributive issues. Radicals usually are egalitarians. They give high priority to greater equality for its own sake and often affirm that there is no necessary conflict between faster growth and a more equal distribution of wealth and income. Orthodox economists give priority to increasing production ('you can't redistribute nothing') and postulate a trade-off between growth and equity.

There is considerable evidence from a number of countries that the domestic economic and social policies that have been followed have resulted in greater inequality and, indeed, in some instances, in an accentuation of poverty. In some cases (Chad, Zaire, Uganda, Somalia, Madagascar, Niger, Sudan, Ghana and Senegal) the incidence of poverty has increased primarily because national income per head has fallen.[40] In other countries, however, the incidence of poverty failed to decline and quite possibly rose despite growth in aggregate output per head. This view was first put forcefully by the ILO in a study which covered rural poverty in the Philippines, Indonesia, Malaysia, Sri Lanka, Bangladesh, Pakistan and the Indian states of Tamil Nadu, Bihar, Uttar Pradesh and the Punjab.[41] A later study suggests that in Nepal too the standard of living of the rural poor has declined.[42] A similar phenomenon seems to have occurred in several African countries notwithstanding the growth they have experienced, viz. Tanzania, Sierra Leone, Zambia, Malawi and most likely the Ivory Coast.[43]

These findings have been disputed by a number of orthodox economists. Some assert that it is not true that poverty has increased, or that 'in a sense, there are no facts'.[44] Others believe that the case is not proven, the data being unreliable or not comparable over time.[45] Still others, that the phenomenon affects only a few countries or has occurred only over limited periods.[46] Or alternatively, that the problem is not serious and can be corrected by larger doses of present policies leading to faster growth;[47] a modified trickle-down approach is advocated.[48]

One can accept that the data are not as abundant, reliable or comparable as one would wish or the time series long enough to reach definitive conclusions. The evidence often is fragmentary and based on a mixture of household sample survey data, information on wage rates (but not on the number of days of employment) and on changes in the relative price of food, the most important wage good. The fact, however, that so much of the data points in the same direction increases the probability that in a distressingly large number of countries a rise in average income per head has been accompanied by the further impoverishment of some groups. Again, it is not possible to identify precisely which groups have been affected and how large they are. Landless agricultural labourers appear to be the most seriously affected and are increasing both absolutely and probably relatively in many countries.[49] Small peasants producing some cash crops for export (jute, sugar, coffee) have experienced a sharp fall in their sales price in recent years and have consequently suffered a fall in income. In those countries in which the relative price of food has increased, deficit food producers (who supplement their own production with purchases from the market) have also been under pressure. The heterogeneity of the poor makes simple generalisations impossible, but in not a few cases a substantial minority of the poor are worse off today than they were, say, 20 years ago.

Yet it is clear that even the poorest countries are in principle capable of alleviating the worst forms of poverty. China demonstrates this beyond any shadow of a doubt. For example, life expectancy in China is 67 years whereas it is 52 in India; the infant mortality rate is 71 per thousand in China whereas it is 121 in India.[50] It is also clear that the policies necessary to do this need not result in a lower rate of growth. For instance, South Korea has achieved an unusually equal distribution of income, Tanzania has had a remarkably successful literacy programme and Sri Lanka has had an equally successful health and nutrition programme.[51] At the same time the growth in GNP per capita during the period 1960–81 was 6.9 per cent per annum in South Korea, 1.9 per cent in Tanzania and 2.5 per cent in Sri Lanka; this can be compared with the average growth rate in low-income countries other than China and India of 0.8 per cent per head per year.[52]

These and other considerations of a similar sort underlie the advocacy of direct redistributive measures, of policies which focus on the creation of more productive employment opportunities[53] and of policies oriented toward the satisfaction of basic human needs.[54] Such an approach to development policy implies the de-thronement of GNP as an aggregate measure of well-being.[55] It also possibly requires a larger role for the state than one finds in most Third World countries and certainly requires a state with a rather different orientation.

That, of course, is the rub. Given the nature of the state, the domestic policies needed to reduce poverty and inequality quickly are unlikely to be introduced. This presents the radical with a dilemma. Either he addresses his analysis to those few revolutionary governments where peasants and workers have obtained power or else he must assume, naively, that existing states can be persuaded by force of argument to cater to the interests of the poor. Whichever he chooses the radical economist is vulnerable to the charge of irrelevance. In the longer run, however, the radical can console himself with the thought that ideas can help to change the world and what is radical today may seem a commonplace tomorrow. Meanwhile, he can direct his analysis to whichever groups are willing to listen – political parties, students and academics, trade unions and peasant organisations, international organisations, and even groups inside the government, for the heterogeneity of the ruling classes ensures that the state is not altogether monolithic or completely intolerant of divergent views.

POLICY APPROACHES

The number of specific policies in principle available to governments to reduce rural poverty is extremely large and clearly cannot be discussed one by one in a relatively short chapter. In order to make the subject manageable we shall ignore completely (i) all macroeconomic policies such as monetary, fiscal and aggregate expenditure policies; (ii) foreign trade policies, including exchange rate policy, controls on capital movements, measures to regulate the behaviour of multinational enterprises and tariffs, quotas and other measures intended to influence the volume and pattern of overseas trade; and (iii) domestic sectoral policies for industry, transport, energy, etc. which have little direct impact on the rural areas although their indirect impact may of course be considerable and highly important. Thus a great deal will be left out of our discussion.

Those policies which remain to be discussed are grouped into four categories. The categories are chosen to emphasise a progression from the most fundamental to the least, from measures which can be expected to have a large direct political or economic impact to those which, while still beneficial, are likely to have a smaller and more delayed effect. Thus we start with measures which affect the distribution of political power, i.e. with policies which enable the voice of the poor to be heard more loudly and which give them an opportunity to influence the distribution of wealth and income. We then consider measures which alter the distribution of productive assets, i.e. the stock of the means of production. Next, we examine policies designed to divert more of the flow of income to the poor and finally, we mention policies designed to divert a larger fraction of the flow of investment to benefit the rural poor.

I The balance of political power

In most Third World countries the poor are not only economically deprived, they are politically oppressed. Especially in the countryside, where the population is scattered, isolated and unorganised, the poor are victims of discrimination (on tribal, caste, ethnic or linguistic grounds), of manipulation (by landowners, moneylenders and merchants) and of exploitation. They are socially and politically repressed, routinely intimidated and frequently threatened by violence or actually harmed. Normally all of this escapes the attention of outside observers – it is part of the quiet crisis of the Third World[56] and represents merely 'the day-to-day repression of "normal" society'[57] – but occasionally the level of violence becomes so intense that it cannot be ignored and indeed becomes an international scandal. Attention in recent years has focused on South and Central America, particularly Argentina, Chile, El Salvador and Guatemala, where the army, the police and right-wing death squads have engaged in mass murder, kidnapping and torture of sections of the rural (and urban) population. Such practices, however, are not limited to Latin America; similar phenomena can be found, for example, in the Philippines and in all South Asian countries.

In India, for instance, the number of recorded incidents of violence against the so-called scheduled castes is high and possibly rising. This is reflected in the figures in Table 2.1 which refer to cases of murder, rape, grievous hurt, arson and 'other offences' as classified under the Indian Penal Code, and cover the five years from 1976 to 1980. As can be seen in the table, most of the recorded incidents occurred in Uttar Pradesh, Bihar, Madhya Pradesh and Rajasthan, but this may reflect a greater accuracy of statistics in these four states rather than a higher level of violence against members of the scheduled castes. Given that 52 per cent of scheduled caste workers are agricultural labourers, 28 per cent small farmers, sharecroppers and tenants, and most of the rest primary leather workers, fishermen and weavers, it is evident that the violence against the scheduled castes is in essence a class conflict between, on the one hand, middle and large landowners and, on the other, the landless and near-landless.

Any serious effort to improve the well-being of the poor should begin by ensuring their freedom from violence and repression. No

Table 2.1 Number of Incidents of Violence Against Scheduled Castes: India, 1976–80

	1976	*1977*	*1978*	*1979*	*1980*
Uttar Pradesh	n.a.	4 974	5 560	4 122	4 279
Bihar	n.a.	681	1 911	2 452	1 890
Madhya Pradesh	n.a.	3 316	3 240	3 866	3 877
Rajasthan	n.a.	261	886	760	1 180
Sub-total	n.a.	9 232	11 597	11 200	11 226
All India	5 968	10 879	15 070	13 861	n.a.

Source: Commission for Scheduled Castes and Tribes, *Annual Report*, 1979 and 1980. Thanks are due to K. S. Subramanian for supplying this data.

need is more basic than the need for personal and group security. In most countries, however, a change in the balance of political power at the national level will be necessary if the basic need for security is to be met. The poor, moreover, are entitled not only to personal security, they also are entitled to bread, i.e. to a minimum of economic security. Ideally, in a decent society in which every person's voice counts, the poor should be able to influence the policies which determine whether or not they enjoy economic security, the most fundamental of which are those policies which affect the distribution of wealth and income. These objectives imply that the rural poor be incorporated into national political movements, gain a voice in national political, judicial and economic institutions and exert influence commensurate with their numbers in all major national decision-making bodies.

This may be impossible to achieve in the short term and it is therefore worth while to consider measures which would change the balance of political power not nationally but simply in the countryside. No doubt there are a great many such measures, but only three will be mentioned to illustrate the type of changes that may be possible in a particular locality.

Power at the local level often is effectively monopolised by landowners and their allies. Their economic influence is, of course, considerable and this in itself may enable them to exert political control over village councils, local elections and the like. In addition, the larger landowners usually have considerable influence over government-appointed officials, notably, district officers, local magistrates and the police. Disputes between landowners and the poor almost always are resolved in favour of the former, be they administrative decisions of district officers, legal judgements by magistrates or physical repression by the police or hired gangs of thugs. A small step toward redressing this imbalance would occur if the police were disarmed and the possession of weapons by private individuals made illegal.[58] The poor would benefit considerably by such measures, for it is the poor and not the landowners who are on the receiving end of most official and privately organised violence.

Next, the rural poor should be allowed to organise themselves politically and their right to do so should be protected by the courts. There are numerous examples throughout Asia of small, locally based political movements which developed more or less spontaneously and which were suppressed as soon as they succeeded in articulating the demands of the poor, recruiting significant numbers of members and posing a threat to the political hegemony of the landed elite. Yet these attempts to establish a countervailing power in the countryside are essential not only to the poor but also to the reformers in the provincial and national capitals, for the reformers need an organised constituency to which they can appeal and a source of information about development priorities. Without political organisations that embody the ambitions of the poor it will be difficult, if not impossible, to translate good intentions into good policies and effective implementation.

Third, more narrowly defined economic organisations also are needed, such as cooperatives composed exclusively of the poor or other groupings of poor people. Let us consider trade unions as an example. It is notoriously difficult to form trade union organisations in rural areas, for fairly obvious reasons. Labour is abundant and cheap and sometimes unemployed for considerable periods of time; the labour force is dispersed over wide areas and among a number of employers; because of their poverty individual workers are unable to resist the demands of employers and for the same reason can contribute little to a collective union fund; and the multiplicity of occupations in which individual workers are often engaged (e.g. as a farmer on their own and on tenanted lands, as a part-time hired agricultural labourer, and as a seasonal or occasional migrant worker in the cities or other rural areas) makes single-interest organisation more difficult. In practice the rural union movement has been most successful in organising plantation workers and even there its success has been limited.

None the less, further progress may be possible, particularly among landless and near-landless workers, who derive most of their income from wages as permanent hired agricultural workers, and among seasonal agricultural workers, who are recruited regularly by contractors or agents of the ultimate employers. The state of Kerala in India indicates perhaps the limits of the feasible.

It is doubtful that rural trade unions can significantly raise either total employment or the real wage rate, and to the extent that they do the latter, this may be partly at the expense of other workers who fail to obtain jobs, or even of small, poor peasants who supplement family labour with some hired labour. Unions may be more successful, however, in bargaining for improved working conditions, helping to ensure that labour laws are enforced, ending the physical abuse of workers by landowners, reducing the incidence of child labour (and thereby encouraging rural children to attend school), and agitating for public policies (such as food rationing schemes) which help to raise the standard of living of the mass of the poor. Too much should not be expected of rural trade unions – the economic environment is too unfavourable for them to flourish – but instead of condoning violence toward trade union leaders and their members, it would be of some help, to at least some groups of the poor, if government policy were supportive of the union movement and protective of its members.

II The distribution of productive assets

If the objective is a rapid reduction in rural poverty and inequality, the centrality of purposeful government intervention is inescapable. Government intervention in favour of the poor is unlikely to occur to a sufficient degree unless the poor are organised. Hence a change in the balance of political power probably is a necessary condition for more narrowly defined economic measures. In most countries a continuation of present policies will not suffice to enable all of the poor to satisfy their basic needs within, say, a generation, either because the trickle-down effects of growth are not working and poverty is increasing, or because trickle-down is working much too slowly.[59] Either way, governments must intervene and the most effective way to intervene, in the sense of achieving the desired result most quickly and efficiently, would be to reallocate the means of production. The purpose of such a reallocation would be to ensure that productive assets are distributed evenly across the entire rural population.

Such a programme has two major advantages. First, since the distribution of income depends to a great extent upon the distribution of productive assets, a redistribution of the means of production would result immediately in a much more equal distribution of income and in a substantial improvement in the living standards of the poor. Only if one assumed, contrary to much historical evidence, that a redistribution of assets would result in a catastrophic fall in output, would the poor fail to benefit. This can easily be demonstrated with a simple example.

Assume that the heterogeneous groups which comprise the poor account for 40 per cent of the rural population. Assume, too, that the poor receive 12 per cent of total rural income while the richest 10 per cent of the population receives 40 per cent of total rural income. The distribution of income in the rural areas would then be as follows:

Percentage of population	*Percentage of income*	*Normalised income per head*
10	40	4.00
50	48	0.96
40	12	0.30
100	100	1.00

If asset redistribution results in complete equalisation of incomes among all classes, and if total output remains unchanged, the income per head of the poor would rise by 233 per cent, that of the middle 50 per cent of the population would increase marginally by 4 per cent and the top 10 per cent would suffer a 75 per cent fall. Even if total output declined, however, the poor still would benefit provided only that total output did not fall by more than 70 per cent! Since this is extremely unlikely, one can be confident that a thorough redistribution of the means of production would indeed go a very long way towards eliminating poverty.

The second advantage of a programme of asset redistribution is that it can be reversed only with great difficulty and is essentially a once-and-for-all measure. There will be little need for government to intervene in the rural economy after the completion of the programme. Having destroyed the economic base of the previously dominant classes in the countryside, the government will no longer have to contend with unrelenting pressure from the rural rich to protect and enhance their privileged position; and having given the poor the means to produce their own income, it will be less necessary for the government to introduce further measures to channel income towards them.

This assumes, of course, that the redistribution of productive assets is complete. That is, all assets must be included: arable land, grazing land, orchards and woodlands, water resources, livestock and major pieces of machinery. A government which embarks upon such a redistribution must then decide what system of economic organisation to adopt. Broadly speaking, there are two choices: a small peasant farming system or some form of communal organisation. In principle either system can work equally well, as the experiences of South Korea and China illustrate, but in practice communal land tenure systems have several features which are worthy of consideration.[60]

First, it is possible within collective systems to ensure that labour is fully employed. Second, communal systems not only create a high degree of income equality, they also tend to perpetuate it over time. Third, communal systems contain a high potential for capital accumulation. Fourth, communal systems provide a framework for industrialising the countryside. They also represent, fifth, an institutional framework for the provision of public services such as health and education. Finally, they provide an institutional framework for local participation in political affairs. Similar features can be incorporated into the design of a small peasant farming system but they are not inherent to such systems.

Few governments will be prepared to contemplate as radical a programme of asset redistribution as we have been discussing and the question of establishing a communal tenure system or a fully fledged small peasant system consequently will not arise. There are, however, a range of alternative measures which do entail at least a partial redistribution of productive assets and which can be of benefit to some sections of the rural poor. These measures include the imposition of land ceilings or the redistribution of 'uncultivated' or 'inefficiently' cultivated holdings. The problems with such policies are that they are easy to evade, difficult to enforce, costly to administer, prone to become entangled in prolonged legal controversy and of very limited effect in reducing hard core poverty. The main beneficiaries tend to be households which already own some land and in many cases the landless are wholly excluded. Where the amount of land to be redistributed is small, a better policy would be to provide each landless household in the rural areas with a house plot or homestead on which vegetables and fruit could be grown, poultry raised and, of course, a house with clear title erected. Such a policy would have the virtue of providing a minimal level of economic security to everyone, although its contribution to reducing poverty would be modest. More ambitious reforms, such as in West Bengal today, may achieve more significant results.

Less ambitious still are policies which leave the distribution of land ownership intact but try to alter the contractual relationship between a landlord and his tenant. Common examples are policies which make sharecropping illegal, or which specify the minimum share to be received by the tenant, or which attempt to give tenants security of tenure. In practice these policies seldom succeed in significantly improving the position of the intended beneficiaries. If landlords are not allowed to evict an unsatisfactory tenant, they will simply switch to a wage labour system of farming. If landlords are told what the minimum crop share must be, they will simply require the tenant to supply more of the material inputs, or take advantage of interlinked factor markets by charging the tenant more for credit or offering him a lower price for the tenant's output that the landlord transports and markets for him, or switch to a fixed rental system. If sharecropping is prohibited by law, the landlord will simply switch to either a fixed rental system of farming or a system based on hired labour. The truth of the matter is that such contractual reforms offer no real substitute for a change in the ownership of the means of production.

III The distribution of the flow of income

If a government is unwilling or unable to alter property rights, it may attempt to alleviate poverty by changing the distribution of income. This is not easy for two reasons. First, income is a flow of output per unit of time valued at a set of prices. In a capitalist system the flow of output is controlled by those who possess the stock of the means of production which generates the output. Any attempt by government to divert the flow towards the poor runs a risk that adjustments by the owners of the means of production will partly neutralise the policy. For example, if government introduces price controls on wage goods in order to reduce the cost of living for the poor, the response may be (i) a reduction in the output of wage goods, (ii) a reduction in the proportion of some wage goods, especially food, that is marketed, (iii) a diversion of the marketed output into the black market, or (iv) a reduction by employers in the nominal wage rate such that real wages remain unchanged.

Second, assuming the above problem does not arise or can be overcome, attempts by government to alter the flow of income require permanent and sustained intervention. This is likely to lead, in turn, to permanent and sustained opposition to the policies by those who lose from them, particularly property owners. That is, the battle to assist the poor will have to be continuous; the war with the capitalist and landowning classes will be never-ending. Moreover, in this war the odds will favour the opposition because governments will come and go, and their policy priorities will change, but as long as the means of production remain in the hands of a minority, the class opposition to redistributive measures will remain. Those who survive will win in the end.

Moreover, in the battle against poverty the government will not be able to count on the support of all the poor. The reason for this is that many of the specific policies designed to redistribute flows of income will be beneficial to some groups of the poor but harmful to others. As we have seen, the poor are not a homogeneous class and their heterogeneity makes income redistributive policies especially difficult. For instance, minimum wage policies are beneficial to those employed in organised urban labour markets but do nothing for the urban unemployed and those in the informal sector, are probably unenforceable in rural areas except in plantations, and may actually harm small and poor employers. A similar problem arises, as we saw, with policies which result in higher producer prices of wage goods. Consumer subsidies on wage goods would have the opposite effects, helping those who purchase wage goods from the market (ignoring general equilibrium interactions mentioned above), harming those among the poor who produce wage goods, and having no effect on those outside the market nexus.

Income transfers to the poor normally do not take the form of cash grants but rather are transfers in kind. The most important transfers in kind consist of provision by the state of free or subsidised health and educational services. These services were discussed above in another context and there is nothing further that need be said here.

Something should be said about food rationing systems, however. They exist in a number of countries and in principle could be used to alleviate hunger and malnutrition. In practice, however, the public distribution of foodgrains has accentuated inequality rather than reduced it. In Burma the system is intended to benefit low-income government employees; in Bangladesh, the army and civil servants; in Pakistan, Thailand, Egypt and most of India the beneficiaries are largely the inhabitants of the urban centres. The orientation of these schemes, including their pronounced urban bias, reflects the nature of class interests and the lack of serious commitment by the governing groups to the reduction of poverty. Only in Kerala, Sri Lanka, Cuba and China has the food rationing system clearly been of benefit to large numbers of poor people.[61]

Thus in general the record of Third World governments in improving the distribution of income is mediocre. This is hardly surprising given the abundant evidence that inequality has actually increased. The tax and expenditure policies associated with Western welfare states have been applied to a limited extent only and have benefited middle and upper income groups primarily; the rural poor have been excluded from these programmes almost entirely. Except in the socialist countries, there has been very little asset redistribution, but where this has occurred, notably after the land reforms in Taiwan and South Korea, the impact on rural poverty has been substantial. Elsewhere, government intervention to divert the flow of income toward the rural poor has had little success: compared with the colonial era the rural poor now receive more education and better public health services and water supplies but not much else. The gains they have enjoyed, where there have been long-term gains, as in Thailand and the Punjab, are a result of growth, not of redistributive government policies. This being so, it is natural to consider whether investment, the most important source of sustained growth, can be used to reduce rural poverty and inequality.

IV The pattern of investment

The possibility of alleviating poverty by channelling a large portion of the flow of investment toward projects of direct benefit to the poor might commend itself to governments. At first glance this option appears to have several attractions. It would not require an immediate change in the distribution of personal consumption or a fall in the standard of living of the dominant groups in society. It would not require a rise in total investment but merely a change in the pattern of investment. And it would not require a change in property rights or in the ownership of the means of production. Such a strategy clearly is a gradualist one: it operates only on the margin, change occurs slowly over a long time and the disturbance to social relations is kept to a minimum. Good is done by stealth and in some countries it may be thought that this is all that is possible.

It is important to recognise, however, just how small is the margin on which one is operating. Total gross investment varies from an average of 14 per cent of GDP in the low-income countries other than China and India to 25 per cent in the middle-income countries.[62] The share of investment allocated to the agricultural sector rarely is as high as 20 per cent and seems to average about 10 per cent.[63] This being so, investment in agriculture in a typical Third World country accounts for only 1.4–2.5 per cent of GDP. Of course investments in other sectors are beneficial to the rural areas, but the fact remains that only a very small proportion of the national product is allocated to investment projects which are intended to raise output and income in the countryside.

Unfortunately, no information exists on the division of agricultural investment between the private and public sectors, but let us be very generous and assume that a third of the investment is undertaken by the state and the remaining two thirds is private investment in such things as machinery, irrigation and drainage, fences, terraces, fish ponds, livestock, dwellings and other buildings. Only state investment can of course be diverted to help the poor since, given an unchanged distribution of income and of land and other means of production, the private sector would have no incentive to alter its pattern of investment. Again, let us be generous and in the absence of data assume that half the existing state investment in agriculture is directed toward the poor. This implies that roughly 0.2 to 0.4 per cent of GDP, at most, is allocated to investment of direct benefit to the rural poor.

The magnitudes in question are pitifully small and even if government policy resulted in doubling the amount of investment intended to benefit landless workers, small tenant and peasant farmers, fishermen, artisans and similar groups in rural areas, the impact on the incidence of poverty would be small. What would be needed is a truly massive increase in public investment.

It has been taken for granted so far that government investment projects intended to benefit the poor do in fact achieve what they set out to do. Alas, there is considerable evidence that rural development projects financed by governments and international agencies often fail to reach the poor or even to attain their goals of increasing agricultural production. Studies of rural development projects in several African countries, namely, Tanzania, Kenya, Ghana, Niger, the Sudan and Nigeria, have demonstrated this quite clearly.[64] Comparable studies have not been done in Asia, but there is no reason to believe that the results would be markedly different. Indeed, recent analyses of rural development policies and programmes (but not of projects) in Asia concluded that 'involvement of the rural people in some way is a precondition for success in rural development' and because of the absence of this precondition, 'rural development successes . . . on a national scale are likely to be glaring exceptions.'[65]

In practice, then, it is the middle and upper income groups in rural areas that capture most of the benefits of government financed investment projects, even when the projects are aimed at the poor. Moreover, in some cases it is impossible to design a project which even in principle could reach the poor. For example, when small peasant farms are interspersed among large holdings as in parts of Bangladesh, the only feasible way to invest in irrigation may be in the form of deep tubewells on the large farms. Deep tubewell investment on the small and scattered peasant farms may be virtually impossible because of the difficulty of forming tubewell cooperatives. Even more difficult are labour-intensive irrigation projects entailing the construction of earth dams and dikes, drainage ditches and field levelling. Yet from the point of view of efficiency, growth and equity, the best project would be the labour-intensive irrigation project: it would provide more employment during the construction period, it would permit a larger area to be irrigated, it would represent a high rate of return on the investment outlay and it would generate more direct benefits for poor peasants. Next best would be tubewell investment within a cooperative framework. Investment in deep tubewells has the disadvantage of being capital-using rather than labour-using, but if this is done within a genuine cooperative framework at least it would be possible to ensure that a reasonably high proportion of the benefits reached small farmers. The least desirable project would be tubewell investments on large farms since neither the advantages of efficiency nor equity would be obtained.

Thus both social and economic criteria suggest that the three projects should be ranked in the following order: (i) labour-intensive irrigation using surface water, (ii) capital-intensive tubewell irrigation centred on peasant cooperatives and (iii) tubewell irrigation on large farms. Yet the combination of private property rights and the spatial distribution of farm sizes has the effect of reversing the order of practical feasibility, with the result that a less efficient technology is used and a more inequitable distribution of income is produced. It simply is not the case that state investment directed toward the poor can be increased substantially without any need to change property rights or the ownership of land.

One exception to this statement, it might be claimed, is labour-intensive rural public works schemes. In principle there is little doubt that such investment programmes can create large numbers of jobs and undertake useful projects which raise labour productivity and farm output by constructing a wide range of productive assets. Apart from China, however, most rural employment schemes in practice have been essentially emergency relief programmes improvised in times of harvest failure and famine. Organisation has been inefficient, resources have been wasted on a vast scale, few permanent additions have been made to the stock of capital in the countryside and only a marginal contribution has been made to alleviating poverty.

If rural employment programmes are to make a permanent contribution to alleviating poverty, two changes are necessary.[66] First, the focus of the schemes must switch from charitable relief of distress to the construction of durable assets. That is, the schemes should come to be viewed as a means of deploying labour to accelerate investment. Second, the assets created by such schemes should become the property of the labourers who construct them. In a communal agricultural system this happens more or less automatically in most cases, but in a capitalist system the value added by the use of new assets rarely accrues to the workers who distributed them. If the asset is paid for and owned by a private capitalist, the net income accrues to him as profit or rent. If it is owned by the state and its services are provided free of charge, as is often the case, 'externalities' are generated and usually these are captured by property owners. For example, the benefits of public highways or soil conservation works or drainage and irrigation facilities are reflected in part in a higher price of land and in part in higher returns to farmers and higher rents charged by landlords.

On the other hand, in principle it would be possible to combine capital formation with progressive income redistribution by ensuring that when assets are constructed by the poor, e.g. by landless labourers, upon completion the ownership of the assets is vested in a cooperative consisting solely of those who supplied their labour. This cooperative would then manage the assets and charge for their use, distributing part of the income to the members and retaining part to finance future capital accumulation. In this manner the productive base of the poorest households could be strengthened on a continuing basis. This policy, while marginalist and gradualist, combines institutional reform, a change in the distribution of productive wealth and capital accumulation in a way which, if implemented on a large enough scale and if sustained for a long enough period of time, could help to transform the economic position of large sections of the rural poor. If, for political reasons, one can attempt to alleviate poverty solely by changing the pattern of investment, this is perhaps the most effective way to do it.

There are a great many projects which could be undertaken which could yield a permanent flow of income to organised groups of the rural poor. Examples include the rehabilitation or construction of fish ponds, the reclamation of waterlogged or salinated land, construction of irrigation tanks, tubewells and other irrigation facilities, construction of bridges and roads, planting of timber forests, coconut plantations, fruit orchards and mulberry bushes for silk-worm cultivation. Income from projects such as these would be derived from the sale of products (fish, fruit), fees for services provided (irrigation water and drainage facilities) and tolls for the use of social infrastructure (bridges, roads). Reclaimed land could either become commercial property and cultivated under the authority of the cooperative or sold and the proceeds reinvested in other activities. Similarly, the products produced by the cooperative could be sold on the market, distributed among the members for direct consumption or used to provide the major input into communally owned processing enterprises such as canneries, timber mills and silk weaving establishments.

Linking asset creation by the poor with asset ownership by institutions organised for the poor provides both a mechanism and an incentive for the works constructed under employment programmes to be maintained and improved. In this way the chronic problem of inadequate or non-existent maintenance could be overcome. Moreover, some of the net income generated by the cooperatives of the poor could be set aside as savings for investment in other productive activities, thereby initiating a sustained if modest process of cumulative expansion. Public land could be leased by the cooperative and private land could either be bought by the cooperative from the landowners at the unimproved site value or rented, or the landowner could be offered a share of the output. Members presumably would participate in the distribution of income in proportion to the number of days of work contributed.

The problems of starting such a scheme are not primarily technical and organisational; these can surely be overcome with a bit of imagination. The main problem is likely to be political and social, namely, to compel those who hold power locally and nationally to permit the poor to become organised and to accumulate productive wealth. In some countries this problem may be insuperable, in which case the poor can either emigrate, hope that growth will do the trick or wait for a social revolution.

Notes

1. Andre Gunder Frank, 'The Development of Underdevelopment', *Monthly Review*, September 1966.
2. Keith Griffin, *Underdevelopment in Spanish America*, London: Allen and Unwin, 1969, p. 38. For some of the early studies see R. C. Dutt, *The Economic History of India Under Early British Rule*, Delhi: Manager of Publications, Government of India, 1963; J. S. Furnivall, *Netherlands India*, Cambridge University Press, 1967; M. Caldwell, *Indonesia*, Oxford University Press, 1968; A. Moorehead, *The Fatal Impact*, London: Hamish Hamilton, 1966; C. O. Sauer, *The Early Spanish Main*, University of California Press, 1966; A. G. Frank, *Capitalism and Underdevelopment in Latin America*, New York: Monthly Review Press, 1967.
3. For a readable account of the attitudes of the imperialists towards the niggers, Kaffirs, blackfellows, Chinks and Wogs they conquered, see V. G. Kiernan, *The Lords of Human Kind: European Attitudes to the Outside World in the Imperial Age*, London: Weidenfeld and Nicolson, 1969.
4. See Colin Clark, *Population Growth and Land Use*, London: Macmillan, 1967.
5. See, for instance, Sauer, *The Early Spanish Main*; Moorehead, *The Fatal Impact*; Stanley J. and Barbara H. Stein, *The Colonial Heritage of Latin America*, New York: Oxford University Press, 1970.
6. A. G. Hopkins, *An Economic History of West Africa*, Harlow: Longman, 1973; C. R. Boxer, *The Portugese Seaborne Empire 1415–1825*, Harmondsworth: Penguin, 1973; W. Rodney, *How Europe Underdeveloped Africa*, Washington DC: Howard University Press, 1973; Ruth First, *South-West Africa*, Harmondsworth: Penguin, 1963.
7. Charles van Onselen, *Chibaro: African Mine Labour in Southern Rhodesia*, Gwelo: Mambo Press, 1977; Colin Bundy, *The Rise and Fall of the South African Peasantry*, London: Heinemann, 1979; Stanley Trapido, 'Landlord and Tenant in a Colonial Economy: the Transvaal 1880–1910', *Journal of Southern African Studies*, vol. 5, no. 1, October 1978; Colin Leys, *Underdevelopment in Kenya*, London: Heinemann, 1975, Ch. 2; G. Arrighi, 'Labour Supplies in Historical Perspective: A Study of the Proletarianization of the African Peasantry in Rhodesia',

Journal of Development Studies, vol. 6, no. 3, April 1970; Francis Wilson, *Labour in the South African Gold Mines*, Cambridge University Press, 1972; J. B. Knight and G. Lenta, 'Has Capitalism Underdeveloped the Labour Reserves of South Africa?', *Oxford Bulletin of Economics and Statistics*, vol. 42, no. 3, August 1980.

8. See Victor D. Lippit, 'The Development of Underdevelopment in China', in Philip C. C. Huang (ed.), *The Development of Underdevelopment in China*, New York: M. E. Sharpe, 1980; and the comments on Lippit's paper in the same volume.
9. See W. Arthur Lewis, *Growth and Fluctuations 1870–1913*, London: Allen and Unwin, 1978.
10. Richard D. Wolff, *The Economics of Colonialism: Britain and Kenya, 1870–1930*, New Haven and London: Yale University Press, 1974, Ch. 5 and Ch. 6.
11. See the references in note 7. Also see Keith Griffin, *Land Concentration and Rural Poverty*, 2nd edn, London: Macmillan, 1981, Ch. 5 and E. E. Rich and C. H. Wilson, *The Cambridge Economic History of Europe*, Vol. IV, *The Economy of Expanding Europe in the Sixteenth and Seventeenth Centuries*, Cambridge University Press, 1967, Ch. 6.
12. John Hicks, *A Theory of Economic History*, Oxford University Press, 1969, pp. 52 and 51.
13. Amiya Kumar Bagchi, *The Political Economy of Underdevelopment*, Cambridge University Press, 1982, p. 119.
14. Ibid. Also see by the same author 'De-industrialisation in India in the Nineteenth Century: Some Theoretical Implications', *Journal of Development Studies,* vol. 12, no. 2, January 1976.
15. Lloyd Reynolds, 'The Spread of Economic Growth to the Third World: 1850–1980', *Journal of Economic Literature*, vol. XXI, September 1983, p. 957.
16. Bagchi, *The Political Economy of Underdevelopment*. Also see George Beckford, *Persistent Poverty: Underdevelopment in Plantation Economies of the Third World*, New York: Oxford University Press, 1972.
17. Richard D. Wolff, 'Modern Imperialism: The View from the Metropolis', *American Economic Review*, May 1970. See also James O'Connor, 'The Meaning of Economic Imperialism', in K. T. Fann and D. C. Hodges, *Readings in US Imperialism*, Boston: Porter Sargent, 1971.
18. The ease with which unpleasant facts can be dismissed as 'special cases' is at times breathtaking. Undivided India, i.e. today's Pakistan, India and Bangladesh, accounts for 71 per cent of what the World Bank classifies as low-income countries (excluding China). Yet Lloyd Reynolds blandly remarks, 'The case of India, which did not achieve intensive growth during the colonial era, has tended to dominate the anti-colonial literature; but India is rather a special case . . .' Reynolds, 'The Spread of Economic Growth', p. 956.
19. R. B. Sheridan, 'The Wealth of Jamaica in the Nineteenth Century', *Economic History Review*, Second Series, vol. 18, 1965, p. 306.
20. Bagchi, *The Political Economy of Underdevelopment*, Ch. 4.
21. W. Arthur Lewis, 'Economic Development with Unlimited Supplies of Labour', *The Manchester School*, vol. XXIII, no. 2, May 1954.

22. Keith Griffin, *International Inequality and National Poverty*, London: Macmillan, 1978, Introduction and Ch. 1. Also see Samir Amin, *Accumulation on a World Scale*, two volumes, New York: Monthly Review Press, 1974.
23. Others, however, have defined classes in terms of the ways various groups appropriate the economic surplus. This enables them to focus on exchange and the circulation of income as well as on the production of output. See, for example, G. Kitching, *Class and Economic Change in Kenya*, New Haven: Yale University Press, 1982.
24. Barrington Moore, Jr, *Social Origins of Dictatorship and Democracy: Lord and Peasant in the Making of the Modern World*, London: Allen Lane, 1964.
25. See, for example, M. Simonsent, *A Experiencia Inflacionaria no Brasil*, Instituto de Pesquisas e Estudos Socials, 1964; T. E. Davis, 'Eight Decades of Inflation in Chile, 1879–1959: A Political Interpretation', *Journal of Political Economy*, August 1963.
26. Ashok Mitra, *Terms of Trade and Class Relations*, London: Frank Cass, 1977.
27. Alain de Janvry, *The Agrarian Question and Reformism in Latin America*, Baltimore: Johns Hopkins University Press, 1981.
28. Amartya Sen, *Poverty and Famines: An Essay on Entitlement and Deprivation*, Oxford University Press, 1981.
29. See, for example, Kaushik Basu, 'The Emergence of Isolation and Interlinkage in Rural Markets', *Oxford Economic Papers*, vol. 35, no. 2, July 1983.
30. See, for example, A. Bhaduri, 'Agricultural Backwardness Under Semi-Feudalism', *Economic Journal*, March 1973; A. K. Ghose and A. Saith, 'Indebtedness, Tenancy and the Adoption of New Technology in Semi-Feudal Agriculture', *World Development*, vol. 4, no. 4, April 1976; P. K. Bardhan and A. Rudra, 'Interlinkage of Land, Labour and Credit Relations: An Analysis of Village Survey Data in East India', *Economic and Political Weekly*, February 1978; P. K. Bardhan, 'Interlocking Factor Markets and Agrarian Development: A Review of Issues', *Oxford Economic Papers*, vol. 32, no. 1, March 1980. Also of interest is Kalpana Bardhan, 'Economic Growth, Poverty and Rural Labour Markets in India: A Survey of Research', ILO, World Employment Programme, Working Paper, Geneva: March 1983.
31. Keith Griffin and Jeffrey James, *The Transition to Egalitarian Development*, London: Macmillan, 1981.
32. I. M. D. Little and J. A. Mirrlees, *Project Appraisal and Planning for Developing Countries*, London: Heinemann, 1974.
33. Frances Stewart, 'A Note on Social Cost–Benefit Analysis and Class Conflict in LDCs', *World Development*, vol. 3, no. 1, January 1975.
34. It is becoming recognised that even in the advanced industrialised countries the major improvements in health were due not to unconventional medical interventions but to improvements in the environment and in living conditions. See T. McKeown, *The Role of Medicine: Dream, Mirage or Nemesis?*, Oxford: Basil Blackwell, 1979; Alastair

Gray, 'Health and Society: Reflections on Policy', IDS *Bulletin*, vol. 14, no. 4, October 1983.

35. WHO/UNICEF, *Primary Health Care*, report of the international conference at Alma Ata, Geneva: WHO, 1978. Also see WHO, *Formulating Strategies for Health for All by the Year 2000*, Geneva: WHO, 1979.
36. Malcolm Segall, 'The Politics of Primary Health Care', IDS *Bulletin*, vol. 14, no. 4, October 1983, p. 32.
37. A comparison in 1980 of the two largest underdeveloped countries, China and India, is instructive.

	China	*India*
Adult literacy rate (%)	69	36
Percentage of age group enrolled in:		
primary education	117	76
secondary education	34	28
higher education	1	9

Source: IBRD, *World Development Report 1983*, New York: Oxford University Press, 1983.

38. Ian Little, Tibor Scitovsky and Maurice Scott, *Industry and Trade in Some Developing Countries*, Oxford University Press, 1970.
39. I. M. D. Little, *Economic Development: Theory, Policy and International Relations*, New York: Basic Books, 1982, p. 373.
40. The countries listed, according to the World Bank, experienced a fall in GNP per head during the period 1960–81: IBRD, *World Development Report 1983*, New York: Oxford University Press, 1983.
41. ILO, *Poverty and Landlessness in Rural Asia*, Geneva: ILO, 1977. Also see Keith Griffin and Azizur Rahman Khan, 'Poverty in the Third World: Ugly Facts and Fancy Models', *World Development*, March 1978.
42. Rizwanul Islam, Azizur Rahman Khan and Eddy Lee, *Employment and Development in Nepal*, Bangkok: ILO (ARTEP), 1982.
43. Dharam Ghai and Lawrence Smith, 'Food Policy and Equity in Sub-Saharan Africa', ILO, World Employment Programme Working Paper, Geneva: August 1983.
44. Little, *Economic Development*, p. 210.
45. Sudhir Annand, *Inequality and Poverty in Malaysia: Measurement and Decomposition*, New York: Oxford University Press, 1983.
46. The debate over whether the increase in rural poverty is episodic or secular has centred on India. Cf. M. S. Ahluwalia, 'Rural Poverty and Agricultural Growth in India', paper presented to the IBRD workshop on Analysis of Distributional Issues in Development Planning, Bellagio, Italy, 22–27 April, 1977: Ashwani Saith, 'Production, Prices and Poverty in Rural India', *Journal of Development Studies*, vol. 17, no. 2, January 1982; Keith Griffin and A. K. Ghose, 'Growth and Impoverishment in the Rural Areas of Asia', *World Development*, vol. 7, nos. 4/5, 1979.

47. M. S. Ahluwalia, 'Inequality, Poverty and Development', *Journal of Development Economics*, vol. 3, no. 3, 1976; M. S. Ahluwalia, 'Rural Poverty and Agricultural Performance in India', *Journal of Development Studies*, vol. 14, no. 3, April 1978.
48. Compare this, however, with the assertion that 'no reputable development economist ever, explicitly or implicitly, entertained any such theory of trickle-down in any of its alleged versions'. (H. W. Arndt, 'The "Trickle-Down" Myth', *Economic Development and Cultural Change*, vol. 32, no. 1, October 1983, p. 1.) This sounds suspiciously like a disclaimer after the event: now that trickle-down has been shown not to work, we are told that no one ever seriously believed in it!
49. But see Mead Cain, 'Landlessness in India and Bangladesh: A Critical Review of National Data Sources', *Economic Development and Cultural Change*, vol. 32, no. 1, October 1983.
50. IBRD, *World Development Report 1983*.
51. Amartya Sen, 'Public Action and the Quality of Life in Developing Countries', *Oxford Bulletin of Economics and Statistics*, vol. 43, no. 4, November 1981.
52. IBRD, *World Development Report 1983*.
53. Frances Stewart and Paul Streeten, 'Conflicts Between Output and Employment Objectives in Developing Countries', *Oxford Economic Papers*, vol. 23, no. 2, July 1971.
54. ILO, *Employment, Growth and Basic Needs*, Geneva: ILO, 1976.
55. Dudley Seers, 'The Meaning of Development', *International Development Review*, vol. II, no. 4, 1969.
56. See Betsy Hartmann and James Boyce, *A Quiet Violence: View From a Bangladesh Village*, London: Zed Press, 1983.
57. Barrington Moore, Jr, *Social Origins of Dictatorship and Democracy: Lord and Peasant in the Making of the Modern World*, Harmondsworth: Penguin, 1967, p. 505.
58. This is essentially the situation in Great Britain, a country widely regarded as having a sharply defined class system.
59. See ILO, *Employment, Growth and Basic Needs*, Ch. 2.
60. Keith Griffin, 'Communal Land Tenure Systems and Their Role in Rural Development', a paper presented to the Development Policy Seminar for UNDP Executives, Institute of Social Studies, The Hague, 21 November 1983.
61. See Griffin and James, *The Transition to Egalitarian Development*, and James D. Gavan and Indrani Sri Chandrasekera, *The Impact of Public Foodgrain Distribution on Food Consumption and Welfare in Sri Lanka*, IFPRI Research Report No. 13, Washington, DC: December 1979.
62. IBRD, *World Development Report 1983*.
63. E. F. Szczepanik, 'The Size and Efficiency of Agricultural Investment in Selected Developing Countries', *FAO Monthly Bulletin of Agricultural Economics and Statistics*, December 1969; J. A. Mollett, 'Agricultural Investment and Economic Development – Some Relationships', *Outlook on Agriculture*, vol. II, no. 1, 1982.
64. Judith Heyer, Pepe Roberts and Gavin Williams (eds), *Rural Development in Tropical Africa*, London: Macmillan, 1981.

65. David A. M. Lea and D. P. Chaudhri, *Rural Development and the State*, London and New York: Methuen, 1983, pp. 337 and 338.
66. This paragraph and the next one are taken from Griffin, *Land Concentration and Rural Poverty*, pp. 312–13.

3 Communal Land Tenure Systems and Their Role in Rural Development

Dispassionate analysis of land tenure systems and their role in rural development has been hampered by ideological conflict. Political rhetoric in North America and Western Europe reflecting a general hostility towards the Soviet Union has helped to create a widely held view that communal tenure systems invariably result in stagnation of production, inefficiency of resource allocation and coercion of the peasantry. Where they survive, communal systems are thought to do so partly because of large imports of food from the West and partly because of the existence of a tiny private sector which somehow manages to flourish despite attempts by governments to suppress it.

These claims may, of course, be true and we shall want to examine them below. Before doing so, however, it is important to recognise that there are many different kinds of communal land tenure systems and a great deal of experience has been gained in the operation of these systems from all over the globe. In twelve countries, accounting for nearly a third of the world's population, collective agriculture in one form or another can be said to be dominant. These twelve countries include the world's largest (China) and two of the smallest (Albania and Mongolia), one country which has had over 50 years of experience in running a collective system (the USSR) and one which has had less than half that time (Cuba). The full list of the twelve, ranked in descending order by size of population, is as follows: China,[1] the USSR,[2] Vietnam,[3] Romania, North Korea,[4] East Germany, Czechoslovakia, Hungary, Cuba,[5] Bulgaria, Albania and Mongolia.

In addition, there are many other countries which have a small collective sector in agriculture or where experiments have been tried or where it is government policy to encourage the development of a communal land system. These countries include Poland and Yugoslavia in Europe; Israel and Algeria in the Mediterranean basin;[6] Kampuchea and Laos in Asia; Mexico[7] and Nicaragua in Latin

America; and Tanzania,[8] Mozambique[9] and Ethiopia in Africa. We exclude from consideration countries where traditional forms of communal tenure continue to exist, as for example in parts of western and southern Africa, since these fall outside our purview. Even so, it is clear that interest in communal land tenure systems is widespread and possibly increasing.

This does not imply, of course, that the adoption of a communal tenure system is open to any country regardless of its political system. One must beware of the fallacy of eclecticism[10] in this as in other areas of social and economic policy. Regime types evidently must be taken into account whenever one analyses a land tenure system or land reform,[11] including of course a communal land system. All that we hope to have established at this point is that communal systems deserve careful study by scholars and should not be dismissed by economists and other specialists in development as unworthy of attention.

THE GROWTH OF PRODUCTION

Data on the average annual percentage rate of growth of agricultural output are presented in Table 3.1. The table contains data not only on the twelve countries where communal agriculture predominates but also on countries (or groups of countries) where individual tenure systems predominate. As indicated in the notes to the table, the period covered by the data is not the same in each country and hence caution must be exercised when drawing conclusions. Our objectives, however, are modest and the data certainly are good enough to test many commonly voiced propositions such as, for instance, that 'collective farming has proved to be the surest way of reducing agricultural production in many countries'.[12]

Let us begin by considering the data for the twelve countries which practise some form of collective agriculture. As can be seen, their growth performance varies widely. At one extreme is North Korea where the rate of growth since the middle of the 1960s has been 5.1 per cent a year, while at the other extreme is Mongolia where the rate of growth has been only 1.3 per cent. The unweighted average rate of growth of the twelve countries is 2.7 per cent a year. This compares with an annual rate of growth during 1960–81 of 1.5 per cent a year in what the World Bank calls the industrial market economies and 2.5 per cent in the 'other low-income countries', i.e. in low-income

Table 3.1 The Growth of Agricultural Production (per cent per annum)

Countries with communal tenure systems		*Countries with individual tenure systems*	
USSR	1.7	USA	1.1
East Germany	1.7	West Germany	1.4
Czechoslovakia	2.3	Belgium	0.1
Hungary	3.1	France	1.1
Bulgaria	1.4	Netherlands	3.4
Romania	3.7	United Kingdom	1.9
Albania	2.9	Italy	2.0
China	4.6	India	1.9
North Korea	5.1	South Korea	3.7
Vietnam	3.2	Other low-income countries	2.5
Cuba	2.1	Middle-income countries	3.2
Mongolia	1.3		

Notes: The periods covered are the following:
Romania and Hungary, 1960–81; China, 1950–81; all other countries with communal tenure systems, 1966–81; countries with individual tenure systems, 1960–80.
The category 'other low-income countries' includes countries with a per capita GNP of US$ 410 or less (at 1981 prices) other than China and India.

Sources: FAO, *Production Yearbooks*; IBRD, *World Development Report 1983* New York: Oxford University Press, 1983; and official Chinese sources.

countries other than India and China. Thus by international standards, agricultural growth rates in countries which have adopted communal land tenure systems appear to be high. Far from suffering from stagnation, our twelve countries have done relatively well.

This impression is confirmed when one compares similar countries or groups of countries, in one of which communal systems are the dominant form of land tenure while in the other, individual tenure systems dominate. The countries selected for comparison are listed on the right-hand side of Table 3.1.

The general pattern that emerges is fairly clear. Thus agriculture in China grew much faster than in India (4.6 versus 1.9 per cent); half again as fast in the Soviet Union as in the United States (1.7 versus 1.1 per cent); and half again as fast in our six Eastern European countries as in the six major Western European countries of France, UK, West Germany, Italy, Netherlands and Belgium (2.5 versus 1.7

per cent a year). Indeed not even South Korea, one of the four 'baby tigers' of the developing world, which enjoyed an agricultural growth rate of 3.7 per cent a year, could match North Korea's rate of 5.1 per cent.[13]

Within our group of twelve countries, the seven low- and middle-income countries grew significantly faster than the others. That is, the average rate of growth of agricultural production in Vietnam, China, Mongolia, Albania, North Korea, Cuba and Romania was 3.2 per cent a year whereas it was only 2.0 per cent a year in Bulgaria, Hungary, USSR, Czechoslovakia and East Germany. Evidently it cannot be claimed that communal land tenure systems are appropriate only in more advanced economies practising mechanised farming. If anything, the evidence suggests that the poorer the country, the better the growth performance is likely to be of its communal tenure system. In fact the rank correlation between per capita income and the rate of growth of agriculture in our twelve countries is –0.38.

On the whole, the larger countries appear at first glance to have done better than the smaller. That is, China, Vietnam, Romania and North Korea enjoyed noticeably faster rates of growth of agriculture than did Cuba, Bulgaria and Mongolia. There are exceptions of course: the Soviet Union, a large country, grew relatively slowly while Albania, a small country, grew slightly faster than average. The general tendency, however, is evident from the fact that when growth rates are weighted by size of population the average annual rate of growth rises from 2.8 to 4.0 per cent. China, however, with its huge population, obviously makes a big difference to the outcome of the calculation, and if one excludes China (thereby giving the Soviet Union a huge weight) the weighted average growth rate becomes less than the unweighted average (2.2 versus 2.6 per cent). It seems safe to conclude therefore that there seems to be no systematic tendency for large countries to enjoy faster growth rates than small.

THE GROWTH OF OUTPUT PER HEAD

Of course the growth of production is only half the story; the other half is the growth of population. If one focuses not on the rate of expansion of production unadjusted for population increase, but on the growth of output per head, the superiority of our twelve countries with communal land tenure systems becomes even more apparent. The reason for this is that in most cases the rate of demographic

Table 3.2 Population Growth Rates, 1960–81 (per cent per annum)

Countries with communal tenure systems		*Countries with individual tenure systems*	
USSR	1.1	USA	1.2
East Germany	−0.1	West Germany	0.5
Czechoslovakia	0.6	Belgium	0.4
Hungary	0.4	France	0.8
Bulgaria	0.7	Netherlands	1.1
Romania	0.9	United Kingdom	0.3
Albania	2.7	Italy	0.5
China	1.9	India	2.2
North Korea	2.8	South Korea	2.1
Vietnam	3.0	Other low-income countries	2.6
Cuba	1.6	Middle-income countries	2.5
Mongolia	3.0		

Notes: The figure for West Germany refers to 1960–70. The category 'other low-income countries' includes countries with a per capita GNP of US$ 410 or less (in 1981 prices) other than China and India.

Sources: IBRD, *World Development Report 1983*, New York: Oxford University Press, 1983.

expansion in our sample countries is slower than in similar countries where individual tenure predominates (see Table 3.2).

Thus in China during 1960–81 the population expanded by 1.9 per cent a year whereas in India it grew by 2.2 per cent; in consequence per capita agricultural production rose in China while in India it tended to fall about 0.3 per cent a year. Similarly, the population growth rate in the Soviet Union, is about 0.1 per cent per annum less than in the United States and as a result, per capita agricultural output per head has been rising slowly but steadily in the Soviet Union and (a fact not widely known) falling about 0.1 per cent a year in the United States (because of government policies to restrict output).

In the six Eastern European countries the population is growing marginally faster than in the six Western European countries with which we previously compared them, namely, 0.9 versus 0.6 per cent a year.[14] Even so, agricultural production per head is growing about

45 per cent faster in Eastern Europe (1.6 as compared to 1.1 per cent a year).

The population of North Korea is growing much faster than that of South Korea, namely, by 2.8 compared to 2.1 per cent a year. None the less, agricultural output per head appears to have grown much faster in the North than in the South (2.3 versus 1.6 per cent a year). Vietnam can perhaps best be compared with the average of the World Bank's 'low-income countries other than China and India'. If one does this it transpires that the population growth rate in Vietnam exceeds the average of other low-income countries (3.0 versus 2.6 per cent a year), but whereas output per head has increased by 0.2 per cent per year in Vietnam, it has fallen by 0.1 per cent on average in the other low-income countries.

Cuba and Mongolia are 'middle-income countries' and can be compared with them. The population growth rate in the middle-income countries is, on average, 2.5 per cent. This is faster than the rate in Cuba (1.6 per cent) but slower than the rate in Mongolia (3.0 per cent). Agricultural production per head, however, has increased by 0.7 per cent per annum in the middle-income countries and this is faster than in Cuba (0.5 per cent) or Mongolia (where indeed output per head has fallen sharply by 1.6 per cent a year).

In summary, during the period 1960–81, agricultural output per head fell by about 0.3 per cent a year in India and 0.1 per cent a year in the 'other low-income countries'. It rose by about 0.7 per cent a year in the 'middle-income countries' and by 0.6 per cent a year in the 19 industrial market economy countries. We cannot give an exactly comparable figure for our twelve countries with communal land tenure systems, but it is clear that on average they performed far better than any of the above. For example, for what it is worth, an unweighted average of our data suggests that agricultural output per head in the twelve countries increased by about 1.2 per cent a year during a broadly comparable period. No importance should be attached to any of the specific figures we have presented – the data are too crude for that – but there can be little doubt that whether measured in terms of the growth of production or in terms of the growth of output per head, agricultural performance in countries where communal tenure systems dominate has in general been significantly better than in countries where individual tenure systems dominate.

THE GROWTH OF LABOUR PRODUCTIVITY IN AGRICULTURE

Another possible indicator of performance is change over time in the productivity of labour in the agricultural sector. Unfortunately, however, we do not have direct measurements of labour productivity and the estimates of trends presented in Table 3.3 should be regarded as rough approximations only.

In the Soviet Union and Eastern Europe other than Albania, the agricultural labour force actually declined during the period 1960 to 1980. A similar phenomenon occurred in the United States and Western Europe. As a result, in both groups of countries the productivity of labour in the agricultural sector increased more rapidly than total output in the sector. The rise in labour productivity was broadly comparable in both sets of countries and was quite impressive. Hence there is nothing in these data to suggest that the performance of countries with communal tenure systems is inferior to those with individual tenure systems.

The same general conclusion is true of the underdeveloped countries. The productivity of the agricultural labour force in China grew much faster than in India, even if one uses an upward biased estimate of the rate of growth of the agricultural labour force in China and hence produces a downward biased estimate of the rate of growth of labour productivity in Chinese agriculture (see the notes to Table 3.3). North and South Korea performed equally well; Vietnam did better (again, even with a downward biased estimate of the growth of labour productivity) than the average of the 'other low-income countries' while Mongolia performed noticeably less well; Cuba out-performed the average of the 'middle-income countries' by a significant margin. Thus the record of the Third World countries with communal tenure systems does not compare unfavourably with the record of the other Third World countries, and in the case of China, North Korea and Cuba, labour productivity in the agricultural sector has increased much faster than in the typical underdeveloped country with an individual tenure system.

INTERNATIONAL TRADE IN AGRICULTURAL PRODUCTS

Despite the relatively good growth performance, it has often been claimed that the weakness of communal tenure systems can be seen by examining the figures on international trade. Some have gone so far as to argue that 'countries that were once food exporters tend to become food importers'.[15] That is, it is widely believed that countries which practise some form of collective agriculture have been forced to rely on massive imports of agricultural products to feed their population and satisfy domestic demand. This claim is not as simple as it seems and raises two issues, one of interpretation and another of fact.

First it is doubtful that a country's balance of trade in agricultural products can tell us anything useful about the effects of a country's land tenure system. For example, a trade surplus might reflect nothing more than planners' preferences, as embodied perhaps in a compulsory delivery scheme, rather than the virtues of a communal tenure system. Alternatively, a trade deficit in agricultural products could reflect a demand pattern with a high propensity to consume food, perhaps because socialist countries tend to have a more equal distribution of income and tend to place more emphasis on the satisfaction of basic needs. Conversely, a country may be a net exporter of foodstuffs while its population starves (as in nineteenth-century Ireland during the famine) or at times when the nutritional needs of a large section of the population are unmet (as in India today) or during periods when the per capita availability of food is declining (as in several African countries). Of course, a negative balance of trade in agricultural products could be due to unsatisfactory performance of the agricultural sector, but it could equally well be a reflection of the fact that the country in question has a comparative advantage in non-agricultural activities such as manufacturing. No one would be so foolish as to claim that the UK trade deficit in food is evidence of inefficiency in British agriculture, yet such claims often are made when it comes to countries where communal tenure systems dominate.[16] In general, the products a country exports and imports are far more likely to reflect its resource endowment and level of development than the strength or weakness of its land tenure system.

Second, even if one does not accept the point about comparative advantage, it simply is not correct to claim that countries with communal tenure systems must rely heavily on imports of agricultural products. This can readily be seen by inspecting the data in Table 3.4. The data refer to our twelve sample countries for the years 1981 and 1982 and cover all international trade in agriculture, fishing and forestry products.

Table 3.3 The Growth of the Agricultural Labour Force and Labour Productivity (per cent per annum)

	(1) *Total labour force, 1960–80*	(2) *Percentage of labour force in agriculture* *1960*	*1980*	(3) *Agricultural labour force, 1960–80*	(4) *Labour productivity in agriculture*
Countries with communal tenure systems:					
USSR	1.0	42	14	−2.4	4.1
East Germany	0.2	18	10	−1.9	3.6
Czechoslovakia	0.9	26	11	−2.1	4.4
Hungary	0.5	37	21	−2.2	5.3
Bulgaria	0.5	56	37	−1.2	2.6
Romania	0.8	67	29	−2.0	5.3
Albania	2.5	71	61	1.7	1.2
China	1.9*	n.a.	69	n.a.	2.7**
North Korea	2.6	62	49	1.1	4.0
Vietnam	1.9*	79***	71	n.a.	1.3**
Cuba	1.4	39	23	−1.0	3.1
Mongolia	2.3	70	55	1.0	0.3

Countries with individual tenure systems:					
USA	1.7	7	2	−2.3	3.4
West Germany	0.5	14	4	−2.7	4.1
Belgium	0.5	8	3	−2.5	2.6
France	0.9	22	8	−2.4	3.6
Netherlands	1.5	11	6	−1.2	4.6
United Kingdom	0.5	4	2	−2.1	4.0
Italy	0.3	31	11	−2.4	4.4
India	1.6	74	69	1.3	0.6
South Korea	2.9	66	34	−0.4	4.1
Other low-income countries	2.1	82	73	1.5	1.0
Middle-income countries	2.2	62	45	0.6	2.6

Notes: *The figure refers to 1970–80.
**Estimate obtained by subtracting the rate of growth of the total labour force from the rate of growth of agricultural output, and hence understates the rate of growth of labour productivity in agriculture.
***The figure refers to North Vietnam only.

Sources: Column (1): IBRD, *World Development Report 1982*; Column (2): IBRD, *World Development Report 1983*; and for North Vietnam, 1960, 'Report of the Central Census Commission Concerning the Result of the Census in the Whole North', *Nhan Dan*, 2 November 1960, p. 3; Column (3): inferred from columns (1) and (2); Column (4): Table 3.1 minus column (3).

Table 3.4 Balance of International Trade in Agricultural, Fishery and Forestry Products, 1981 and 1982 (US$ millions)

	1981	*1982*
USSR	−16 292.2	−14 585.0
East Germany	−1 934.1	−2 010.9
Czechoslovakia	−1 173.5	−1 060.5
Hungary	870.6	1 160.4
Bulgaria	312.0	682.5
Romania	199.2	513.1
Albania	14.0	15.4
China	−4 261.6	−4 420.0
North Korea	−117.8	−76.6
Vietnam	−207.6	−20.2
Cuba	3 155.0	2 564.4
Mongolia	97.4	96.6

Source: FAO, *Trade Yearbook 1982*, Vol. 36, Rome: 1983. The figures for China are estimates made by the FAO. It may be of interest to note that of the nine countries previously compared with the twelve above, five had a trade deficit in agricultural products (West Germany, Belgium, the UK, Italy and South Korea) and four a surplus (USA, France, Netherlands and India).

The first thing to note about Table 3.4 is that six out of the twelve countries had a positive balance of trade in agricultural products in 1981 and in 1982. These six countries were Hungary, Bulgaria, Romania, Albania, Cuba and Mongolia. Thus they covered three continents (Europe, Asia and Latin America) and included both poor countries and rich. Since these countries were net exporters of foodstuffs, the criticism of food import dependence clearly cannot be applied to them. This leaves us with the six countries which are net importers of agricultural products.

The next thing to note about the table is that two thirds of the countries with a negative trade balance in agriculture are highly industrialised. In Czechoslovakia, 75 per cent of net material product originates in industry; in East Germany 70 per cent; and in the Soviet Union 62 per cent.[17] One cannot be so precise for North Korea, but it is well known that prior to partition agriculture predominated in the southern part of the country while industry was located largely in the north. One estimate suggests that already by 1970 industry accounted for 74 per cent of North Korea's national product.[18] In each of these four countries, hence, it is hardly surprising that there are net imports of agricultural products. The composition of aggregate output strongly suggests that these countries should have a comparative advantage in the export of manufactured goods and consequently should import foodstuffs and some raw materials. If this view is accepted, it follows that nothing can be inferred from the trade figures about the performance of their communal tenure system.

Vietnam, one of the remaining two countries with a negative balance of trade in agricultural products, obviously is a special case. Its economy has been so badly disrupted by war that it is impossible to tell whether the present trading pattern will persist or not. Vietnam certainly was once a net exporter of rice and it may well become so again – the tendency for gross imports of agricultural products gradually to decline is encouraging – but for the time being the picture remains unclear. All one can say is that the latest figures (for 1982) are encouraging.

Finally, there is China. In general, foreign trade turnover accounts for only about 10 per cent of China's GNP. The country is basically self-sufficient in food, fuel and manufactured consumer goods. Until 1976 the country had an export surplus in agricultural, fishery and forestry products, but since then the balance of trade in those products has become negative. The major reason for this is the abrupt change in the composition of China's exports that occurred between 1970 and 1975 when China first became a significant supplier of petroleum. (A similar transformation occurred in Nigeria in roughly the same period.) A subsidiary reason may be a rise in the volume of food imports and fall in food exports on response to government measures to raise real incomes and consumption of both peasants and workers.

In 1970 fuels accounted for only 1 per cent of China's exports; by 1975 they accounted for 14 per cent and the proportion continued to rise steadily so that by 1980 they accounted for 22 per cent. That is, between 1970 and 1980 the share of fuels in China's total exports increased by 21 percentage points. The opposite occurred with regard to exports of food and raw materials other than fuel. In 1970 these products (SITC 0, 1 and 2) accounted for 48 per cent of China's total exports whereas by 1980 they accounted for only 27 per cent, a fall of exactly 21 percentage points. In other words, during the decade of the 1970s China reduced substantially her dependence on exports of food and raw materials other than fuel.

Turning to imports, it is noteworthy that something broadly similar has been happening here as well. There has been a gradual tendency for the share of foodstuffs in total imports to fall and for the share of machinery to rise. Thus between 1970 and 1980 imports of machinery (SITC 7) rose from 15 to 28 per cent of the total while imports of food (SITC 0 and 1) declined from 19 to 14 per cent of the total. That is, during the decade of the 1970s China actually reduced her dependence on imported food (while increasing her dependence on imported machinery).

Thus the data for China in Table 3.4 can be quite misleading. The negative trade balance in agricultural, fishery and forestry products is due to a change in the country's comparative advantage as reflected in a changed composition of both exports and imports; it has nothing to do with an alleged inability of the country to feed itself. Indeed, net international trade in food represents a tiny fraction of China's total trade[19] and, more important, of domestic food consumption.

RESOURCE UTILISATION AND ALLOCATIVE EFFICIENCY

A general criticism made of communal land tenure systems is that they tend to be inefficient. Some writers seem to believe that communal tenure is an inherently inefficient way of organising rural development and that collective agriculture must inevitably result in a waste of resources. This, however, is clearly wrong. As the respected American agricultural economist D. Gale Johnson has stated, 'It now seems quite evident that any form of land tenure can be made efficient.'[20] Indeed, as he says, 'in terms of efficiency, it makes little difference whether the land is owned by the state (all of the people), by the members of collective farms or by private persons, either as landlords or operators.'[21] Recent research has clearly demonstrated that there can be no *a priori* presumption that one form of tenure system is more efficient than all others.

This being so, the issue comes down to the actual practice of collective agriculture in the countries which have adopted this system. The evaluation of historical experience, however, is never as conclusive as the results of an exercise in theory and, hence, judgement inescapably influences one's assessment. This judgement, moreover, is based not only on what one knows about the behaviour of a particular system over time but also on how it compares with other systems, in our case with individual tenure systems. There can be little doubt that there is considerable inefficiency in countries which have adopted individual tenure systems. In Western Europe and

North America, farming is heavily subsidised, an excessive amount of resources has been allocated to agriculture and, despite attempts by governments to restrain output through acreage controls, there are large production surpluses combined with relatively high food prices for consumers. In Third World countries with individual land tenure systems the problems are rather different. In many cases the internal terms of trade have been turned deliberately against agriculture.[22] Within the agricultural sector, factor markets function far from perfectly,[23] access to government-provided services such as technical assistance is very uneven[24] and as a result there often are large differences in productivity across farm sizes.[25]

There are analogous problems in the countries which have communal land systems. Farm prices often have been kept low in order to provide cheap food for the urban population. Decision-making sometimes is highly centralised – as in the USSR, East Germany, Czechoslovakia and Bulgaria – and this has introduced unnecessary rigidity into the sector. Frequently, communal systems have been built on the assumption that there are economies of large scale in agriculture and that efficiency can be increased through mechanised operations on large fields.[26] The Russian system in particular appears to have been built on this assumption, yet there is little empirical evidence to support it.

More generally, it is widely believed that there are economic advantages in conducting field operations collectively, i.e. ploughing, sowing, weeding and harvesting. The system used in Tanzania's *ujamaa* villages, for instance, to the extent that it is not derived entirely from ideological preferences, seems implicitly to be based on this belief, yet there is no evidence that this assumption is correct and lots of evidence that peasants tend to resist this variant of collective cultivation. Be that as it may, in countries where emphasis is placed on large-scale collective farming there is a problem about the composition of output. The reason for this is that some crops lend themselves more readily to this method of production than do others. Wheat and cotton growing, sheep and cattle ranching, tea and coffee plantations are examples of activities which can be undertaken efficiently on a large scale. More difficult, given the existing known technology and the resource endowments of most poor countries, are such things as rice cultivation, pig raising, horticulture and the management of soft-fruit orchards.

This problem of the appropriate scale of production can be overcome by creating an institutional hierarchy within the collective system whereby those activities which benefit from economies of scale are undertaken at the collective (or commune) level and those which are best done on a small scale are assigned to individual households or to groups of households (e.g. in China until recently, to production teams). It is misleading to think of communal systems as necessarily being institutionally homogeneous. In fact in most systems the household economy and its private sector form an integral part of the communal land tenure system.[27] The private sector should not be regarded as a residual vestige of an earlier individual tenure system, that perhaps is tolerated only reluctantly, but as an essential component of an efficient communal system. The private sector is largely complementary to the collective sector: it absorbs labour that could not otherwise be employed; it occupies a relatively small amount of land to grow products that are of great value and which require great care; it engages in small-scale livestock and poultry raising; and it produces handicrafts and other articles using labour-intensive methods of production.

A well organised communal system, with a flexibly designed institutional hierarchy, should in principle be more efficient than the individual tenure systems one actually encounters in most Third World countries. One particular advantage of a communal system is that it can ensure that resources are fully utilised, that is, that every scrap of land is cultivated, that irrigation water is allocated efficiently and, above all, that labour is fully employed. Of course not all communal systems have in practice achieved this ideal, but the potential is there and at least one country has had some success in translating this potential advantage into concrete reality.[28]

One characteristic of all communal land tenure systems is that they are intensive in their use of management skills. Collective farming, narrowly defined, requires skilled management because important decisions have to be made about the allocation of labour among various tasks, the optimal timing of agricultural operations and the appropriate use of heterogeneous pieces of land. Decentralising decision-making to the level at which economies of scale are exhausted obviously will help, but even if this is done a scarcity of good managers is likely to be a problem.

If decentralisation takes the form of dividing the communally owned land between a private and a collective sector, as it does in the great majority of communal systems, a further problem is raised about the optimal allocation of labour between the private plot or field and the collective field. It is commonly observed that a disproportionate amount of agricultural labour is devoted to the private sector and too little to the collective sector, with the result that yields are much higher in the private sector than in the collective sector, while the productivity of labour is much higher in the collective sector than in the private. The phenomenon is analogous to one noted earlier in countries with individual tenure systems, namely, a tendency for there to be large differences in productivity of land and labour across farm sizes. This source of allocative inefficiency is not easy to eliminate, although the introduction of the 'production responsibility system' in China and other economic reforms can be regarded as an attempt to achieve this.

A related managerial problem of communal systems is labour incentives in the collective sector. The task is to devise a set of work incentives to ensure that everyone contributes the right quantity and quality of effort. This is a problem which, of course, is common to any organisation larger than the single person enterprise – and is known in the economics literature as the free rider issue – but it is especially important in communal systems because members cannot normally be fired for poor performance. No general solution to this problem has been found in either capitalist or socialist enterprises: both rely on a changing blend of monetary rewards, non-material incentives and commands, and both never seem to achieve more than a partial success. If the individual tenure systems have sharper material incentives, this may be because they are more tolerant of inequality and unemployment. If the communal tenure systems are more successful in eliminating extreme forms or poverty, this may be because they are more willing to use commands and restrict so-called bourgeois freedoms.

Yet another, and very important, managerial problem arises from the fact that by their very nature communal systems are multipurpose development institutions. They often combine (i) the functions of local government, e.g. local policing and the administration of justice; (ii) the provision of social services, and in particular health and elementary education services; (iii) the development of industry and other non-agricultural rural activities; and (iv) responsibility for ensuring a high rate of saving and capital accumulation and an efficient pattern of investment. These numerous and very different tasks undoubtedly place severe demands on the limited supplies of managerial ability. At the same time, it is likely that any alternative system designed to achieve the same results would be at least as demanding of managerial skills as are communal systems. For example, a rural development strategy based on small peasant farms and individual land tenure will be highly intensive in its use of management skills and, moreover, because these skills will have to be supplied by government rather than by the commune or collective, they are likely to be much more costly. Hence, in the majority of cases the true alternative to the communal system is likely to be not less management but less development.

TENURE SYSTEMS AND COMPREHENSIVE RURAL DEVELOPMENT

This, of course, is the ultimate test. Do communal land tenure systems possess advantages which individual tenure systems lack when it comes to promoting all-round economic, social and political development in rural areas? Alas, there is no unambiguous answer to this question since objectives vary from one country to another and any particular objective can almost always be achieved in more than one way. Nevertheless, communal systems are characterised by a set of features which makes them attractive to those concerned with combining sustained growth of output, the alleviation of poverty, the provision of basic needs and the creation of an egalitarian society. The adoption of a communal land tenure system does not guarantee that any of these objectives will be attained, but it does make their attainment somewhat easier.

First, as we have seen, it is possible within a collective system to ensure that labour is fully employed. In much of the Third World seasonal unemployment is common and it is widely believed that much labour is 'surplus' to the needs of production. In countries with communal tenure systems, in contrast, labour tends to be largely a fixed cost – its marginal cost to the collective certainly is low, even if not zero – and consequently it 'pays' the collective to employ labour even on projects which have a low rate of return. As a result, output is higher and poverty lower than would otherwise be the case. Second, the distribution of income in rural areas tends to be more equal in countries where communal systems predominate than in countries where individual tenure is the rule. The reason for this is that in communal systems there is little or no income from property – there is only income from labour – and hence a major source of inequality no longer exists. The combination of a higher level of output and a more equitable distribution of income can make an enormous difference in reducing the extent of malnutrition and acute

Table 3.5 Capital Accumulation in Hebei Province, 1962–78

	Collective accumulation as a percentage of net collective income	*Collective accumulation per capita* (yuan)
1962	7	3.3
1965	12	7.0
1970	14	9.9
1973	18	13.6
1977	21	15.4
1978	19	18.0

Source: M. S. Marshall, Jr, 'Institutional Transformation and Economic Growth in Rural China', D. Phil. thesis, Oxford, 1982, Table 7.10, p. 257.

poverty in a low-income country. Furthermore, communal tenure systems have an advantage over small-scale, egalitarian, individual peasant farming systems in that they are more likely to be successful in preventing inequalities from reappearing once the land reform has been completed. That is, communal tenure systems not only create equality, they also tend to perpetuate it.[29]

Third, communal systems contain a high potential for capital accumulation. In the early stages of rural development a high level of investment can most easily be achieved by mobilising labour with low opportunity costs for capital construction projects. In this case investment is 'financed' not by reducing current consumption but by reducing leisure. In the later stages of development investment can be financed by allocating a portion of collective income to a collective accumulation fund. Given a measure of collective self-discipline, the annual flow of funds into investment can rapidly become a significant proportion of total collective income. In fact it is this feature of communal systems which accounts for the relatively rapid rates of growth they have enjoyed.

In Hebei province, China, for example, the rate of savings and investment on the communes rose very rapidly during the period 1962–78. At the beginning of the period collective accumulation accounted for only 7 per cent of net collective income, the rest being distributed to commune members for consumption. By the end of the period, however, the rate of accumulation had increased nearly three times, to about 19 per cent of net collective income, and accumulation per capita had risen from 3.3 yuan to 18 yuan (see Table 3.5).

Some governments, however, give high priority to urban development and particularly to promoting the expansion of heavy industry. Where this occurs, they are able through compulsory delivery schemes to extract a marketable surplus of food from collectives to feed the urban population. Some analysts regard this as an important advantage of collective agriculture, and it certainly was important historically in the Soviet Union; but it obscures an even more important advantage of a communal system, namely, that it provides a framework for industrialising the countryside and thereby diversifying the rural economy. In contrast to most Third World countries, where the level of rural industrialisation is low and its geographical distribution is very uneven, manufacturing activities are widely spread in countries where communal systems dominate, and income from manufacturing and construction often accounts for a substantial part of the total income of many rural households. This is a fourth advantage of communal systems of considerable significance.

In the majority of Third World countries the public administration is highly centralised and bureaucratic, expensive in relation to available resources and ill-suited to reaching those in poverty, particularly the poor who inhabit the rural areas.[30] As a result there are few social services available in the coutryside and such services as do exist tend to be concentrated in the relatively more prosperous regions and to be monopolised by the better-off households in those regions. Some of these tendencies can be counteracted by devolving responsibility for the provision of basic services to the local community, encouraging a high degree of participation by local people in the organisation and running of social services and by constructing strong linkages between the grass-roots organisations and higher levels of administration. It is one of the virtues of a communal system that it provides an institutional framework in which this can be done.

This fifth feature helps to explain why countries which have adopted communal tenure systems seem to have done so much better than most other countries in meeting the basic needs of their population and distributing public services in an equitable way. Communal systems are well designed to assist in the administration of health and nutrition programmes, to deliver potable water and basic sanitation facilities, to promote family planning programmes, to provide primary and secondary education and to assist those in need in their old age.

The data in Table 3.6 illustrate this, although in each case they refer to the nation as a whole and not just to the rural population. Even so, they suggest that in practice the seven underdeveloped

Table 3.6 Health, Education and Life Expectancy

*Country**	*Infant mortality rate (aged 0–1), 1981*	*Population per nursing person, 1980*	*Adult literacy, 1980* (%)	*Secondary school enrolment, 1980* (% of age group)	*Life expectancy at birth, 1981* (years)
Vietnam	97	2930	87	48	63
China	71	1890	69	34	67
Mongolia	53	240	95**	89	64
Albania	48+	310	n.a.	63	70
North Korea	33	n.a.	n.a.	n.a.	66
Cuba	19	360	95	71	73
Romania	29	270	98	75	71
Low-income countries	99	4668	52	29	58
Middle-income countries	81	1769	65	39	60

Notes: * Countries are ranked by level of GNP per capita. The 'low-income countries' include Vietnam and China while the 'middle-income' countries include the other five in our list.
** The data refer to 1960.
+The data refer to 1980.

Source: IBRD, *World Development Report 1983*, New York: Oxford University Press, 1983.

countries in our sample of twelve have a superior record to the average Third World country in reducing the infant mortality rate, providing basic health services (as measured by population per nursing person), ensuring basic literacy, providing a secondary education and enabling people to enjoy a long life. These are advantages which deserve careful consideration when assessing the role of communal land tenure systems in promoting rural development.

Finally, communal systems provide an institutional framework for local participation in political affairs. The average peasant family living on a Chinese commune, say, has a much bigger voice in local affairs than does the typical landless labourer, tenant or small peasant farmer in, say, Pakistan or Bangladesh. Indeed, in most Third World countries the mass of the rural population is oppressed by local landlords and their allies in government and they have no effective political influence at the local level. They might or might not have a vote in national elections, depending on whether the government is a dictatorship (as was the case until recently in the Philippines) or a democracy (as in India), but their power to alter matters which most directly impinge upon their daily lives is negligible.

The macro-political regimes in countries where communal land tenure systems predominate are authoritarian and are no more desirable to a liberal than authoritarian regimes in countries where individual tenure systems prevail. From the point of view of the rural population, however, the former have been successful in greatly reducing 'the day-to-day repression of "normal" society' [31] and in virtually eliminating the overt violence directed against the peasantry that is a commonplace elsewhere in the Third World.

There is little truth in the proposition that peasants invariably oppose communal systems and must be coerced into accepting them. There was of course coercion in the Soviet Union in the 1930s at the time of collectivisation and it is from that period that communal systems have been associated in the West with rural terror and violence. The objective of the Soviet government, however, was not to promote rural development but to squeeze wage goods out of the countryside to supply the cities and to finance a huge defence expenditure programme. The peasants predictably resisted fiercely. In Eastern Europe conditions were very different and the Russian example was not followed. For a start, the tempo of collectivisation was slower; indeed it was a fairly gradual process, lasting several years or even a decade. In Hungary, for example, collectivisation began in 1949 and, because of peasant resistance, was not completed until 1962. Furthermore, in Eastern Europe there was less pressure from the central government to collectivise and in Poland and Yugoslavia most of the cooperatives were dissolved because of resistance from the peasantry. In Hungary collectivisation came to a halt between 1953 and 1955 and 500 collectives were actually disbanded. Landowners throughout Eastern Europe were of course dispossessed but there was no significant 'liquidation of kulaks' and in fact the majority of the landowners were subsequently employed in the collective sector. The landless joined the collectives voluntarily although many of the more prosperous peasants did not. Today, however, there is little evidence that the rural population of Eastern Europe is hostile to communal land tenure systems although there is abundant evidence that they (and their urban fellow citizens) are hostile toward their Russian overlords.

In Cuba the land reforms of 1959 and 1963 were very popular and there 'seems to have been no move among the agricultural labour force for dividing the land of the estates into separate, small units'.[32] The North Korean land reform of 1946, which created small peasant holdings, was carried out with popular support and mass participation and has been described as the fastest and most peaceful land reform of any post-revolutionary society in Asia or Europe.[33] Collectivisation was carried out between 1953 and 1958, i.e. not until after the Korean War, and was a response to the problems caused by the devastation and heavy loss of life (particularly among adult males) that occurred during the war. Indeed 'the war had anyway caused a kind of co-operative agriculture to be introduced'[34] and it was not difficult to obtain the consent of the peasantry to build on this foundation. Finally, in China the commune system was created by a government which came to power as a result of a peasant revolution. The major objective of the system in China has always been rural betterment and it would be very difficult to argue that the commune system as it has evolved in that vast country does not enjoy the support of the great majority of the rural population.[35] The present shift towards assigning responsibility to households for cultivating collectively-owned land should not be interpreted as a rejection of communal land tenure systems in general.

Thus the claim that communal tenure systems always are resisted by the peasantry and hence always entail massive coercion will not stand up to even cursory examination. It is true, of course, that the agrarian reforms leading to the establishment of communal systems have been no less violent than other types of land reform, and the losers naturally have resisted whenever they could, but it would be wrong to argue that landless workers and small peasants, who were the intended beneficiaries of the reforms, have resisted communal systems where they would have welcomed an individual tenure system. Indeed in countries where they are well established it appears that communal systems are accepted largely without question and are recognised as having contributed to rural development. Increasingly this is recognised in other countries too, and many governments in the Third World have responded by attempting to create islands of communal production in a sea of individual tenure. Alas, however, historical experience does not augur well for the success of these attempts.

More often than not in such cases, the communal sector is starved of resources, denied credit and technical assistance, and confined to inhospitable terrain. It is subjected to continuous political harassment by the defenders of individual tenure and given little chance to develop within a favourable environment. Either its growth is nipped in the bud or it is forced to endure a lingering and painful death. Examples of the latter include the collective *ejido* in Mexico, and of the former the *asentamiento* in Chile. On occasion a communal system has been implanted in part of the agricultural sector and has brought measurable gains to its members. Where this has occurred there is a danger that the members of the collective will become a new vested interest and will try to prevent other sections of the rural population from acquiring the benefits of membership. This happened, for instance, on the workers' self-managed farms (*unités d'autogestion*) in Algeria and on the *asentamientos* in Chile until they were destroyed in General Pinochet's counter-revolution.

Thus the problem small communal systems face is how to avoid becoming either an endangered species or a privileged minority. Few countries have solved this problem. In most instances, but certainly not in all, peaceful coexistence is unlikely to be viable in the long run and a choice will have to be made between a communal or individual tenure system. It would be idle to pretend that such a choice is straightforward, or that one system is clearly superior to the other. In fact, in principle, both systems are capable of achieving the same results. Guatemala, for example, has achieved a rapid rate of growth of agricultural output; Brazil has enjoyed a high rate of growth of agricultural income per head; Taiwan has been remarkably successful in industrialising the countryside and diversifying sources of income in rural areas; Sri Lanka has an enviable record in delivering social services in rural areas and ensuring that the basic needs of her people are satisfied; and after the land reform, South Korea appears to have achieved an equitable distribution of income in the countryside. These are all countries where individual land tenure dominates.

Communal systems have two things working in their favour, however, which make them an attractive instrument for rural development. First, the system brings together many desirable features under a single institutional framework. This makes it possible, once the system is established and functioning properly, to combine sustained rapid growth of agricultural production, rural industrialisation, rising per capita consumption, a high rate of investment, an equal distribution of income, the provision of essential social services and a high degree of participation in local affairs. It is the combination of all these things, rather than marked superiority in achieving any one particular objective, that makes communal systems worth considering seriously.

Secondly, the performance of communal systems in attaining each of the objectives mentioned above is better than the average performance in countries where individual tenure systems prevail. It is not the case that communal systems perform better in some respects and worse in others; they perform better in all respects. Thus there is no need to sacrifice one goal to achieve another. Of course the performance of the communal system in a particular country may be inferior to the average performance of countries where individual tenure systems dominate. Similarly, the performance of the individual tenure system in a particular country may be superior to the average performance of countries where communal systems dominate. In general, however, communal systems have done better than individual tenure systems. Hence, in terms of probabilities of success, the communal land tenure system is the better vehicle for promoting rural development.

Critics of this view could argue that the achievements cited should be attributed not to communal land tenure systems narrowly defined but to a comprehensive set of socialist agricultural policies of which communal tenure forms only a part. Rapid accumulation, for example, may be due to a system of centrally planned savings, and this may require communal tenure as a precondition, but a high rate of investment does not spring from communal tenure automatically. Similarly, the achievements in health, education and welfare may reflect not sectoral but national social and economic priorities, and communal structures may simply be a vehicle for implementing these policies. While this argument is true as far as it goes, it stops short of the central point, which is that it is misleading to separate communal systems from their wider context. Policies necessarily are interrelated and when examining a set of policies and institutions the question is whether or not they are coherent and reinforce one another. The evidence that we have assembled in this chapter suggests that in countries in which communal systems are dominant, institutional arrangements and government policies in practice have tended to be coherent. The result has been a considerable improvement in the well-being of the rural population.

Notes

1. The commune system in China is undergoing rapid change. For a recent analysis see Keith Griffin (ed.), *Institutional Reform and Economic Development in the Chinese Countryside*, London: Macmillan, 1984.
2. Much of the controversy surrounding Soviet agriculture originated during the period of collectivisation during the early 1930s. A good discussion is contained in Alec Nove, *An Economic History of the USSR*, Harmondsworth: Penguin 1969, Ch. 7. For an analysis of the role of collective farming in the development of an economically backward part of the Soviet Union see Azizur Rahman Khan and Dharam Ghai, *Collective Agriculture and Rural Development in Soviet Central Asia*, London: Macmillan, 1979.
3. Very little is known about collective agriculture in Vietnam. See, however, Nguyen Huu Dong, 'Collective and Family Agriculture in Socialist Economies', IDS *Bulletin*, vol. 13, no. 4, September 1982.
4. The best study is Joseph Sang-hoon Chung, *The North Korean Economy: Structure and Development*, Stanford: Hoover Institution Press, 1974.
5. See Arthur MacEwan, 'Cuban Agriculture and Development: Contradictions and Progress', in Dharam Ghai *et al.* (eds), *Agrarian Systems and Rural Development*, London: Macmillan, 1979.
6. For a discussion of the attempt in Algeria to establish workers' self-managed farms see Keith Griffin, *Land Concentration and Rural Poverty*, 2nd edn, London: Macmillan, 1981, Ch. 1. On Israel see Haim Barkai, *Growth Patterns of the Kibbutz Economy*, Amsterdam: North Holland Publishing, 1977 and Yehuda Don, 'Dynamics of Development in the Israeli Kibbutz', in Peter Dorner (ed.), *Co-operative and Commune: Group Farming in the Economic Development of Agriculture*, Madison: University of Wisconsin Press, 1977.
7. There is a large literature on the Mexican *ejido*. One excellent study that is often overlooked, however, is Cynthia Hewitt de Alcantara, *Modernizing Mexican Agriculture: Socioeconomic Implications of Technological Change 1940–1970*, Geneva: UNRISD, 1976, Ch. V.

8. See Dharam Ghai and Reginald Herbold Green, 'Ujaama and Villagisation in Tanzania', in Ghai *et al.* (eds), *Agrarian Systems and Rural Development.*
9. See R. K. Srivastava and I. Livingstone, 'Growth and Distribution: The Case of Mozambique', in Dharam Ghai and Samir Radwan (eds), *Agrarian Policies and Rural Poverty in Africa*, Geneva: ILO, 1983.
10. Keith Griffin, *The Political Economy of Agrarian Change*, 2nd edn, London: Macmillan, 1979, Ch. 8. The phrase was coined originally by Marshall Wolfe.
11. For an excellent example of how this should be done see Alain de Janvry, *The Agrarian Question and Reformism in Latin America*, Baltimore: Johns Hopkins University Press, 1981. An early attempt at a comparative analysis is Jack Dunman, *Agriculture: Capitalist and Socialist*, London: Lawrence and Wishart, 1975; see especially the chapters on the GDR (Ch. 4), Poland (Ch. 5), Hungary (Ch. 6) and Yugoslavia (Ch. 7). Z. Kozlowski argues that agricultural growth in Eastern Europe has been relatively slow given the very rapid rate of growth of industry, and this has resulted in a chronic disequilibrium between supply and demand for foodstuffs. See his 'Agriculture in the Economic Growth of the East European Socialist Countries', in Lloyd Reynolds (ed.), *Agriculture in Development Theory*, New Haven: Yale University Press, 1975.
12. Doreen Warriner, *Land Reform in Principle and Practice*, Oxford University Press, 1969, p. 67.
13. The other three 'baby tigers' are Hong Kong, Singapore and Taiwan.
14. These are unweighted averages and the figure for Eastern Europe is strongly influenced by Albania where the population is growing by about 2.7 per cent a year.
15. Lloyd G. Reynolds, *Image and Reality in Economic Development*, New Haven: Yale University Press, 1977, p. 400.
16. Conversely, few people claim that Poland's deficit in agricultural trade indicates the weakness of individual tenure systems. Yet of the seven largest importers of cereals, five are countries with individual tenure systems (Japan, Italy, Poland, UK and Brazil) and two are countries with communal tenure systems (USSR and China).
17. See IBRD, *World Development Report 1982*, New York: Oxford University Press, 1982. The figures in the text refer to 1980.
18. Jon Halliday, 'The North Korean Model: Gaps and Questions', *World Development*, September/October 1981, p. 894.
19. The value of food (SITC 0,1) as a percentage of total exports and imports was as follows:

	Exports	*Imports*
1966	31	27
1970	29	19
1975	30	12
1980	18	14

20. D. Gale Johnson, 'Agriculture in the Centrally Planned Economies',

American Journal of Agricultural Economics, December 1982, p. 845.
21. Ibid. There is a large literature on the theory of collective enterprise. For recent contributions see Louis Putterman, 'Voluntary Collectivization: A Model of Producers' Institutional Choice', *Journal of Comparative Economics*, vol. 4, June 1980 and Louis Putterman, 'On Optimality of Collective Institutional Choice', *Journal of Comparative Economics*, vol. 5, December 1981.
22. See, for example, Michael Lipton, *Why Poor People Stay Poor: Urban Bias in World Development*, London: Temple Smith, 1977 and I.M.D. Little, *Economic Development: Theory, Policy and International Relations*, New York: Basic Books, 1982, pp. 160–1. Recently, however, it has been argued that relative food prices have increased and this has led to the further impoverishment of landless labourers and small peasants who are net buyers of foodgrains. See the paper by K. Griffin and A. K. Ghose reprinted in Griffin, *Land Concentration and Rural Poverty*, Ch. 8.
23. Griffin, *The Political Economy of Agrarian Change*.
24. See, for example, the special issue of *Development and Change*, vol. VI, no. 2, 1975.
25. R. Albert Berry and William R. Cline, *Agrarian Structure and Productivity in Developing Countries*, Baltimore: Johns Hopkins University Press, 1979.
26. Michael Ellman, 'Agricultural Productivity Under Socialism', *World Development*, September/October 1981. Even if one agrees that given the factor proportions prevailing in most Third World countries, the economies of scale in crop cultivation are limited, a communal system may be able to exploit economies of scale in marketing output, purchasing material inputs, acquiring technical knowledge and, as we argue later, managing rural development. In addition, large units may be able to spread risks by diversifying output, assuming the collective is large enough to contain a variety of soil types and growing conditions.
27. See Griffin (ed.), *Institutional Reform and Economic Development in the Chinese Countryside*, Ch. 2.
28. See Keith Griffin, *International Inequality and National Poverty*, London: Macmillan, 1978, Ch. 9 on 'Efficiency, Equality and Accumulation in Rural China: Notes on the Chinese System of Incentives'; and Thomas G. Rawski, *Economic Growth and Employment in China*, Oxford University Press, 1979, Ch. 4.
29. Louis Putterman, 'A Modified Collective Agriculture in Rural Growth-with-Equity: Reconsidering the Private, Unimodal Solution', *World Development*, February 1983.
30. See Keith Griffin and Jeffrey James, *The Transition to Egalitarian Development*, London: Macmillan, 1981, Ch. 5; Norman T. Uphoff and Milton J. Esman, *Local Organization for Rural Development: Analysis of Asian Experience*, Ithaca: Cornell University, Rural Development Committee, 1974.
31. Barrington Moore, Jr, *Social Origins of Dictatorship and Democracy: Lord and Peasant in the Making of the Modern World*, Harmondsworth Penguin, 1967, p. 505. Professor Ken Post of the Institute of Social Studies in The Hague has suggested that one advantage of collective

systems is that the peasantry sometimes can use them to protect themselves against the state.

32. MacEwan, 'Cuban Agriculture and Development', p. 333.
33. Halliday, 'The North Korean Model', p. 890.
34. Ibid. p. 893. It is ironical that the first agrarian reform in North Korea was a Jeffersonian redistributive reform carried out during the Russian occupation, whereas the second reform consisted of socialist collectivisation and was carried out in response to the suffering inflicted by the Americans during the Korean War.
35. This does not imply that every reform in post-liberation rural China has enjoyed the support of the peasantry or that every reform has led to rural betterment. The Great Leap Forward and the accompanying disasters and starvation are examples of what can happen when things go wrong. It does not follow, however, that such errors are intrinsic to communal tenure systems or that events would have been less disastrous if no attempt had been made to introduce communal land reforms.

4 The Chinese Economy after Mao

Chairman Mao died in September 1976, and with his death an era in Chinese and world history came to an end. Nearly a quarter of mankind was directly affected by Mao's politics, and in this sense he undoubtedly was the greatest revolutionary leader of this or any other century. He was also the architect of a distinctive strategy of socialist economic development. Yet within two or three years of his death China embarked upon a major series of economic reforms which, if implemented in full, will profoundly alter the way the Chinese economy functions. Indeed the reforms currently under discussion, when combined with those that have already been introduced, are far more radical than anything previously even considered, let alone implemented, in any other communist country. These reforms are the subject of this chapter.

But first it is necessary to put the country into perspective. China is by far the world's largest underdeveloped country. The recent census revealed that there are over a thousand million Chinese living on the mainland. This is half again as large as India, the next most populous country, and it is nearly double the size of the other 31 lowest-income underdeveloped countries. In global terms, nearly a quarter of mankind lives in the People's Republic of China.

According to conventional measures of national income, China is also one of the poorest countries on earth, having an average income per head comparable to that of India and Pakistan but significantly lower than that of Indonesia, Nigeria or Brazil. As we shall see, however, there are indications that China has done much better than most other Third World countries in alleviating the worst forms of poverty.

China is, of course, a socialist country. All large enterprises belong to the state, agricultural land is collectively owned, private property in productive assets is of relatively little significance, and the provision of many basic needs – including food, shelter, health and education – is largely the responsibility of the state. Some of these features currently are being modified – and we shall consider whether these modifications signal an end to socialism in China – but it is evident that the Chinese economy is organised on principles very different from our own.

How well has this economy performed? Let us begin with growth and accumulation and focus on the period between 1970 and 1982.[1] During that period China's domestic product grew by 5.6 per cent a year. This exceeds by a considerable margin the rate of growth achieved in India and the other low-income countries and is about the same rate of growth as in the middle-income countries.[2]

What is true of aggregate output is true also of the two most important sectors of agriculture and industry. Chinese agriculture grew by 2.8 per cent a year, half a percentage point faster than the low-income economies as a whole and nearly as fast as the growth in middle-income countries. As a result, food production per head in China was 24 per cent higher at the end of the period than at the beginning, compared to 1 per cent higher in India, minus 3 per cent in the other low-income countries, and 11 per cent in the middle-income countries.[3]

In industry, China grew nearly twice as fast as India, more than twice as fast as the other low-income countries and 43 per cent faster than the middle-income countries. Thus the growth performance in China compares very favourably with the rest of the Third World.

Reasons are not hard to find. First, China devotes a larger share of its domestic product to investment than other underdeveloped countries. For example, in 1982 the percentage investment rate was 28 per cent in China, 25 per cent in India and 13 per cent in the other low-income countries. Secondly, the rate of growth of investment in China is high; in fact it is much higher than in the other low-income countries and not much below the rate currently achieved in the middle-income countries.

Not only has production increased more rapidly in China than in most other Third World countries, but the population has increased significantly *less* rapidly than the average. As a result, output per head has tended to rise much faster in China than elsewhere. The recent census indicates that the rate of demographic expansion in China is about 1.5 per cent a year and is projected to fall further. This compares favourably with population growth rates in India (2.3 per cent), other low-income countries (2.6 per cent) and the middle-income countries (2.4 per cent).

Indeed, combining the estimates of the rates of growth of domestic product and population results in estimates of the rate of growth of output per head between 1970 and 1982 of 4.2 per cent a year in China, 1.3 per cent in India, 0.8 per cent in other low-income countries and 3 per cent in the middle-income countries. Clearly, China has done much better than the great majority of Third World countries.

Other indicators show that the benefits of rapid growth have been spread widely and have reached all sections of the population. For example, both the birth and death rates in China are much lower than in most other underdeveloped countries. The infant mortality rate, at 67 per 1000, is well below that of India, less than 60 per cent that of the other low-income countries and lower even than the infant mortality rate in the middle-income countries where average incomes are five times higher than China's.

Indeed, China enjoys a demographic profile more like that of a rich country than a poor. Life expectancy is 67 years compared to only 55 in India and even less in the majority of the other low-income countries. The adult literacy rate is nearly double that of the low-income countries and marginally higher than that of the middle-income countries.

Equally significant is the secondary school enrolment ratio. In China, more than 4 out of 10 children of secondary school age are in school; in India, 3 out of 10; in the other low-income countries, 2 out of 10. These differences underline in the most vivid way possible the differences in development priorities between China and most of the Third World.

The purpose of presenting the above statistics is to demonstrate that the motives behind the economic reforms in China cannot have been primarily economic or demographic; the motive must have been largely political. Economic growth rates were relatively high; average incomes were rising and were equitably distributed; population expansion was under control and there was no danger of a Malthusian crisis. The reforms may or may not improve the long-run performance of the economy, but it is evident that they were not introduced in response to an economic crisis or in response to a failure of the Maoist strategy for economic development.[4]

REFORMS IN THE AGRICULTURAL SECTOR

Whatever the reasons were, radical changes have occurred, particularly in the countryside, and it is appropriate therefore to begin with the reforms in the rural areas, the place where 80 per cent of the Chinese live.

This section concentrates on the four most important reforms. First, the prices received by farmers have been raised sharply while the prices paid by farmers for industrial products have been held down. As a result, agriculture's terms of trade improved by at least 37 per cent between 1978 and 1982 – 'at least' because this calculation does not take into account prices in the free market, which are usually higher than the official prices.[5]

Second, the policy of local grain self-sufficiency has been relaxed and producers now have greater freedom in deciding what to grow and how best to grow it. That is, both the output mix and the input mix are determined locally on the basis of profit calculations rather than centrally on the basis of administrative calculations. Regional comparative advantage is beginning to be exploited. Some effects already can be seen, notably in the reduction in the amount of land devoted to grains and an increase in the acreage allocated to industrial crops such as cotton and rapeseed.

Third, the private household economy has been liberalised. The private plot has been enlarged (from 5 per cent to 15 per cent of the collectively owned land), private non-agricultural or 'sideline' activities have been encouraged and most restraints on the free market have been removed. The result has been an enormous surge in private incomes in rural areas. Between 1978 and 1982 average private income rose nearly three-fold and the share of private income in total peasant income rose from 27 to 38 per cent.

Finally, collective farming has been abandoned and instead the collectively owned land has been turned over, under contract, to individual peasant households. The production team, the smallest collective unit in each commune, no longer is responsible for cultivation: its main task today is to allocate land among households and ensure that they comply with contractual agreements. The peasants no longer receive work points for cultivating the collective fields but instead receive whatever they produce from the land allocated to them after discharging their contractual obligations to their production teams. China, thus, has adopted a small peasant farming system – which they call the production responsibility system – under which the peasantry has been converted into tenant farmers paying fixed rents in kind. The commune system as it was known for over 20 years has ceased to exist.

Two questions immediately arise: have the reforms worked and were such radical changes necessary? That is, have the economic results of the reforms been positive and, if so, could the results have been achieved within the earlier economic and institutional framework?

There is no doubt that there has been an acceleration in the rate of growth of agricultural output. In terms of production, the short-run effects clearly have been positive. Moreover, the incomes of the rural population have increased even faster than output, thanks to the improvement in the agricultural terms of trade. This rise in average rural incomes, contrary to what was feared, has not been accompanied by a sharp rise in inequality in the distribution of income. Land and other productive resources have been evenly distributed and the initial impact of the reforms, at least at the local level, has often resulted in less rather than more inequality. Thus far the reforms deserve high marks.

As time passes, however, a few problems may emerge. These problems are likely to centre on the level of capital accumulation, the long-run rate of growth of production and the distribution of income.

I Capital formation

There are five sources of investment and savings in rural China: (i) investment undertaken by the state, (ii) investment undertaken by the commune organising seasonally available labour on public works projects, (iii) investment financed from the profits of collective enterprises owned by the commune or its production brigades, (iv) investment financed by the production teams from their collective accumulation funds and (v) private household savings and investment. Each of these is considered below.

(i) State investment

State rural capital formation in China as a whole seems to have declined slightly, possibly reflecting national policy decisions to reduce aggregate investment in order to raise consumption levels quickly. One of the major political objectives of the economic reforms was to 'mobilise the enthusiasm of the people'; another was to restore the status and prestige of the Communist Party. Both could be achieved, it was thought, by raising living standards more quickly and thereby showing that the Party had not lost touch with the masses and was concerned about the well-being of the people, and above all the rural people. In the short run the easiest way to improve the standard of living of the majority of the people was to reduce the high level of investment and channel these resources into consumption, and this was the strategy that was adopted.

It is unlikely, therefore, that the decline in total state investment, or of that part directed to the rural areas, will be reversed in the near future. The significance of this for the countryside should not be exaggerated, however, since state investment in rural areas before the reforms usually was little more than 10 per cent of total state investment.

(ii) Labour-investment

Labour-investment by communes and brigades was much more important. Indeed, China is known throughout the world for its success in mobilising seasonally unemployed and other 'surplus' labour for investment in rural areas. An enormous amount of work was undertaken – field terracing and levelling, irrigation and flood control projects, tree planting, road and bridge building – and these projects changed the face of the Chinese countryside. Some of the work was of poor quality and required frequent repair and maintenance and the return on investment often was long delayed and disappointingly meagre. None the less, much good was achieved.

Under the new reforms, however, the emphasis formerly placed on labour-investment has been reduced. This form of investment has not disappeared entirely, but the new institutional arrangements built around small peasant farms have undermined the sense of solidarity and communal participation that used to be such a striking feature of the commune system, and have weakened incentives for collective labour-investment. Sadly, the decline in labour-investment is likely to be felt most strongly in the poorer communes rather than the rich.

(iii) Investment from profits of collective enterprises

The richer communes tended to rely relatively little on labour-investment to achieve high rates of capital accumulation. The engine of growth in their case usually was the reinvested profits of commune and brigade-run enterprises. Unfortunately for these communes the profits of collectively owned enterprises have been squeezed through a combination of higher wages, higher taxes and higher raw material prices. To make matters worse, the proportion of profits retained by the enterprises for reinvestment has fallen. This is a deliberate act of policy and is one of the methods that has been used to increase consumption standards of the peasantry.

The joint effect nationally of a falling profit rate and a lower reinvestment ratio has been to reduce the rate of increase of fixed assets in commune- and brigade-run enterprises. Indeed, between 1978 and 1982 the rate of fixed asset formation declined precipitously, that is, by about two-thirds.

(iv) Investment from collective accumulation funds

Increasingly, then, the burden of collective accumulation in the rural areas will fall upon the collective accumulation funds of the production teams. Here, too, however, there are worrying trends. Many teams have begun to sell their assets to individual households and in most cases the money thus obtained has not been reinvested but has been held in the form of idle balances. As a result there has been a decline in the stock of collectively owned means of production.

In principle, it would be possible to adopt a strategy whereby teams sold off their draught animals and small items of collectively owned capital equipment, and reinvested the proceeds in larger pieces of equipment, in which economies of scale are important, and generated new investment through the collective accumulation fund. Such a strategy would permit a change in the composition of collectively owned assets while ensuring that the stock of productive assets continued to increase. But alas, this has not been done. Assets are being liquidated and not replaced and the rate of collective investment has been reduced.

(v) Private sector investment

This means that if investment is to be maintained at a high level the private sector will have to shoulder more responsibility for rural savings and investment. Whether the private sector can shoulder this responsibility remains to be seen. So far, all we know is that private savings have increased sharply – often to 25 per cent of total household income – that a high proportion of these savings are channelled to housing and the purchase of consumer durables and that only a relatively small proportion is used for investment in fixed productive assets. Moreover, the productive investment undertaken by households often consists of purchases of assets from the production teams.

This transfer of ownership does not represent an increase in the stock of the means of production in the countryside, since what the household gains the team loses.

Of course, other corporate forms could emerge that are compatible with the new Chinese socialism – and one must not underestimate the inventiveness of the Chinese – but so far, at least, private corporations or joint private–state corporations have not arisen in the rural areas. Thus the private sector remains restricted largely to the household economy and private savings are amassed and largely invested by individual households.

On balance, then, it is likely that the overall rate of investment in rural areas will fall. State investment probably will decline slightly; labour-investment will fall sharply but there may be an offsetting rise in the efficiency of such investment; investment financed from the profits of commune- and brigade-level enterprises is certain to fall, as will collective accumulation by production teams. Investment by households, on the other hand, surely will rise and the productivity of that investment is likely to be high. It is possible that the rise in private investment and in the average productivity of investment will not fully compensate for the fall in various forms of collective investment. There is thus a danger that the long-run rates of capital formation and of agricultural growth may decline slightly.

II Long-run growth

Much of the recent spectacular growth of output is due to a once-and-for-all increase in efficiency. The benefits of an improved allocation of resources have not been exhausted, but it is virtually inevitable that the additional gains will diminish year by year and hence this source of growth is bound to be of declining importance in the longer run. Added to this is the danger that the new institutional arrangements will make it more difficult for farmers to exploit economies of scale where they exist. The old communes had weaknesses, but one of their strengths was the ability to take advantage of economies of scale. That strength may have been sacrificed in order to obtain what the reformers regard as the even greater advantages of a small peasant farming system.

Quite a separate issue is the maintenance of the existing stock of large, lumpy collective assets: such things as irrigation channels and drainage ditches, terraced fields and anti-erosion works. There is a risk, to put it no stronger, that if the administrative structure of the commune is weakened, these valuable collective assets will fall into disrepair. If that happens the long-run rate of growth will be adversely affected.[6]

In summary, there is a danger – not a certainty but a danger – that the reforms may have the unanticipated and unwelcome effect of lowering the trend rate of growth of agricultural production. This could occur because of a combination of a lower investment ratio, diminishing gains from an improved allocation of resources, an inability fully to exploit economies of scale and a deterioration in parts of the collectively owned and constructed rural infrastructure.

III Distribution of income

Speculation about future trends in the distribution of income in rural areas is even more difficult than assessing future agricultural growth rates. In principle, inequality need not increase. To avoid it happening, however, a number of conditions will have to be fulfilled. For example, land must continue to be allocated equitably and reallocated periodically as households change in composition and size. Ideally the 'rent' or the amount paid to the team by each household should reflect the true scarcity rent of the land allocated to that household. Failing this, sub-contracting or sub-tenanting of land between households should be prohibited and all land not wanted or required by a household should be returned to the team for reallocation. When land is returned, the team should fully compensate the household for any immovable assets and any improvement made to the land.

Comparable conditions would have to apply in the capital and labour markets.

In practice the necessary conditions are not being applied in full and there is a genuine likelihood that inequality will increase somewhat in future. Land 'rents' are well below true scarcity values and consequently farming households receive large unearned incomes. This would not matter too much if land were reallocated fairly frequently, but in fact the period of a contract recently has been extended to 15 years. More remarkable, land reclaimed by peasants from previously uncultivated areas is classified as 'private land' and becomes virtually the property of the household that organised the reclamation. Similar phenomena have been observed in the capital market. For example, the sale or rental to households of tractors and other collectively owned assets have been at prices substantially below market clearing rates. This of course enables the lucky buyer to earn large quasi-rents with little exertion. In such cases inequality increases merely because of the way the reforms were introduced, not by intent.

These, then, are some of the possible consequences of the reforms. Let us now consider whether they were necessary.

IV Were the reforms necessary?

The debate centres on the institutional reform of the commune system and the reintroduction of a small peasant farming system. Three of the four major reforms could have been implemented without having to dismantle the communes, namely, the raising of farm prices, the exploitation of regional comparative advantage and the liberalisation of markets and the household economy. The issue is whether the large recent gains in output could have been achieved with these three policies alone, within the framework of collective farming by production teams.

The official view is that the production teams were inefficient because they did not provide adequate material incentives to their members. Small peasant farms, in contrast, give an incentive to people to work longer hours than before, to work with greater intensity per hour and also to work with greater intelligence, imagination and creativity. This argument is persuasive, but only if one compares the present system with the previous one, warts and all. It is not necessarily the case that production teams are inherently less efficient than small family farms.

Three points of criticism are made about the structure of incentives in the production teams. First, an excessive proportion of the income of the team was distributed 'according to need' rather than 'according to work'. Consequently everyone received enough to eat whether or not they made a full contribution to production. Second, the wage (or strictly speaking work point) differentials were very narrow and hence there was little encouragement to work harder to obtain a higher income. Everyone was paid much the same regardless of the effort expended. Third, such differentials as existed were arbitrary and did not reflect the difficulty of the task, the skill required or the worker's marginal product. The link between effort and reward was weak, not least because differentials were often based on such personal characteristics as sex, age and political attitude.

Assuming all these points are valid, it none the less would have been possible in principle to modify and improve the incentive structure without altering the essential nature of the production team. For example, the amount of grain distributed 'according to need' could have been reduced, thereby making more grain available for distribution 'according to work'; work point differentials could have been widened to stimulate greater effort; and the criteria by which work points were awarded could have been changed, possibly switching to a piece-rate from a time-rate payment system. No doubt some problems would have remained, but it is perhaps a pity that China did not experiment with alternative incentive schemes within the framework of the production team to see if it were possible to retain the advantages of the commune system while enjoying the growth of output achieved under the new household production system.

THE REFORM OF STATE INDUSTRIAL ENTERPRISES

The reforms in industry have followed those in agriculture with a lag of about five and a half years. The motives behind the reforms are several. A chief motive has been a desire to reverse the tendency for the rate of growth of industrial output to decline gradually over time, notwithstanding the fact that by world standards the present rate of growth continues to be impressive. In addition, the authorities are keen to introduce new technology, to raise the quality of industrial products, to expand the range of goods offered and to improve the marketing and distribution systems in order to eliminate both acute shortages of some products and unsaleable stockpiles of others.

In the initial period the reforms have concentrated on increasing the autonomy of state enterprises and giving managers greater freedom and responsibility in decision-making. In this respect the industrial reforms are analogous to the production responsibility system in agriculture.

It is not hard to understand why enterprise autonomy has been singled out for priority attention, since the situation before the reforms was one of almost total centralisation and little discretion allowed to managers. Production targets were specified in the plan; material inputs were allocated by the state; labour, too, was allocated by the state, as was credit and foreign exchange. All profits were remitted to the government where they formed a vast pool of financial resources available for allocation in accordance with plan priorities. Finally, all fixed investment by state enterprises was determined centrally and the necessary funds were provided at virtually no cost. Enterprises thus were responsible for neither profits nor losses and managers consequently had little incentive to use resources efficiently.

The reforms, introduced in 1984, still require most managers to meet a production quota, but once the quota is fulfilled managers are free to produce additional output and sell it where and how they wish at whatever price it will fetch, provided only that the price neither exceeds nor falls below the fixed state price by more than 20 per cent. Managers also are given greater freedom in selecting workers and administrative staff, in designing (within specified limits) pay and bonus systems, in determining the internal organisation of the enterprise and in forming joint ventures or mergers with other enterprises. Finally, firms now are allowed to retain 70 per cent of their depreciation funds and, in theory, 45 per cent of their profits. This all sounds like common sense run riot.

There is, however, a difficulty. As the reform process has proceeded the need to change the methods by which prices are determined has assumed growing importance. Decentralisation and the relaxation of administrative controls and physical, quantitative planning imply that decisions increasingly will be taken in response to price signals. That being so, it is vital that the price signals received by managers reflect true scarcities, true costs. Otherwise resources will be misallocated and decentralisation will lead to a decline in efficiency rather than to an increase. It matters little if, say, coal is underpriced and refined petroleum products are relatively overpriced when production, distribution and investment decisions in these industries are based on non-price criteria. But if prices are used to guide decisions, underpricing of coal will result in sub-optimal levels or production and investment in mining and excess demand by users; the converse will, of course, occur in the petroleum industry.

The Chinese leadership, for understandable reasons, has been unwilling to reform the price system while other major changes are occurring. They fear that a general overhaul of relative prices could lead to inflation, since it probably will be easier to raise the prices of products experiencing excess demand than to lower the prices of products suffering from excess supply. They fear, too, that a radical change in relative prices may introduce considerable uncertainty into the economic system and make planning at the enterprise level exceedingly difficult. This, in turn, could result in a fall in industrial output and a decline in employment. Finally, the authorities recognise that a change in relative prices will alter the distribution of income, possibly in ways that cannot readily be foreseen, and they wish to avoid creating unjustified inequalities or undermining political support for the reform process as a whole.

Price reform thus is likely to occur gradually, on a step-by-step basis. Indeed, several changes have already been introduced and China today has a multiple pricing system. Some output continues to be determined in accordance with planned quota targets and is sold at official fixed prices established by the state. Some output is produced under indicative plans and state guidance, and above-quota production is freely sold by the enterprise at any price within the range of plus or minus 20 per cent of the official price. Finally, some products, mostly consumer goods, are sold on totally free markets at whatever price is determined by the forces of supply and demand.

There is a debate in China today about what principles should in future be used in setting prices. Several different strategies are possible and it will be fascinating to see what procedure ultimately is agreed upon. One expectation is that the Chinese will continue to be highly pragmatic and that decisions will be taken largely on a case-by-case or category-by-category basis.

One possibility would be to begin with the commodities China exports and imports, and to adjust gradually the prices of these goods to a moving average of world prices. Next, one could tackle the non-traded commodities currently subject to official pricing regulations. Here, it would be desirable to allow domestic demand and supply to operate and to adjust the official price gradually each year until a market clearing price is established. Thereafter, prices could reflect domestic market conditions without further official intervention.

No doubt some residual price controls or price ceilings will be necessary for state enterprises which enjoy a monopoly position. And some subsidies will continue to be necessary for some goods and services for reasons of social policy and an equitable distribution of income. Housing, medical services and urban transport are cases in point.

Turning now to industrial products sold under a guided or indicative plan, the objectives should be (i) to continue to reduce compulsory quotas, (ii) to abolish immediately the fixed official price where this is higher than the floating price and (iii) where the floating price is higher than the official price, to raise the latter in stages until the two coincide, thereafter allowing supply and demand to clear the market.

The price for foodgrains raises difficult problems because grain is the most important wage good and any change in grain prices will have widespread implications for living standards in both the cities and the countryside. The official retail price of grain in urban areas has remained roughly constant for the last decade whereas the purchase price paid to peasant producers increased by about 26 per cent between 1978 and 1982.

As a result a wide gap has emerged between the price paid by the state for grain and the price at which it is sold to consumers. This gap is filled by subsidies financed out of general state revenues. In 1982 these subsidies were equivalent to 7.5 per cent of the national income. This represents an enormous sum and, moreover, one which will continue to grow as grain production expands. Clearly some adjustment is essential.

The adjustment process, however, is bound to be delicate and will have to occur over a number of years. What is required is (i) some combination of a lower compulsory production quota, (ii) a reduction in the quantity of grain urban consumers can obtain through the rationing system, (iii) a higher price of rationed grain and (iv) abolition of the price premium on above-quota grain deliveries to the state in favour of purchases at the free market price. The latter, in turn, should slowly be brought into line with world prices as previously mentioned. These changes will raise the average cost of foodgrains to urban consumers and hence lower their standard of living. This, almost certainly, is undesirable and it surely will be necessary to compensate workers for a higher cost of living through an appropriate increase in their nominal wages.

Finally, there are the commodities traded on free markets. The number of such commodities is few, probably no more than 10 per cent of the total, and every opportunity should be taken to increase the volume of transactions on unregulated markets. Indeed, the presumption should be that all commodities are traded on open markets at prices determined by supply and demand unless the government has strong reasons to insist on regulated prices. Probably strong reasons will not often be forthcoming and if the reformers keep their nerve it should be possible to combine greater autonomy of state industrial enterprises with widespread liberalisation of prices. In fact if price liberalisation is not possible, greater autonomy may be undesirable. There may be no comfortable stopping place between, on the one hand, centralised planning and quantitative controls and, on the other, enterprise autonomy plus rational market prices. Either system can work reasonably well but a hybrid of the two is likely to fail.

CONCLUSION

Let us assume the reforms in industry and in agriculture are carried through to completion. What sort of economy will China have then? Will China still be a socialist state? Many observers in the West, both those who admire what is happening and those who deplore it, believe China is rapidly creating a capitalist economy. They cite as evidence the abandonment of collective farming, the enlargement of the private plot and the switch to a small peasant farming system with long-term security and rights which in some respects are similar to those normally associated with private property. They adduce, too, the reduced emphasis on central planning and quantitative controls, the reinstatement of profit as a management yardstick in the state industrial enterprises and the intention to expand the role of prices and the market mechanism in allocating resources. Finally, a topic we have not touched upon, they mention the greater integration of China into the world economy and the tentative steps taken to encourage foreign investment in China.

Does all this mean that China is no longer a socialist country? Perhaps the answer depends on one's definition of socialism. If by socialism one means a society in which ownership and control of the instruments of production are in the hands of the community as a whole, then China most definitely is a socialist country. Agricultural land continues to be collectively owned, large-scale industry is almost entirely in the hands of the state, and most small and medium enterprises, in both rural and urban areas, are collectively owned. In the cities, almost all housing is owned and allocated by the government. By the criterion of ownership, then, China is clearly socialist, not capitalist.

Some people regard the defining characteristic of socialism to be central direction of the economy by the government. By this test, too, China remains a socialist country. Certainly central planning will be less detailed than before and the instruments of planning will become increasingly refined, subtle and indirect, but central guidance and direction will remain: there is no likelihood that anything approaching laissez faire will be allowed to operate for long in China.

Finally, some people, particularly those who come from the social democratic tradition of Western Europe, judge a country by its social policies and the degree of equality in the distribution of income these help to produce. It is perhaps a little artificial to compare China to the welfare states of Northern and Western Europe, since the differences in levels of income are so large, but there is no doubt that the relative degree of equality in China is remarkable by any standard and is matched by very few other countries in the world.

In the last analysis one need not be too concerned about what label is put on China. Following Deng Xiao Ping, it does not really matter whether the cat is white or black so long as it catches mice. Whatever the colour, the Chinese economy after Mao is an unusual cat and, for a Chinese mouse, the chances of being caught are more than negligible.

Notes

1. The best official data on the Chinese economy are provided by the State Statistical Bureau, *Statistical Yearbook of China*, published annually and available from Economic Information and Agency, 342 Hennessy Road, Hong Kong. The data cited below, however, are taken from the World Bank's annual *World Development Report*, New York: Oxford University Press, in order to facilitate comparison with other Third World countries. The period selected for comparison, viz. 1970–82, is essentially arbitrary, and conforms to the World Bank's presentation. Inclusion of the decade 1960–70 would not alter the qualitative conclusions, while extension of the period beyond 1982, when the effects of the economic reforms became dramatic, would greatly favour China in comparison with the rest of the world, by then suffering from the effects of widespread international recession.
2. Following the World Bank's classification, low-income countries are defined as those with a GNP per capita of less than $410 in 1982, and middle-income countries as those Third World economies with a GNP per capita of $410 or more.
3. Population growth rates in 1970–82 were 1.4 per cent per annum in China, 2.3 per cent in India, 2.6 per cent in the other low-income countries and 2.4 per cent in the middle-income countries.
4. The reformers in the Chinese government, in this interpretation, were reacting to what they regarded as the excesses of the Great Leap Forward, the Cultural Revolution and the period of the Gang of Four and, particularly in agriculture, were attempting to remodel the economy so that it conformed more to the pattern that prevailed in the early 1950s. An unkind critic could label this movement as literally reactionary, an attempt to return to an earlier golden age of socialist development.

5. It is difficult to obtain accurate estimates of the size of the free market. One indication of the rapid growth of such transactions is the fact that 'retail sales by peasants to non-agricultural residents' rose from 31 100 million yuan in 1978 to 110 800 million yuan in 1982, of which 28 000 million yuan was food in 1978 and 96 500 million yuan was food in 1982.
6. Of course irrigation companies could be formed to maintain and expand irrigation facilities, but the author is not aware of any such company. An easier solution would be to maintain a strong commune administrative structure for the management of collective assets such as irrigation systems, or to turn responsibility over to the townships (*xiang*) which have replaced the communes, and the latter seems increasingly likely in many parts of China.

5 Industrial Reforms in China

China has had an enviable record of industrial development since liberation in 1949. In aggregate terms the rate of growth of industrial output in China since 1960 has been about twice as fast as in the rest of the world and China's performance has easily exceeded that of the other large Third World countries such as India, Brazil and Mexico. This is shown in the first column of Table 5.1. In per capita terms China's performance compares even more favourably because of its below-average rate of growth of population. Thus, for example, in aggregate terms China's industrial output grew 38 per cent faster than the average of the middle-income economies, whereas in per capita terms China grew 68 per cent faster (see the second column of Table 5.1).

Gross domestic product also increased rapidly in China, but industry was by far the 'leading sector' and consequently its share of total output jumped from about a third in 1960 to 46 per cent in 1981. Indeed the share of gross domestic product attributable to industry is higher in China than in the much-heralded 'newly industrialising countries' of Latin America and East and South-east Asia (see column three of Table 5.1). Even so, China still is a very poor country. The level of mechanisation remains low and the country continues to rely on human beings for the carriage of goods in cities and for much of its motive power. In absolute terms, as can be seen in the final column of the table, industrial output per head in China, although more than twice as high as in India, is well below the level of output in the middle-income economies. China is gaining quickly, but there is a long way to go.

One advantage China has over many other Third World countries is that its system of economic planning, and the rather closed nature of the economy, have enabled the country to avoid the impact of the current world recession and to insulate itself from cyclical fluctuations originating in Europe and North America. There has been nothing in China comparable to the industrial depression and debt crisis that have afflicted the more industrialised economies of Latin America in recent years.

Despite this apparent success the Chinese leadership has become

Table 5.1 Industrial Performance

	Growth of industrial production, 1960–81		Share of GDP originating in industry, 1981	Industrial output per head, 1981
	Total (% p.a.)	*Per capita* (% p.a.)	(%)	(US$)
Low-income economies:	5.1	3.0	34	n.a.
China	9.8	7.9	46	123
India	4.9	2.7	26	54
Other low-income	4.9	2.3	17	n.a.
Middle-income economies:	7.1	4.7	38	n.a.
South Korea	15.6	13.5	39	659
Brazil	9.1*	7.0*	34	594
Mexico	6.4	3.2	37	1242
Industrial market economies	4.3	3.4	36	n.a.

Note: * 1970–81

Source: IBRD, *World Development Report 1983*, New York: Oxford University Press, 1983.

dissatisfied with certain aspects of the country's industrial performance and, following the reforms in agriculture,[1] has decided to embark upon a series of reforms in industry, focusing in particular upon the state enterprise sector. The reasons for dissatisfaction include the following:

(i) a tendency for the rate of growth of industrial output to decline gradually over time, although by world standards the present rate of growth remains high;
(ii) a tendency to continue to use methods of production long after they have become technologically obsolete and an associated tendency to lag behind in the introduction of new and better technologies;
(iii) a tendency for the quality of many manufactured goods in China to be well below world standards;
(iv) a restricted range of product choice, limited variety, infrequent model changes and sluggish responsiveness to customer preferences in both the consumer goods and capital goods sectors; and
(v) a poorly developed marketing and distribution system which has led to acute shortages of some products and large, unsaleable stockpiles of other products.

It should be said straight away that industrial reform is not a new topic in China. Previous reforms, however, of which there have been four, have been little more than oscillations between decentralisation and recentralisation, i.e. between moves to shift responsibility for state industrial enterprises to the provincial level (1958 and 1970) and moves to concentrate power in the central ministries in Beijing (1961–3 and 1977). In contrast, the reforms begun in 1979, and now being accelerated, go much deeper than this and in principle entail a radical change in China's system of economic management.[2]

THE RESEARCH TRIP

In August and September 1984 a group[3] from Oxford visited China in order to study at first hand the reforms currently underway, to assess the results achieved and difficulties encountered and to discuss likely future developments. This chapter is based on material collected on that trip. Academic discussions were held with colleagues in Beijing, Shenyang, Shanghai and Guangzhou, while numerous meetings with

Table 5.2 Regional Location of Industrial Production, 1982

	Gross output value (100m.yuan)	(%)
Shanghai	636.70	11.4
Jiangsu	503.21	9.0
Liaoning	476.31	8.5
Guangdong	272.18	4.9
Beijing	228.69	4.1
Sub-total	2117.09	37.9
China	5577.45	100.0

Source: State Statistical Bureau, *Statistical Yearbook of China, 1983.*

senior government officials were organised in all of the above mentioned places plus Changzhou and the Shenzhen Special Economic Zone adjacent to Hong Kong. Arrangements were made to visit commune- and brigade-run enterprises, urban collective enterprises and state enterprises, at each of which there was an opportunity to discuss the implementation of the reforms with experienced managers. Our visits to factories covered both heavy industry (iron and steel, mining equipment, diesel engines, small walking tractors) and light consumer goods industries (pharmaceuticals, a printing works, textiles, electronics, watches and a factory that made combs).

Although the area that could be covered in the time available was necessarily limited, we did manage to visit the major industrial regions of the country. Indeed the three provinces (Liaoning, Jiangsu and Guangdong) and the autonomous municipalities visited (Beijing and Shanghai) account for 38 per cent of China's industrial output (see Table 5.2). Even so, it must be recognised that conditions can vary quite a bit from one region to another and hence one must be cautious in drawing general conclusions from a small, non-random and geographically restricted sample. The more wide-ranging discussions held in Beijing with central government officials, however, hopefully enable biases arising from the choice of regions to study to be anticipated and corrected.

The discussion of the industrial reforms begins with measures designed to increase the autonomy of state enterprises and to give managers greater freedom and responsibility in decision-making. This is followed by consideration of labour payment systems, i.e. the wage structure, bonuses and floating wages. We then turn our attention to returns to and charges for the use of capital, i.e. profits, depreciation and interest rates. Next, we discuss commodity price reforms and the criteria that might be used in future in setting relative prices. This is followed by a section on transitional arrangements. We conclude, finally, with a few reflections on the Special Economic Zones.

ENTERPRISE AUTONOMY

There has been a tendency in China to plan as if the economy were one large factory or, alternatively, as if state enterprises were merely a department of a government ministry. Everything is centralised and little discretion is left to the manager. Production targets are specified in the plan; material inputs are allocated by the state; labour is allocated by the state; credit is distributed by the banking system according to predetermined norms for working capital; foreign exchange allocations also are determined centrally. No profits are retained by the enterprise but instead are remitted to the centre where they form part of a vast pool of finance capital available for allocation in accordance with centrally determined priorities. Finally, all fixed capital investment by state enterprises is determined centrally and the necessary funds are provided at virtually zero cost. Enterprises thus are responsible for neither profits nor losses: everyone (as we were frequently told) eats out of the big iron pot of the state. This, at least, was the tendency until recently, although the situation differed in practice depending upon the sector or area.

The reforms are intended to end this state of affairs. Enterprises are being given more autonomy; administrative methods of management are giving way to indirect methods of control; managers and workers are being encouraged to exercise more initiative; and obligatory targets are being reduced and in some cases abandoned. State enterprises now are allowed to retain some of their profits and a system of profit taxation will replace the old system whereby 100 per cent of profit was subject to remission. Similarly, the income of workers will henceforth be more closely related to the performance of their enterprise and of the work groups to which they belong.

Managers in future will be expected to take managerial decisions and the Party committee will cease to interfere in day-to-day decisions. Similarly, it is intended that ministries should begin to confine mandatory quotas to products that are badly needed, in short supply or which are regarded as basic necessities of the people. Production of other products will be 'guided' by the plan by using 'economic levers' (taxes, subsidies, prices) while production of an increasing number of goods and services is expected to be regulated by market forces. The rigid pricing system – under which it takes three years to adjust the price of a small commodity – is intended gradually to be replaced by a more flexible system which permits larger and more speedy changes in relative prices.[4]

On 12 May 1984 the government published a list of 10 principles which illustrates the degree of enterprise autonomy envisaged by the reformers. The ten principles are described below.

(i)

Having fulfilled state mandatory quotas, managers of state enterprises are free to use any remaining productive capacity to produce additional output. The commodity composition of above-quota output and the quality standards desired are left to the discretion of the enterprise.

(ii)

Above-quota output can be marketed by the enterprise in whatever way it wishes and need not be sold to the state. That is, the enterprise may sell directly to other enterprises, or set up its own marketing outlets or sell to wholesalers or retailers.

(iii)

Managers of state enterprises are free to sell above-quota output at prices which reflect market forces, provided only that the sales price neither exceeds nor falls below the fixed state price by more than 20 per cent.

In principle these three provisions could increase the autonomy of state enterprises quite considerably as they give managers much more freedom to make production, marketing and pricing decisions. In practice, however, everything will depend upon the relationship of mandatory production quotas to the productive capacity of the firm. If output targets are high in relation to capacity, the incentive effects will be weak and the reforms will achieve little. Although it is still too early to tell, it appears that planned output, even in experimental enterprises, accounts for a high percentage of total production. Thus in the Capital Iron and Steel Co. in Beijing, above-quota output was only 2 per cent of the total; in the No. 2 Watch Factory in Shanghai, it was 4–8 per cent; in the Changzhou Tractor Factory, 5 per cent; and in the Shanghai Diesel Engine Factory, 5–10 per cent. Only in the Shenyang Heavy Machinery Co. was above-quota output a high proportion of the total, at 50 per cent.

These figures suggest that the implementation of the reforms has been cautious so far. If eventually the impact of the reforms proves to be disappointing, it would be sensible for the government to consider reducing planned targets significantly below the productive capacity of the enterprise. Alternatively, the government should at least not raise output quotas in future, so that on the margin 100 per cent of additional output is produced, marketed and priced at the discretion of the manager. In fact, marketing systems already are more flexible than they once were and some state enterprises are allowed to sell part of their planned output directly to customers rather than delivering everything to the state. Similar flexibility in setting output targets would be desirable.

(iv)

Managers are now allowed to obtain a fraction of their inputs directly from other enterprises, thereby by-passing the state supply system. This is a corollary of (ii) above and applies to both planned and above-plan output. A number of enterprises visited have taken advantage of this provision and it seems to have worked well; further liberalisation of the input marketing system almost certainly would be desirable.

(v)

State enterprises are free to sell or rent unneeded fixed assets, provided the capitalised value of the firm is not reduced. Receipts from the sale of fixed assets may be put on deposit with the banking system, where they earn a low rate of interest, or they may be used to purchase new equipment. Cases of asset disposal were found, e.g. the Shenyang Heavy Machinery Co. sold some old equipment to small collective enterprises, but this seems to be uncommon. As the reforms gather pace, however, it is likely that managers will wish to get rid of their out-of-date equipment and replace it with capital of a more recent vintage; there will for a long time be enterprises in areas of labour surplus or where industry can complement agriculture which will be willing buyers.

(vi)

Managers also are allowed to retain 70 per cent of the depreciation funds of their enterprise, although the rate of depreciation is fixed by the state. Previously firms were allowed to retain only 50 per cent of their depreciation funds, so there has been a modest increase in the resources that can be deployed by managers without having to seek the prior permission of state authorities.

In principle this seems to be a sensible change. There is a danger, however, that if depreciation funds are retained by the enterprise and reinvested in physical assets for the same enterprise, the existing industrial structure may become ossified. Depreciation as a cost of capital should in theory be kept distinct from depreciation funds as a source of finance for investment. Of course, on many occasions, perhaps most occasions, it will make sense for an enterprise to reinvest its depreciation funds in its own business, but sometimes it might make more sense for the depreciation funds to flow from one enterprise to another in order to facilitate industrial expansion elsewhere. This will not happen unless either the state retains some control over the allocation of such funds or a capital market is allowed to develop in which managers can place unneeded funds at an attractive rate of return. Hence there is a connection between changes in interest rate policy (discussed below) and in the treatment of depreciation funds.

(vii)

Managers are to become free to determine the internal organisation of the enterprise, without interference from government ministers or Party secretaries. This, when implemented, will be an important change from past practice when the manager was under the leadership of the Party. Undoubtedly this reform will improve economic efficiency, although, of the enterprises visited, only at the Changzhou Tractor Factory was a major internal reorganisation implemented shortly after this provision came into effect. One can anticipate, however, that many more such reorganisations will be introduced in future.

(viii)

The managers of state enterprises can choose not only the organisational structure of the firm, they are also given greater initiative in selecting the management team and individual workers employed by the enterprise. The number of workers is still controlled by the state, but the selection of individual workers will become the responsibility of management. In most of the enterprises which we visited the manager put first in the list of benefits from the reform, the power to weigh technical competence above political record. The adverse consequences of the past slogan 'more Red than expert' are thus being overcome. In that connection there has been a distinct weakening of local Party influence over strictly managerial decisions.

For example, at the Shenyang Heavy Machinery Co. the manager can select his own management staff, he can recruit and hire technicians on his own initiative, he can discharge people for criminal behaviour or gross misconduct and he can demote employees for persistent lack of competence or failure to perform their duties to a necessary standard. At the No. 2 Watch Factory in Shanghai some management personnel have been changed – by negotiated retirement, by elevation to an advisory position or by transfer to another job without loss of pay. Similar changes occurred at the Changzhou Tractor Factory, where those who lost posts became advisers with the same salary and privileges as before. This is, evidently, a humane way to handle a difficult problem; it does of course increase the cost of management, but these costs are likely to be low compared to the gains in efficiency achieved by a better management team and consequently the enterprise ought to be able to carry the extra costs without too much difficulty.

In any case, it is very difficult in practice to fire workers in China. This is regarded, rightly, as an extreme step and is never done until other possibilities have been exhausted. Preferred methods are encouragement, persuasion, retraining and reassignment of tasks as alternatives to dismissal and as a result, managers rarely sack an employee. Managers can dismiss workers only for major violations of safety regulations (which endanger the lives of others), persistent absenteeism and such serious violations of rules as to constitute criminal conduct. Idleness and incompetence are not grounds for dismissal – they are grounds for demotion, a cut in wages or a reduction in bonus. Similarly, general redundancy is not considered adequate grounds for dismissal, despite the overmanning that undoubtedly exists.

We found only one case of an enterprise which terminated the employment of a relatively large number of workers. This was the Changzhou Stocking Factory, a state enterprise which recently came under collective management, and 73 persons were affected: 64 were transferred from the factory to its retail outlets (where they received income on a commission basis), seven were seasonal employees who were not re-hired the following season and two were dismissed outright.

The general policy on recruitment and dismissal, thus, is clear and sensible, although it does discourage labour mobility. It is doubtful that managers need more power to fire workers: the present system appears to work well and is far more humane than the system that prevails for instance in the United States. Equally, the new policy which enables the enterprise to recruit its management team and workforce directly is a step forward. The next step should be to relax controls over the total number of employees so that managers can decide on the optimal size of firm.

(ix)

One major change is that managers are allowed to introduce any bonus scheme of their choice and to modify the wage structure, subject to an overall limit on the total wage bill (excluding bonuses). In particular, managers can use up to 3 per cent of the total wage bill each year to promote deserving staff. The labour payment system, in fact, has become quite complex and is the topic of the next section of this chapter.

(x)

Finally, state enterprises are allowed to form joint ventures or combines with other enterprises, be they in the state, collective or private sectors. The intention is to permit vertical integration where this makes economic sense and to facilitate coordination and specialisation horizontally. In practice, joint ventures are likely to be used by state enterprises to help ensure supplies of raw materials and components or to find a productive use of spare capacity. For example, the Changzhou Stocking Factory recently entered into a joint venture with three other factories in which it agreed to use its facilities to design socks while its partners use their capital equipment to produce them.

Table 5.3 Wage Differentials in State Enterprises (yuan per month)

	Capital Iron and Steel Co.	*Shenyang Heavy Machinery Co.*	*No. 2 Watch Factory*
Highest wage	108	215	180
Average wage	n.a.	60	64
Lowest wage	36	43	45
Range	3:1	5:1	4:1

Source: Field notes.

LABOUR PAYMENT SYSTEMS

The wage structure in China was introduced in the 1950s, based on a Soviet model, and has remained essentially unchanged ever since. The structure provides for eight nationally determined grades and has been widely criticised as excessively rigid and centralised. The state controls every person's wage and the wage received by a worker is entirely divorced from his productivity or the general performance of the enterprise in which he works. Moreover, the wage structure is highly compressed and consequently income differentials among factory employees are narrow. This is illustrated in Table 5.3.

It is notable that in all three enterprises the range of wages (excluding bonuses) is rather narrow. The widest range, in the Shenyang Heavy Machinery Co., is only 5:1, a much smaller wage differential than would be found in a capitalist country. Moreover, there are very few persons at the top of the wage scale and hence the average wage is not all that much higher than the lowest wage. The absolute difference between the lowest and average wage is 17 and 19 yuan per month in the Shenyang Heavy Machinery Co. and No. 2 Watch Factory, respectively, while the proportional differential is about 40–45 per cent. Finally, the highest wage is not necessarily received by the manager. For instance, at the No. 2 Watch Factory an apprentice earns 45 yuan per month, the factory director 130 yuan and a senior engineer 180 yuan.

It is not obvious, however, that the wage structure has harmed incentives or, to put it another way, that wider differentials would result in greater effort from workers and hence greater output and higher efficiency. Moreover, it is not clear that it always is possible in a modern, interdependent, complex and mechanised industrial enterprise to relate a worker's remuneration to his productivity or to his contribution to output even if one wanted to, although it may sometimes be possible to do so. A piece-rate system, clearly, has advantages in this respect compared to a time-rate payment system. Finally, an attempt in China to link average wages in an enterprise to the profitability of that enterprise is likely to result not in an improved allocation of resources but in an arbitrary and inequitable distribution of income among the members of the industrial labour force. The reason for this is that profits in state enterprises depend less on technical efficiency in production than on the planned set of relative prices and the latter, in turn, are widely recognised as being arbitrary and irrational. Thus if wage reforms are to enjoy any chance of success they must be accompanied by price reforms.

The first step in reforming the labour payment system has been the introduction of bonuses. At first there was a ceiling on the size of bonus a worker could receive but that ceiling has now been lifted and instead there are three constraints on the enterprise which affect how much can be paid out in bonuses. First, the enterprise must make a profit, part of which is retained. If no profit is earned, no bonus can be paid. Second, not all the retained profit can be distributed as bonuses; a substantial part must be reinvested. The guideline seems to be that at least 50 per cent of retained profits should be allocated to reserves (which in practice have hitherto been minimal) and the development of production (i.e. investment) and no more than 50 per cent to bonuses and welfare funds.[5]

In practice, however, the guideline often is ignored. For example, a study of 29 industrial enterprises and five shops in Chongqing, by the People's Bank of China, indicated that 70 per cent of retained profits are used to improve workers' living standards and less than 30 per cent is reinvested.[6] Similarly, at the Shenyang Heavy Machinery Co., 80 per cent of the retained profits are used for bonuses and only 20 per cent for the development of the enterprise. The reason given for this is that retained profits are so low that 80 per cent of them are needed in order to provide the 'standard' bonus to the workers of two and a half months' wages. This argument implies, however, that the bonus is not discretionary and is not a reward for above average performance but is a regular part of a worker's income. If so, it is unlikely that bonuses are having much of an effect on incentives.

Be that as it may, since July 1984 state enterprises have had a third constraint imposed upon them in the form of a tax on expenditure on above-normal bonuses. The tax is progressive, rising from zero on bonus payments equivalent to no more than $2\frac{1}{2}$ months of the basic wages bill[7] to 300 per cent on total bonus payments greater than six months of the wages bill. The full schedule is as follows:

up to $2\frac{1}{2}$ months' bonus	zero tax
$2\frac{1}{2}$ to 4 months' bonus	30% tax
4 to 6 months' bonus	100% tax
more than 6 months'	300% tax

Individual workers may of course receive bonuses of any size without penalty; the tax falls on the enterprise, not on the workers, and hence managers have a strong incentive to limit the total amount spent on bonuses to about 20 per cent of the basic wage bill.

None the less, the retained profits of some state enterprises are so large that they are able to pay more than $2\frac{1}{2}$ months' wages in bonuses despite the additional taxation this attracts. Thus the No. 2 Watch Factory allocates only 22 per cent of its retained profits to bonuses yet pays a bonus equivalent to 3.1 months; the Changzhou Tractor Factory pays a bonus of 4.2 months; and the Capital Iron and Steel Co., while allocating 20 per cent of its profits to bonuses, pays a bonus equivalent to 5.1 months. The last two enterprises, hence, pay 100 per cent tax on their above-normal bonuses.

There is no doubt that the bonus system gives managers greater flexibility in rewarding workers for good performance or extra effort. Each manager is free to devise a scheme which best suits his factory and consequently the details of the bonus system vary considerably from one enterprise to another. In the Changzhou Tractor Factory, for example, workers receive a basic bonus if their assignment is fulfilled properly; they are then eligible for an extra bonus (equivalent to a progressive piece-rate payment system) if they exceed their production target. In 1984 the range of bonus payments was about 5:1 (or 10–50 yuan) and the effect of the system was probably to widen income differentials slightly. The same probably is true at the Capital Iron and Steel Co., where the range of bonus payments is 4:1 as compared to the range of wage payments in Table 5.3 of 3:1.

Under the old system, bonuses at the No. 2 Watch Factory in Shanghai were an identical absolute amount for each person and hence the distribution of income (i.e. wages plus bonus) among employees at the factory was more equal than the distribution of wages alone. The present system allocates bonuses partly by position held and partly as a reward for exceeding output targets, and the

Table 5.4 Monthly Bonuses at No. 2 Watch Factory, Shanghai, 1984 (yuan per month)

Factory director	30
Vice-director	25
Section leaders	10
Technical staff	12
White collar workers*	8–10
Production workers+	32 max.

Notes: * Some white collar workers have received no bonus at all in some months.
+ Production workers receive bonuses for above-target output on a piece-work basis. The range is zero to 70–80 yuan per month, and the largest bonus received by anyone in one year was 385 yuan in 1983 (equivalent to an average monthly bonus of 32.08 yuan).

Source: Field notes.

question therefore arises as to whether the distribution of bonuses is more or less equal than the distribution of wages. The data presented in Table 5.4 gives some indications on this issue.

The range of wage rates at the No. 2 Watch Factory, as shown in Table 5.3, is 4:1. The range of bonus payments is not absolutely certain, but the data in Table 5.4 suggest that when averaged over a year the range is unlikely to be in excess of 4:1 and it could be smaller than this. It is conceivable therefore that the bonus system reduces income inequality and it is unlikely that it increases it. The director of the factory, for example, receives an annual bonus equivalent to 2.77 months' salary, and this is marginally less than the average bonus of 3.1 months' wages. Given that the director in this case is the second most highly paid employee, it is improbable that bonuses have been used to improve the relative earnings of senior management. More likely, bonuses have altered the distribution of earnings among production workers, favouring those who have succeeded in raising output above planned targets.

More recently, experiments with many variants have begun with so-called floating wages as an alternative to bonuses. There are at least two broad systems of floating wages: one which supplements fixed wages (in many respects similar to a bonus but distinguishable by its greater permanence) and the other as a substitute for fixed wages. In enterprises which are allowed to adopt either of these systems, roughly 30 to 50 per cent of the labour force will find that their wages are directly related to the profitability of their enterprise, rising when profits rise and presumably falling when profits decline. The test of what happens to wages when profits fall has not yet been faced, however, because all the firms selected for the experiment enjoy large and stable profits.

Floating wages, like bonuses, are financed out of retained profits, but unlike bonuses which are determined monthly, a floating wage is fixed for a few years ahead, normally three. Moreover, if all goes well, after a number of years the floating wage is converted into the basic wage and then (unlike a bonus) becomes pensionable. Better still from the point of view of the enterprise, floating wages are not liable to tax no matter how high the wage floats. Of course, the government must agree for an enterprise to have a floating wage system and it must further agree to the amount by which the wage is allowed to float within a given period, e.g. two steps on the national wage scale every twelve months, but even so, there is a danger that floating wages (like bonuses in some enterprises) will get out of control. At the very least, it would seem desirable for expenditure on floating wages to be subject to tax in the same way as above-normal bonuses.

It is arguable, however, that more substantial changes are needed. China has experimented with a number of labour payment systems and perhaps the time has come for a reform of the reforms and the definitive selection of a payment system that will meet the country's needs for the foreseeable future. Such a system could reasonably include four elements.

(i)

It would be desirable to introduce a new national wage scale which applies to all 86 100 state industrial enterprises. The scale would be uniform throughout the country except that adjustments could be made where necessary to take into account differences in the cost of living, e.g. in Guangdong. The number of grades in the scale and the wage differentials built into the scale should, of course, reflect the need to provide adequate incentives to workers to perform at their best. Collective enterprises would be free to adopt the new wage scale if they wish, but they would not be required to do so.

This national wage scale would then form the basis for the remuneration of industrial labour. Control of this scale by the centre would make possible a national incomes policy and would make it easier to avoid the dangers of a cost-push inflation, a danger which will be particularly great during the initial periods of a comprehensive price reform. The existence of a national wage scale will also make it possible to influence the distribution of income in the industrial sector and to prevent an unacceptable degree of inequality from emerging. Finally, control of the national wage scale will enable the planners to maintain control over the investment–consumption balance in industry, or at least over the 78 per cent of gross industrial output value that originates in the state-owned enterprises.

(ii)

Some flexibility in remuneration could be encouraged by allowing enterprise managers to design and implement relatively modest bonus schemes. The amount spent on bonuses should be linked, as now, to the profitability of the enterprise but the payment of bonuses need not be monthly. Managers could be allowed, for instance, to pay bonuses quarterly if they prefer. Floating wages should be disallowed. Such a scheme would enable managers to take local conditions into account and to reward exceptional achievements, yet it would not permit the average level of remuneration in an enterprise to diverge sharply from national norms. Consequently, there would be little risk that the cumulative impact of decisions taken at the level of the enterprise would undermine centrally determined priorities and policies.

(iii)

Existing restrictions on the level of bonuses should be maintained and strictly enforced. Specifically, firms running at a loss should not pay bonuses; firms with retained profits should not be allowed to allocate more than, say, 40 per cent of their profits to bonuses and workers' benefits; and the progressive tax on bonus payments larger than $2\frac{1}{2}$ months' wages should be adhered to and preferably tightened further. Indeed, if the great majority of state enterprises are able to pay large bonuses to their workers, this probably means that the general level of industrial wages is too low and should be raised. On the other hand, if just a few state enterprises are able to pay large bonuses to their workers, this probably means that the prices of the products produced by those enterprises are too high and should be lowered.

(iv)

Indeed price reform is an integral part of wage reform. Without the former, a bonus system can be very unfair. Some enterprises, for example, may be unable to pay their workers a bonus, not because technical performance is poor or because the workers are less productive than average, but because the price of the enterprise's product has been fixed at an irrationally low level. The 'regulatory tax' is, of course, only a temporary expedient and even so some enterprises may be able to pay very large bonuses solely because they enjoy exceptionally high planned prices for their products. Price reform, then, is vital to ensure that the wage reforms are equitable; it is also vital to ensure that the profit reforms make sense.

PROFITS, DEPRECIATION AND INTEREST

Perhaps the most important reforms introduced so far concern the financial management of state enterprises. Previously all profits earned by an enterprise were transferred to the government along with half the depreciation funds. All losses were covered by the state. Hence the enterprise had no incentive to increase efficiency or avoid loss. In 1978, however, the first tentative reforms were introduced when some large-scale enterprises were allowed to retain some profits. A second step was taken in 1980 when 6600 state enterprises practised some form of profit retention. Then in 1982 a beginning was made toward replacing the system of profit remission by a corporate income tax. By 1983 most enterprises had changed over to a corporate income tax system although they were still required to remit some of their after-tax profits as well. Finally, from October 1984 profit remission ended and state enterprises were regulated solely by taxation.

The standard rate of income tax for large state enterprises is 55 per cent. Small enterprises are taxed at a lower rate on an eight-step progressive tax scale which begins at 7 per cent. In principle state enterprises are allowed to retain all profits after payment of the income tax and they may use these retained profits as they like, subject only to the broad guidelines issued by the government, as previously mentioned. The intention, evidently, is to make each enterprise an independent profit-and-loss accounting unit.

Table 5.5 Rate of Profit on Capital by Industry, 1982 (per cent)

Coal mining	0.5
Agricultural machinery	2.3
Iron ore mining	5.0
Construction materials	7.9
Chemical fertilisers	9.1
Rolled steel	20–30
Organic chemicals	21.3
Pharmaceuticals	25.9
Oil refining	40.0

Note: In coal mining 61.9 per cent of the enterprises operate at a loss.
Source: Discussion with officials at the State Planning Commission, Beijing.

Reality does not yet coincide with the reformers' intentions. Loss-making enterprises, for instance, are not normally allowed to become bankrupt. Cases of bankruptcy are not unknown – we came across a small bicycle manufacturer in Liaoning province that was forced by losses to go out of business – but generally speaking the state continues to cover the losses of state enterprises. Similarly, the government does not allow state enterprises to retain super-normal profits but instead scoops them up with the regulatory tax. The justification for this is that the rate of profit on fixed plus circulating capital varies enormously from one sector to another, as shown in Table 5.5, and hence a uniform rate of tax on profits would imply that some enterprises would retain huge sums while others would retain very little.

The regulatory tax, thus, is used to compensate for the effects of price distortions on the profitability of state enterprises. The problem, however, is that the regulatory tax is arbitrary and is negotiated on a case-by-case basis with each enterprise. Hence, where once state enterprises were subjected to detailed physical controls, they now are subjected to detailed financial controls. This tends to negate one of the major purposes of the reform, namely, the substitution of general and indirect economic mechanisms (economic levers) for administrative regulations. The regulatory tax may be acceptable during the transition phase of the reform process, but the sooner prices are reformed and the regulatory tax is abandoned, the better. The objective should be a single tax (or tax scale) on the profits of state enterprises combined with a rational set of relative prices.

Table 5.6 Percentage of Total Profits Retained by State Enterprises

	Year(s)	*Retained profits (%)*
No. 2 Watch Factory	1979–84	5.6 (8.6)+
Shanghai Diesel Engine Factory	1980–84	15.0
Capital Iron and Steel Co.	1983	27.0
Shenyang Heavy Machinery Co.	1983	28.0
Changzhou Stocking Factory	1983	38.2
White Cloud Industrial, Agricultural and Commercial Combines Co.*	1983	90.0 (100.0)+
Average of all state enterprises	1983	17.0

Notes: * Despite the fact that 88 per cent of its output value originates in industry, this enterprise is regarded for tax purposes as an agricultural enterprise and consequently has a contract to deliver a fixed amount of profit to the government.
+The figure in brackets is the retention rate on above-plan profits.

Source: Field notes.

Meanwhile, the proportion of profits retained by enterprises varies widely but the average rate of retention is only about 17 per cent, not the 45 per cent that one might have expected. This is shown in Table 5.6.

Turning to depreciation of capital equipment and buildings, two points can be made. First, in general, rates of depreciation are too low and ought to be increased. Idle capital appears not to be depreciated at all, no account appears to be taken of technological obsolescence and very modest provision is made for ordinary wear and tear. Prior to the reforms, rates of depreciation were as low as 3.0 per cent. They have since been increased to 5.0 per cent at the Shenyang Heavy Machinery Co. and 5.8 per cent at the Shanghai Diesel Engine Factory, but a further rise would be desirable. It is worthy of note that in wholly-owned foreign enterprises, in joint ventures and in enterprises located in Special Economic Zones, buildings are amortised over 20 years and equipment over 10, implying straight-line rates of depreciation of 5 and 10 per cent, respectively. There is no reason to treat state enterprises less favourably than other enterprises and hence a rate of depreciation of machinery of at least 10 per cent for all state enterprises can readily be justified.

Second, depreciation represents a true cost, viz. the cost of using buildings and equipment. This cost is borne by the enterprise and hence it probably would be desirable to allow all funds set aside to cover this cost to be retained by the enterprise. Prior to the reforms, state enterprises were allowed to keep only 50 per cent of their depreciation funds; the proportion recently has been raised to 70 per cent and this clearly is a step in the right direction. Some firms, however, retain 100 per cent of their depreciation funds, e.g. the Changzhou Stocking Factory, a state enterprise under collective management, and consideration should be given to extending this practice to all state enterprises.

The final issue in this section is the rate of interest. Here it appears that two and possibly three reforms would be desirable. First, on average, rates of interest are very low – often between 2.4 and 3.6 per cent – and clearly do not reflect the true scarcity of capital. As an initial approximation to the correct rate, the real average rate of interest might be raised to 6.0 per cent (or perhaps a bit higher) to reflect the long-term rate of growth of the economy. Given a current rate of inflation of about 2 per cent a year, this implies an average nominal rate of interest of 8.0 – 8.5 per cent.

Second, state banks appear to charge very different rates of interest depending upon the sector to which the loan is made. This is undesirable, particularly now that managers have greater responsibility for investment decisions, because the relative price of labour and capital faced by state enterprises will not reflect real scarcities but will vary depending upon the sector of activity. This will introduce distortions into choices about the optimal degree of mechanisation and if continued for long will result in a considerable misallocation of resources. The justification given for favouring certain sectors with low interest rates is the irrational price system, but the latter is an argument for price reform and is not a good reason for subsidising the cost of capital to selected enterprises. In principle the rate of interest ought to be uniform across sectors, after taking risk into account, and it would be desirable if policy were to move in this direction.

Lastly, the spread between lending and borrowing rates appears to be very wide, perhaps of the order of 3:1. It is especially important that state enterprises are offered an attractive rate of interest on their cash deposits so that an active loanable funds market can be created.[8] If this is not done, state enterprises will be tempted to invest all their retained profits in the expansion of the firm, even when the rate of return on additional investment is very low. It is highly desirable that finance capital flows to those sectors and enterprises where profit rates are high and this can be encouraged by raising the average rate of interest and if possible reducing the spread between the banks' lending and borrowing rates.

PRICE REFORM

As the reform process has proceeded, the need to reform the methods by which relative commodity prices are determined has assumed growing importance. Initial priority was given to increasing the autonomy of state industrial enterprises. This probably was the best first step, but it soon became apparent that if the managerial reforms were to be successful, they would have to be reinforced by changes in labour payment systems and in the treatment of capital costs. These, in turn, implied a reform of the entire price system. Indeed, price reform is the heart of the entire reform process.

The authorities have naturally and rightly been unwilling to overhaul the price system all at once. They recognise that changes in the price system can have major repercussions, possibly provoking a generalised inflation or creating instability of production, and they have decided that price reform should occur gradually, on a step by step basis. This surely is correct, although it must be accepted that a gradual reform creates its own problems arising from disparities between reformed and unreformed prices. There are advantages, then, in moving ahead as quickly as possible, consistent with the need to maintain stability and growth.

Several changes have of course occurred already and China today in effect has a multiple price system. Some output continues to be determined in accordance with planned quota targets and is sold at official fixed prices established by the state, often on the basis of price relativities introduced in the 1950s. A prime example is petroleum products. Some output is produced under indicative plans and state guidance, and above-quota production can be freely sold by the enterprise at any price within the range of plus or minus 20 per cent of the official price. An example is mining equipment. Finally, some products are sold on totally free markets and the price is determined by supply and demand. A number of small consumer goods fall into this category. It is impossible to give precise figures for the distribution of industrial sales among the three markets mentioned, but an informed guess is that 40 per cent of industrial production is sold under administrative planning procedures, 50 per cent under a guided plan and 10 per cent in free markets.[9]

The question is, how does one move from this situation to a more desirable one, and what criteria should be used in future in setting prices? Let us consider first commodities sold under official or planned prices. These can be divided into two categories: key commodities traded internationally and non-traded commodities.

As regards the key commodities that China exports and imports, it would be sensible to move gradually, say, over a period of three years, towards unification of domestic and world prices (or, strictly speaking, border prices: f.o.b. or c.i.f. for exports and imports respectively) subject to a unitary exchange rate (to link domestic and foreign purchasing power relations as desired by the authorities). The number of commodities affected will be small since China's exports are just under 10 per cent of the national income and its imports about 8.4 per cent, and trade is concentrated on a relatively few commodities. Well over half the country's exports, for example, consist of mineral fuels, etc. (mostly crude oil and petroleum products), textiles (silk, cotton cloth) and food and animal products (cereals, tea, pork). It would be a relatively simple matter to bring the domestic price of most of these products into line with border prices. A possible exception is energy resources. At present the domestic price is very far below international prices and an abrupt increase in domestic prices might seriously affect the cost structure of the entire economy. Adjustment, hence, will have to be slow, probably through an iterative process, but the ultimate objective should be to unify energy prices at world levels. Similarly, over half the country's imports consist of food (notably cereals and sugar), chemicals (especially fertiliser) and raw and intermediate materials such as cotton and rolled steel, and the domestic prices of most of these goods could readily be equated with the c.i.f. price. The domestic price need not be identical to the border price – in fact a moving average of border prices would be better than the spot price as it would smooth out price fluctuations – but it would be desirable for domestic and border prices to bear a close approximation to one another.

There is no particular reason to attempt to discover or artificially calculate border prices for non-traded commodities currently subject to official pricing regulations. Instead domestic supply and demand can be allowed to operate and the official price adjusted gradually each year until a market clearing price is established. Thereafter, prices should reflect market conditions without official interference.

Three qualifications, however, are necessary. First, the state will wish to retain residual price controls on those products produced under conditions of monopoly. Given the size of the Chinese economy there are likely to be few such products, but some price controls (or price ceilings) may be necessary. Second, where necessary, measures should be introduced to increase competition among state enterprises, either by breaking-up existing state monopolies[10] or by encouraging new firms to enter the market or by permitting imports from abroad. If in future the market is to determine prices, it is essential that markets be as competitive as possible. It is here that the trade centres recently established in Shanghai and elsewhere have a useful role to play.

Third, it may be desirable to continue to subsidise the price of some goods and services for reasons of social policy. An obvious example is urban housing, although medical services, transport, water and cooking gas also are heavily subsidised. Housing construction and maintenance, in fact, are almost free, rents being about one yuan per month for 10 square metres. Given the acute shortage of living accommodation in China's cities, one could not possibly allow rents to be determined by supply and demand unless one were prepared either to allow the standard of living of the urban population to fall sharply or to synchronise changes in rents with adjustments to the national wage scale. Neither course is to be recommended at present. Instead the experiment in Shanghai of creating a limited market in housing[11] should be monitored carefully and if it shows signs of being a success the experiment should be extended to other parts of the country.

Turning now to industrial products sold under a guided plan, the general principles should be (i) to increase the proportion of total output that is above the planned target and (ii) to eliminate the difference between the official price and the so-called floating price. The first principle can readily be implemented by persevering with the announced intention of reducing compulsory quotas and allowing the managers of state industrial enterprises as much freedom as possible to determine the volume and composition of output. The second principle can be implemented by doing two things. First, in cases where the floating price is lower than the official price, the official price should be abolished forthwith. This would apply to a fairly large range of consumer goods, including some pharmaceutical products, combs and, in Guangdong province at least, chicken and pork.

Second, in the important case where the floating price is above the official price, the floating price should be used to guide the direction of adjustment of the fixed price. The intention should be to narrow the gap between the two prices gradually, say, over a period of three years, and then to let supply and demand clear the market. The products that would be affected include coal, steel, timber, petroleum, some types of machinery, cement and some consumer goods. If floating prices were used as signals to planners for price adjustments, within a relatively short time China could have a set of relative prices that reflects domestic supply and demand conditions and a set of prices, moreover, that could readily be linked to the world market, if this were desired, by allowing managers to buy and sell abroad.

The price of grain deserves special consideration because it is the most important wage good and any change in grain prices will have widespread implications for living standards in both rural and urban areas. The official retail price of grain in urban areas has increased hardly at all in the last ten years. The purchase price paid to peasant producers, however, has increased considerably. Between 1975 and 1982, for example, the quota price was raised by 27.1 per cent and increased further in 1983. In addition a price premium of 50 per cent is paid by the state on previously agreed above-quota sales. Sales of grain in the free market usually take place at prices about 85 per cent above the basic quota procurement price or, if such grain is sold at a 'negotiated price' to the state, at a price a shade lower than this.

As a result a wide gap has emerged between the price paid by the state for grain and the price at which it is sold to urban consumers. This gap has had to be filled by subsidies financed out of general state revenues, of which the profit remittances of industrial enterprises accounted for 35.3 per cent in 1982. Between 1978 and 1982 grain subsidies increased by about 300 per cent, viz. from 7–8 billion yuan in 1978 to about 32 billion yuan in 1982.[12] This is equivalent to 28.5 per cent of total government revenue in 1982, or 80.6 per cent of the revenue from industrial enterprises, or 7.5 per cent of the national income! This clearly cannot go on much longer, yet unless policies are changed the situation will get even worse because of the success of the agricultural reforms in stimulating grain output.

The adjustment process is bound to be delicate and will have to occur gradually. A start could be made (i) by reducing the compulsory production quota by, say, a half while leaving the procurement price unchanged and (ii) combining this with an equally sharp reduction in the amount of grain urban consumers can obtain through the rationing system, while leaving the ration price unchanged. Then, (iii) the price premium on above-quota deliveries to the state should be abolished and all additional purchases by the state conducted at the negotiated/free market price. The latter, in turn, should slowly be brought into line with average border prices as previously discussed. The effects of these measures would be to reduce the volume of transactions in the rationing system, to reduce the total amount of money spent on grain subsidies, to reduce the price of grain in the free market and to simplify the price structure.

It would be desirable to complement these measures by (iv) an increase in nominal wages on the national wage scale to compensate workers for a higher cost of living. The average price of grain purchased by urban consumers would, of course, be higher and to this extent the policies suggested are inflationary. In aggregate terms the higher wage payments, however, need not result in higher costs and prices and lower profits elsewhere as the higher wages would be exactly offset by reduced government expenditure on food subsidies and consequently by a reduced government requirement for tax revenue from state enterprises. If handled properly, the relative price of grain will rise but the average price of all commodities should remain unchanged. Individual prices will of course rise or fall depending upon the relationship between wage costs, product prices and profits in the enterprise concerned. Finally, once the initial adjustment has taken place, perhaps in two or three years, the government can consider whether the time has come to end the grain rationing and production quota system. Food in China is abundant now, malnutrition is rare and the population is well able to meet its basic needs. The rationing and procurement system, of immense value in the past, may no longer be necessary or relevant in present conditions.

This brings us, finally, to commodities traded on free markets. The number of such commodities, as we have seen, is few and every opportunity should be taken to increase the volume of transactions in free markets. In fact, a useful point of departure would be that all commodities are traded in open markets at prices determined by supply and demand unless the planners have powerful reasons to insist on regulated prices. There must be thousands of products for which no reason, let alone a powerful reason, can be adduced for controlling their price. At the Changzhou Stocking Factory the price of all 50 varieties of stocking was fixed by the state until recently; now only the 30 per cent of output purchased by the state is sold at official prices and the rest is sold at floating prices; in principle, however, there is no reason why all the stockings should not be sold on the free market. Similarly, the Changzhou Comb Factory produces 1000 different kinds of combs, 100 of which are sold at official prices. This makes little sense; in fact there is no reason at all for government administrators to determine the prices of 100 different varieties of combs produced in Changzhou. Absurdities of this type are repeated daily throughout China and if they were ended consumer welfare, the pace of labour productivity and industrial output would rise more rapidly.

TRANSITIONAL ARRANGEMENTS

China is undergoing major structural changes in the middle of the worst world recession since the 1930s. Yet China not only has managed to avoid a decline in industrial output, the country has continued to expand at a satisfactory rate, both in industry and in agriculture. So far, the transition has been handled skilfully and stability of production and incomes has been maintained. The problems of the transition, however, are likely to increase as the shift from reliance on physical controls to greater reliance on the price mechanism accelerates. The danger is that the large changes in relative prices required to correct the present irrational price structure will result in a large increase in the general level of prices, i.e. in inflation.

Although the dangers of inflation are considerable they must not be exaggerated and it should be possible to devise a set of policies that will reduce the risk considerably. First, it is necessary to ensure macro-economic balance and in particular to maintain firm control over the availability of credit and the rate of interest. The three reforms in interest rate policy suggested earlier should therefore have high priority for implementation at the beginning of the transition period. Second, it is important that in markets where there is excess supply at the official price, the government allows prices to fall. This can best be done by abolishing the official price for such commodities, as previously recommended. If China is not in the situation of general shortage as defined by Kornai, one would expect there to be

Table 5.7 Household Liquidity, 1982

	Rural Areas	*Urban Areas*
Population (million)	797.3	210.8
Savings deposits (million yuan)	22 810	44 730
Savings deposits per head (yuan)	28.61	212.19
Average annual consumption (yuan)	212	501
Savings deposits as percentage of annual consumption	13.5	42.4

Source: State Statistical Bureau, *Statistical Yearbook of China 1983*, pp. 109, 454 and 484.

roughly equal numbers of markets where there is excess demand and markets where there is excess supply, and consequently a general movement in the direction of using market clearing prices is likely to leave the average level of prices unchanged. This assumes, however, that prices are just as flexible downwards as upwards. If they are not, prices will rise in markets where there is excess demand whereas in markets where there is excess supply, adjustment will take the form of a combination of reduced output and an increase in inventories of unsold goods with possibly a slight fall in price. In this case, the change in price structure will be accompanied by inflation, and possibly by a fall in output as well.

Thirdly, it is highly likely that if markets are liberalised, households, particularly urban households, will reduce their deposits with the banking system in order to purchase consumer goods. In this sense it could be said that China suffers from suppressed inflation or an excess of household liquidity, at present distorted market prices and interest rates. This of course is merely conjecture, but the data in Table 5.7 indicate that in 1982 savings deposits in the urban areas were equivalent to about 42 per cent of average urban consumption. One reason for the relatively high liquidity in the cities might be that in rural areas savings have been channelled into private house building whereas in the urban areas such opportunities do not exist. This suggests that the experiments to create a small private housing market in the cities could play a valuable role during the transition phase of the reforms in soaking up some of the excess liquidity in urban areas and thereby reducing inflationary pressures in other markets.

Fourth, particularly during the transition period, it is important that the government maintains control over wage incomes in order to prevent purchasing power in the hands of households from becoming excessive and provoking generalised inflation. An incomes policy centred on a reform of the national wage scale, combined with a modest bonus scheme, is probably a precondition for a successful price reform. Similarly, fifth, the recommended changes in the treatment of depreciation could with advantage be introduced at an early stage so that all charges for the use of capital become more realistic. If these changes in factor prices lead to greater deficits or even losses in some state enterprises which are at present profitable, these deficits will have to be covered by the state out of general revenues pending reform of the commodity price structure.

Finally, it would be desirable to retain the regulatory tax on above-normal profits, but solely as a transitional measure. As soon as the commodity price reform has been completed, say, within five years, the regulatory tax should be abolished. The net profits of state enterprises would then be controlled by a single, uniform corporate income tax scale, which could, of course, be changed from time to time as circumstances require. Meanwhile, it will be necessary to devise and implement a strategy for price reform, perhaps along the lines discussed in the previous section. If this were done, China would be able to look forward to an industrial sector of increasing sophistication and diversity, capable of sustained rapid growth and of competing effectively with the rest of the world.

THE SPECIAL ECONOMIC ZONES

Four Special Economic Zones have been established, one in Fujian province (Xiamen) and three in Guangdong (Shantou, Zhuhai and Shenzhen). The largest by far is at Shenzhen, an area of 327.5 km^2 which is connected to the south to the New Territories of Hong Kong. In addition to the Special Economic Zones, China has selected 14 coastal cities as open economic development zones where trade and joint investment ventures with overseas corporations are encouraged. These zones are intended to serve several purposes, viz. to promote employment in industry, to earn foreign exchange needed for China's modernisation programme, and to raise living standards in what are often relatively economically backward regions. Their primary purpose, however, is to attract new technology and skills to China through the establishment of relatively capital-intensive industries. The output of these industries is largely for export although sales in the domestic market are allowed.[13]

Shenzhen, the Special Economic Zone visited during this study, was established in 1980. Since then, up to the end of 1983, approximately 2.9 billion yuan has been invested: 1.9 billion by the Chinese and 1.0 billion by overseas investors. Industrial investment, however, accounts for only 25–30 per cent of the total, the remaining 70–75 per cent being investment in infrastructure, housing and other non-productive activities. The outlook, none the less, is fairly bright since contracts with foreign investors for another 3.7 billion yuan have been signed and these should result in due course in a large number of additional manufacturing projects. Certainly the Shenzhen Special Economic Zone Development Co., the organisation responsible for foreign investment, joint ventures, trade and land development in the zone, is ambitious and already has plans to build an airport, electrify the railroad between Shenzhen and Guangzhou, construct a nuclear power station and expand further the offshore oil support base which supports exploration in the South China Sea.

Population growth in the zone has been very rapid, rising from almost nothing in 1979 to 320 000 people by the end of 1983. The labour force at that time was 192 000, of which 122 000 represented permanent jobs and 70 000 temporary workers mostly engaged in construction. The target for 1990 is a population of 400 000 and a labour force of 240 000; by the turn of the century these two figures are intended to double.

The main attraction of a Special Economic Zone to an overseas investor is likely to be a low unit cost of labour, i.e. low wage costs in relation to the productivity of labour. This is where China's comparative advantage lies and in the case of Shenzhen the obvious comparison is with Hong Kong. We therefore begin our analysis by comparing wage costs in Shenzhen and Hong Kong.

State enterprises in the Special Economic Zones pay essentially the same wages as outside the zones although there is a cost of living adjustment.[14] Foreign enterprises inside the zones are not subject to wage controls and are free to allow their wage rates to be determined by the forces of supply and demand. In practice, foreign enterprises and joint ventures usually pay slightly more than state enterprises – 5–10 per cent may be typical – and this enables them to attract the more skilled workers and to demand greater intensity of work from their labour force. In addition to the wage received by the worker, however, foreign enterprises are required to allocate 5 per cent of the total wage bill to an internal welfare fund to finance medical services, the training of employees, purchases of uniforms, etc. On top of this the enterprises must pay the equivalent of 25 per cent of the wage bill to a government Labour Service Company to cover the cost of state pensions and social security, costs which in the case of state enterprises are financed by the state out of profit taxes.

The average cost of labour in Shenzhen appears to be only about 40 per cent of the average wage in Hong Kong, and presumably firms in Hong Kong also have non-wage costs of employing labour. That is, the cost of labour in Shenzhen (including allocations to the welfare fund and payments to the Labour Service Company) is approximately HK$800 per month (or 267 yuan) as compared to an average wage received by a worker in Hong Kong of HK$2000 per month. Hence, provided the productivity of labour in Hong Kong is no more than $2\frac{1}{2}$ times that in Shenzhen, enterprises in the zone are likely to be competitive in terms of unit labour costs.

Consider, for example, the Shenzhen Goodyear Printing Co., a joint venture, half of whose equity capital of 6.5 million yuan came from Hong Kong. The average total cost per employee is 325 yuan per month and consists of the following: the average wage[15] of 175 yuan, surcharges of 30 per cent (or 75 yuan) and overtime payments and bonuses of 75 yuan. In Hong Kong a similar person in the printing industry would receive a wage of HK$3500 per month plus bonuses, etc., of approximately HK$500, or the equivalent of about 1333 yuan per month. That is, labour costs in the printing industry are roughly four times higher in Hong Kong than in Shenzhen. Labour productivity in Hong Kong also is higher but not four times higher. Thus the Goodyear Printing Co. is competitive with Hong Kong although its transport costs are slightly higher, it cannot match Hong Kong's speed of delivery and it does not yet have Hong Kong's established commercial links.

Turning now to purchases of raw materials, it is the policy of the government to encourage foreign firms and joint ventures to purchase supplies from China. This encouragement takes the form of sales of raw materials by the state to such enterprises at prices below the official price, viz. at the lower export price or in some cases at a price even lower than this. The implication is that state enterprises in competition with foreign enterprises located in Special Economic

Zones are discriminated against, a curious policy for the government of a socialist country to follow. Moreover, if the price at which raw materials are sold to foreign enterprises is lower than the f.o.b. price in foreign exchange that could have been earned by exporting the raw materials, foreign companies are subsidised by the Chinese people and their government, an equally curious policy. It would seem sensible to supply raw materials to all enterprises, domestic and foreign, at the same price: ideally that price should be the border price in the case of exportable commodities, as previously discussed.

Joint and foreign enterprises that use domestic raw materials are allowed to sell part of their output on the domestic market. The volume of domestic sales permitted is strictly regulated and depends on the proportion of materials obtained from domestic sources. This is an important privilege for foreign companies in Special Economic Zones because profit margins on domestic sales are usually higher than on exports. For instance, one of the products manufactured by the Kilter Electronics Company in the Shekou Industrial Zone of Shenzhen sold for the equivalent of HK$1150 on the domestic market and HK$400 if exported to Hong Kong. At the prevailing exchange rate, the manager of the enterprise naturally fulfilled his domestic sales contract first and then switched to production for export. The October 1984 devaluation of the yuan shows that the authorities are aware of this sort of problem.

There is some evidence that foreign and joint enterprises are able to borrow from the Bank of China at much lower rates of interest than prevail abroad. State enterprises in the Shenzhen Special Economic Zone pay an annual rate of interest of 6 per cent on borrowed funds. The Goodyear Printing Co., a joint venture, pays 8 per cent for loans in local currency and 10 per cent to borrow foreign exchange. This can be compared with the 15–17 per cent charged by banks in Hong Kong. One consequence of this is that foreign equity holders have an incentive to maximise low interest rate borrowing from the domestic banking system to the possible detriment of inflows of capital from abroad. In the case of the Goodyear Printing Co., for example, total fixed assets are 8.2 million yuan, of which 79.3 per cent is equity capital and 20.7 per cent was financed by a loan from the Bank of China. It is of course an open question whether the 1.7 million yuan that was borrowed domestically would have been obtained abroad had the loan not been available, but at the very least, it would seem that interest rate policy applied to foreign and joint enterprises ought to be reviewed.

There certainly is no need to subsidise interest rates paid by foreign corporations, particularly since the rate of taxation on profits is so favourable. Outside the Special Economic Zones, joint enterprises and wholly-owned foreign enterprises pay a 30 per cent profits tax, although the possibility of reducing this rate in the 14 coastal cities chosen to be open development zones already is being discussed. Inside the four Special Economic Zones the rate of tax on profits is 15 per cent, but the full rate usually is not applied until the enterprise is well established. That is, the first two years of profitable operation are not normally taxed and the next 3–5 years are taxed at only 7.5 per cent. These concessions are not automatic – they are subject to negotiation – but a standard pattern seems to have emerged. The package as a whole must be very attractive to foreign enterprises, since the rate of taxation of profits in Shenzhen compares favourably even with the low profits tax of 16.5 per cent that prevails in Hong Kong. Moreover, if profits are reinvested instead of repatriated even the 15 per cent tax is remitted.

The Special Economic Zones, then, offer a good deal to foreign businessmen: freedom to adopt their own techniques of management and to operate within a market economy, absence of customs duties on imported materials if the final product is exported, competitive labour costs, subsidised prices on some domestically purchased raw materials, low interest rates on loans from the domestic banking system (although the banking system itself is underdeveloped) and modest taxation of profits which can be freely repatriated. What does China gain from all this? The answer so far must be not very much. Some new technology has been introduced; some exports have been generated; some exposure to improved methods of management has been obtained. Perhaps the major benefit has been political: reassurance to residents in Hong Kong that it is possible to have 'two systems in one country' and, more generally, the creation of a filter between the capitalism of the West and China's particular form of socialism. The Special Economic Zones, in sum, are experiments on a grand scale: they represent not just attempts at industrial reform but attempts to create a new system of economic management in China.

Notes

1. See Keith Griffin (ed.), *Institutional Reform and Economic Development in the Chinese Countryside*, London: Macmillan, 1984.

2. See the text of the *Decision of the Central Committee of the Communist Party of China on Reform of the Economic Structure*, adopted by the 12th Central Committee at its third plenary session, 20 October 1984, published in Summary of World Broadcasts, FE/7780/C/1 on 22 October 1984.
3. The delegation consisted of Andrea Boltho, Sir Henry Fisher, Keith Griffin (head), Michael Kaser and Cyril Lin. We visited China at the invitation of the Institute of Economics of the Chinese Academy of Social Sciences; our international travel was financed by a grant from the British Academy and additional support was provided by Oxford's George Webb Medley Fund and the Chinese Studies Centre at Wolfson and St Antony's Colleges. We are most grateful to our Chinese and British benefactors for making possible an unusually stimulating research trip.
4. We will comment at considerable length on the price reforms later.
5. There appears to be some confusion about the guideline. Some informants and sections of the press claim that no more than 40 per cent should be spent on bonuses and workers' benefits while the majority claims the maximum is 50 per cent. Evidently this point should be cleared up so that managers know what is expected of them.
6. 'Enterprises Ignore State Guidelines', *China Daily*, 21 August 1984.
7. In Guangdong province the standard bonus is three months' wages and enterprises are not required to pay taxes on above-normal bonuses until this limit is reached. The reason given for this concession is that the cost of living is higher in Guangdong than in other parts of China and hence the application of national wage scales and bonus arrangements would result in a lower real standard of living for workers in the province.
8. We collected very little data on this topic. However, at the Shenyang Heavy Machinery Co. we were informed that their deposit rate recently was increased to 0.6 per cent per month (or 7.4 per cent per annum compound) from 0.4 per cent.
9. This guess was made by a senior official at the State Planning Commission.
10. An example of this is the decision recently taken to divide the Civil Aviation Administration of China (CAAC) into five separate airlines in 1985.
11. In 1981–2 the Shanghai Municipality built 20 000 m^2 of housing for sale to private individuals. The programme increased to 100 000 m^2 in 1983 and the planned figure for 1984 was 200 000 m^2. The price of housing is set at the cost of construction plus the capitalised value of land rent; the average price of a 30 m^2 apartment is approximately 10 000 yuan. Mortgages are not available for private buyers.
12. This information was provided by a senior official at the State Price Bureau.
13. For a general discussion see Ji Chongwei, 'Why China Has Opened Special Economic Zones', *China Reconstructs*, vol. XXXIII, no. 9, September 1984.
14. At the Kilter Electronics Co. Ltd in the Shekou Industrial Zone located one hour's drive from Shenzhen city, nominal wages are a multiple of

those in Beijing (from where the workers are recruited) whereas the real wage is about one third higher. For example, the nominal wage of the lowest paid workers was 39–43 yuan per month in Beijing and 113 yuan in Shekou. Note that Kilter Electronics is a joint venture and hence, unlike state enterprises, may pay whatever wage it wishes.

15. The lowest wage in the enterprise, paid to new recruits, is 140 yuan per month and the highest, paid to the manager, is 262 yuan.

STATISTICAL APPENDIX

All of the tables in this appendix are reproduced from the *Statistical Yearbook of China 1983* (State Statistical Bureau, October 1983) and are included for the convenience of the reader. A copy of the *Yearbook* can be obtained from Economic Information and Agency, 342 Hennessy Road, Hong Kong.

Table 5A.1 Number of Industrial Enterprises (ten thousands)

Year	*State-owned enterprises*	*Collectively owned enterprises*	*Of which: Commune-run*	*Total*
1970	5.7	13.8	4.5	19.5
1975	7.5	18.8	7.7	26.3
1980	8.34	29.35	18.66	37.73
1981	8.42	29.68	18.55	38.15
1982	8.61	30.19	18.58	38.86

Table 5A.2 Gross Industrial Output Value (100 million yuan)

Year	*State-owned enterprises*	*Collectively owned enterprises*	*Of which: Commune-run*	*Total*
1970*	2153.3	267.5	26.6	2420.8
1975**	2678.6	540.2	86.8	3218.8
1980**	3928.4	1034.4	280.5	4992.4
1981+	4054.4	1089.3	323.2	5177.7
1982+	4340.3	1192.8	354.3	5577.5

Notes: * At 1957 constant prices.
** At 1970 constant prices.
+ At 1980 constant prices.

continued on page 144

Table 5A.3 Index of Gross Industrial Output Value (index: 1952 = 100)

Year	*State-owned enterprises*	*Collectively owned enterprises*	*Total*
1950	53.3	63.3	55.7
1960	634.5	214.6	535.7
1970	914.0	370.1	786.0
1975	1338.6	805.8	1216.4
1976	1323.9	914.6	1232.2
1977	1492.0	1107.6	1408.4
1978	1706.8	1213.9	1598.6
1979	1858.7	1297.7	1734.4
1980	1962.8	1541.7	1887.0
1981	2011.9	1686.6	1967.4
1982	2154.7	1846.8	2115.7

Table 5A.4 Composition and Rate of Growth of Gross Industrial Output by Branch of Industry

Branch	*Composition, 1982* (%)	Rate of Growth (% p.a.) *1953–57*	*1958–62*	*1963–65*	*1966–70*	*1971–75*	*1976–80*
Metallurgical	8.7	29.2	7.4	20.4	8.8	5.3	8.4
Power	3.7	20.5	20.7	12.8	11.5	10.9	8.6
Coal	2.8	17.1	11.8	0.1	8.8	5.4	4.8
Petroleum	5.2	32.7	22.2	27.4	18.5	14.6	7.0
Chemical	11.8	31.3	14.4	23.9	17.3	10.4	11.3
Machine building	22.0	29.7	7.6	21.8	15.5	13.6	7.5
Building materials	4.0	20.0	–4.5	30.1	9.4	11.5	12.7
Forest products	2.0	13.7	–4.9	8.1	–1.8	7.5	7.2
Food products	13.6	13.2	–1.7	11.4	2.4	8.4	8.1
Textiles	15.5	8.6	–3.3	21.8	8.0	4.2	13.2
Paper-making	1.3	19.1	2.5	12.1	3.3	6.5	9.1
Total	100.0	18.0	3.8	17.9	11.7	9.1	9.2

Table 5A.5 Labour Productivity in State-owned Industrial Enterprises (1980 prices)

	Yuan per person per year	*Index: 1952 = 100*
1949	3 016	72.1
1952	4 184	100.0
1957	6 362	152.1
1962	4 817	115.1
1965	8 979	214.6
1978	11 130	266.0
1979	11 838	282.9
1980	12 080	288.7
1981	11 863	283.5
1982	12 133	290.0

Table 5A.6 Composition of Employment, 1982 (10 000 persons)

	Total	*Of which: state-owned units*	*Collective and individual workers:*	
			Towns	*Rural areas*
All sectors	44 706	8 630	2 798	33 278
Industry	5 930	3 503	1 548	879
Construction	1 340	678	283	379
Agriculture, etc.	32 013	805	55	31 153
Transport, post and telecommunications	850	515	220	115
Commerce, etc.	1 820	1 180	510	130
Education, health, welfare, culture, etc.	1 646	1 175	113	358
Government and people's organisations	611	563	14	34
Other	496	211	55	230

6 Rural Development in Arid Regions: The Case of Xinjiang

Xinjiang Uygur Autonomous Region is the largest administrative unit in China. It covers a vast area of 1.6 million square kilometres, or 16.7 per cent of China's territory. That is, it is larger than the combined size of France, West Germany, the United Kingdom, Ireland, Italy, the Netherlands, Belgium, Austria and Denmark. The population, however, is small – less than 14 million people live in the region or 1.3 per cent of China's population – and consequently population density is very low, at just under nine persons per square kilometre.

The region is remote and inhospitable and this accounts for the low population density. Physically, Xinjiang is divided into three sub-regions. In the south is the Tarim basin, in the heart of which is the Taklamakan desert. The basin itself is surrounded by high mountains – the Kunlun range to the south, the Karakorums to the south-west, the Pamirs to the west and the Tien Shan to the north – and the climate in the basin is very dry. The fringe of the basin, however, is speckled with oases which use the melted snow from the mountains to irrigate a large variety of crops. Kashgar, the largest oasis, is located in the extreme west of the Tarim basin and has an annual rainfall of 50–60 mm on average and a range of 10 to 100 mm.

The Junggar basin occupies the northern part of Xinjiang. It, too, has a desert at its centre, but the Junggar is less arid than the Tarim although it is considerably colder. Most of the basin consists of grassland and the main rural activity is livestock raising, mostly sheep, by nomadic and semi-nomadic pastoralists. The basin is bounded in the north by the Altai Mountains, on the west by a lower range of mountains and on the south by the Tien Shan.

The Tien Shan thus run from west to east across the whole of Xinjiang and divide the two basins from one another. The range contains peaks as high as 7400 metres and many of the mountains are more than 4000 metres high and are permanently covered in snow. These provide water for irrigating the Ili Valley in the west, the state farms around the regional capital, Urumqi, in the middle of the

Table 6.1 Population and Rural Labour Force in Xinjiang, 1984

Population:	13 440 800
Urban	4 242 400
Rural	9 198 400
Pastoral	774 300
Rural labour force:	3 797 900
Agriculture, forestry, fishery and sidelines	3 018 300
Livestock	264 400
Collectively-run enterprises	115 700
Construction	98 100
Transport and communications	27 200
Trade, commerce and services	51 000
Other	232 200

Source: Xinjiang Academy of Social Sciences

range, and the Hami and Turpan depressions in the eastern section of the range. The oases in the Turpan depression are especially noteworthy since the depression is 160 metres below sea level and is practically rainless, yet Turpan is a major centre in China for the production of grapes and melons.

Demographically, Xinjiang is typical of China as a whole in that a high proportion (68.4 per cent) of the population lives in rural areas. It is distinctive, however, in that about 60 per cent of the people are not Han but are members of minority nationalities, the great majority of whom live in the countryside. There are a dozen minority nationalities in the region,[1] but the two most important are the Uygurs (who are mostly in the oases of the Tarim basin) and the Kazaks (who traditionally led a nomadic life in the Junggar basin). Both the Uygurs and the Kazaks, as well as most of the other ethnic minorities, are culturally Muslims and all are free to practise their religion if they wish.

Politically, Xinjiang is not a province but an autonomous region. This is advantageous to the people of the region for two reasons. First, the Regional People's Congress in Urumqi has the authority to devise local laws and regulations that differ from those prevailing in the provinces; that is, the region has the power to make laws that reflect its peculiar characteristics and the interests of its various ethnic minorities. For example, the legal age of marriage in China is 22 and 20, respectively, for men and women. In Xinjiang, however, the legal age has been reduced to 20 for men and 18 for women. Similarly, the national population policy is one child per couple, but this policy does not apply to members of minority nationalities in Xinjiang, although it does apply to Han living in Xinjiang.[2] Again, Muslim religious festivals in Xinjiang are treated in the region as national holidays.

The regional government has made special provision for the educational needs of its people.[3] Students living in the border areas are not required to pay school fees (which in any case are very low throughout China) and are supplied with textbooks free of charge instead of being asked to buy them. In some areas, particularly where there are significant numbers of nomadic people, boarding schools have been established so that the children of pastoralists are not denied an opportunity to obtain a basic education.

Second, as an autonomous region, Xinjiang is eligible for special assistance from the central government. In practice, this assistance has taken several forms. First, some of the taxes collected in the region are retained for its own use instead of being passed on to the centre. Second, special funds intended for construction and investment projects in border areas have been given to the regional government by the centre. Third, the central government has given funds direct to the county authorities to use as they think best: these grants are common in all border areas of China, in the relatively poor areas of the country and in areas inhabited largely by ethnic minorities. In aggregate the central government currently provides about 1.6 billion yuan a year[4] to Xinjiang in the form either of direct investment in infrastructure or as grants and loans to regional authorities. This is equivalent to about half the capital formation in the region and is a measure of the importance of central government support to economic development in this part of China.

THE STRUCTURE OF THE ECONOMY

Although most of the people in Xinjiang live in the rural areas, only 43 per cent of the gross output value originates in agriculture; the rest is produced in the industrial and mining sectors. Within agriculture the broad composition of the value of output in 1984 was as follows:

crop cultivation	70.3%
animal husbandry	18.2%
forestry	3.2%
fisheries	0.2%
sideline production	8.1%

Fish production, not surprisingly in a desert area, is negligible. Sideline production, including village industrial enterprises, is about half as important as in the rest of China, reflecting the remoteness of the region and, within the region, the low population density and dispersed settlement pattern. At first glance, animal husbandry, at 18.2 per cent of gross agricultural output value, seems rather low, given that in China as a whole livestock products accounted in 1982 for 15.5 per cent of agricultural production. The comparison, however, is misleading because in most areas of China pig production accounts for a large part of the value of output in the livestock sector, whereas in Xinjiang, a Muslim region, pig production is unusually low. The most important livestock in Xinjiang are sheep and goats, of which there were 24.4 million in 1983. Only Inner Mongolia could boast of more.

Grains (maize and, above all, wheat) dominate crop cultivation and account for 69 per cent of the sown area. Grain output per head is now 739 jin[5] and is higher than the national average of 701 jin in 1982. Given this, and the fact that China is now self-sufficient in grain and, indeed, has a relative surplus and a grain storage problem, it would make sense for Xinjiang to consider reducing the area devoted to wheat and maize. Some land in the plains and villages could probably be used for intensive, irrigated pasture and forage production, thereby making it possible to reduce somewhat the grazing intensity on natural pastures in the mountains. The mountain areas affected could in part be reforested in order to control erosion and in part allowed to rest in order to give the grass an opportunity to recover from overgrazing. In some areas the grasslands could be resown with improved grasses, but not until weed infestation was reduced. In a few areas tourism, properly controlled, could be developed in parallel with a reforestation programme, thereby making it possible for more people to enjoy the mountains, rivers, lakes and reservoirs which contribute so much to the beauty of Xinjiang.

The main cash crops are cotton, sugar beet and various types of oil-bearing crops, e.g., rapeseed, sunflower and sesame. Cash crops occupy just over 19 per cent of the sown area. The rest of the land

Table 6.2 Rates of Growth of Gross Output
(per cent per annum in constant prices of 1980)

	Xinjiang, 1975–84	*China, 1975–82*
Total product	9.6	7.8
Industry	11.2	8.2
Agriculture	7.8	6.1

Sources: China: *Statistical Yearbook 1983*, State Statistical Bureau, 1983; Xinjiang: Institute of Economics, Xinjiang Academy of Social Sciences.

(11.7 per cent) is used to grow a very wide range of vegetables and fruits, of which grapes, melons, apples and pears are probably the most valuable. The cropping pattern, as is evident from the above figures, is biased toward low-value, high-bulk products and it clearly would be in the economic interest of Xinjiang to shift the composition of output in favour of crops with a more favourable ratio of value to weight. In effect this means switching from grains to fruit on the margin.

Such a shift in the cropping pattern, however, will require heavy investment in transport facilities, including air transport. The reason for this is that high transport costs and the consequent economic isolation of the farming areas of the oases virtually force each sub-region within Xinjiang to be self-sufficient in basic foodgrains. Conversely, high transport costs make it very difficult to produce specialised, high-value crops for large but distant markets. The result is that for every mu[6] devoted to fruits and vegetables nearly 7 mu are devoted to grains, despite the fact that agriculture is entirely dependent on expensive (compared to rainfall areas) irrigation systems.

Be that as it may, the rate of growth in Xinjiang has been impressive. Historically a remote, isolated and economically backward region, in recent years Xinjiang has grown faster than the rest of China and has experienced rapid improvements in average living standards. This can be seen in Table 6.2, where growth rates in Xinjiang for 1975 to 1984 are compared with growth rates in China as a whole for the slightly shorter period of 1975 to 1982.

Total product in Xinjiang has grown by about 9.6 per cent a year since 1975, or about 1.8 percentage points faster than in China as a whole. This is due in part to the very rapid growth in manufacturing and mining, where Xinjiang has exceeded the national average by 3 percentage points. The most remarkable performance, however, has been in the agricultural sector. China as a whole has done well, growing by 6.1 per cent a year in the seven years after 1975, but Xinjiang has done better still, growing by 7.8 per cent a year in the nine years after 1975, or 1.7 percentage points faster than the national average.[7] This achievement is particularly outstanding when one considers the harsh physical environment farmers and pastoralists confront, the need for substantial investment (notably in irrigation) before crop cultivation is possible and (as discussed) the constraint imposed on the cropping pattern by poor and expensive transport.[8] No region in the world, including the Sahelian countries of Africa, has had to face more difficult obstacles to rapid agricultural growth, yet few regions have achieved faster rates of growth than Xinjiang.

As a result, what was once a very poor region now enjoys a standard of living roughly comparable to the national average, although living standards still are much lower than those in the relatively rich provinces and municipalities of eastern China. Industrial workers in Xinjiang are paid the same as the average in the rest of China, but the standard of living in the countryside is approximately 10 per cent lower than the average in the rest of China. The heartening thing, however, is that agricultural incomes have risen relatively quickly and the difference between rural incomes in Xinjiang and elsewhere in China is rapidly disappearing.

The rural population of Xinjiang is 9.2 million, including 1.8 million people who live in rural townships. The rural labour force is 3.8 million, including those who work on state farms. There are about 774 000 people in the livestock sector or 264 000 workers. The rural economy of the region is not homogeneous but consists of three sub-sectors: the agricultural system of the oases, the state farms on land reclaimed from the desert and the pastoral economy of the semi-nomadic people. We shall examine each in turn beginning with agriculture in the oases.

THE AGRICULTURAL SYSTEM IN THE OASES

In general the institutional arrangements within the oases are similar to those in the rest of China. Virtually all of the production teams have switched to the household responsibility system and to production contracts. The communes have been converted to townships (*xiang*) and the brigades have largely disappeared. The teams continue to exist – although they are often called villages – and in addition to administering the contract quotas, they maintain the collective accumulation and welfare funds. The reforms are relatively recent – they were introduced in the north in 1984 and in the south in 1981 and 1982 – and so far, at least, no serious problems seem to have emerged.

The largest oasis in China is the Kashgar prefecture and, despite its size, it is fairly typical of most oases in Xinjiang. The prefecture covers 11 counties and the city of Kashgar (or Kashi). The population of the prefecture is 2.31 million persons, of which 1.84 million live in rural areas and 470 000 in urban areas. Rural income per head in 1984 was 213.57 yuan. The oasis is surrounded by desert and agriculture is dependent on irrigation water obtained from melted snow that is transported by rivers and canals from the Pamir Mountains.

The total cultivated area is 6.6 million mu, 95 per cent of which is irrigated. The cropping ratio is low, viz. 1.09, indicating that only 9 per cent of the land is double-cropped, the rest yielding a single harvest in the summer. The sown area is thus 7.2 million mu. Nearly 70 per cent of this area is devoted to grains (wheat and maize) and 19 per cent to cash crops (mostly cotton). Relatively little land is used to grow fruit, melons and vegetables. The reason is basically that it does not pay to do so: fruit is in surplus, there are few food-processing factories and the lack of transport makes it difficult to ship fresh produce to markets outside the prefecture. The regional capital, Urumqi, for example, is three days by road from Kashgar.

The prefecture contains 36 million mu of pasture which supports 4 million head of livestock, mostly sheep. It thus requires 9 mu to support one animal. Given that most of the pasture is not irrigated, this is not a high ratio for an arid region, but the intention of course should be to increase the amount of irrigated pasture, thereby permitting an increase in herd size and an improvement in breed quality. Additional water for irrigating pastures could be made available, as we shall see, by more economical use of existing supplies. It is not necessary, and indeed would be undesirable, to invest in canals and reservoirs merely to irrigate pastures; seasonally surplus water should suffice.

Livestock in Kashgar are closely integrated into farming. Four fifths of the animals are owned by farmers who support their small flocks from the grasslands allocated to them, from controlled foraging in the forest areas and from wheat straw. Slightly more than 10

Table 6.3 Land Use in Kashgar Prefecture, Xinjiang (million mu)

Cultivated land		6.6
irrigated	6.3	
unirrigated	0.3	
Pasture		36.0
natural pasture	33.8	
irrigated pasture	2.2	
Forest		5.0
natural forest	2.0	
artificial forest	3.0	
Total		47.6

Notes: 1. Only 0.6 million mu are double-cropped. The sown area therefore is 7.2 million mu.
2. The total irrigated area is 8.5 million mu.
3. The grand total may contain some double counting because some of the irrigated pastures also contain trees and the land is jointly used for forestry and grazing.

per cent of the animals are raised under semi-nomadic conditions, summer grazing in the mountains alternating with winter grazing in the plains. This general pattern is characteristic of livestock in the Tarim basin, and differs considerably from the nomadic patterns more common in the northern parts of Xinjiang.

The oases of the south are large, isolated, self-sufficient economies that revolve around grain and livestock. Kashgar produces all the grain it needs, imports about 12 per cent of its meat (mostly pork for the non-Muslim population) and exports cotton. Very few other agricultural products are either imported or exported to other centres, although manufactured consumer and intermediate goods are, of course, imported.

Although in recent years the rates of growth of agricultural output and rural incomes have been high, two elements operate as constraints on accelerated development. The first, as we have already emphasised, is transport and marketing. The second is the availability of water for irrigation. The second constraint, in turn, can be divided into two components: the size or capacity of the irrigation system and the efficiency with which a given supply of water is used.

The irrigation system of Kashgar consists of 102 reservoirs of all sizes plus 30 000 km of canals of four different sizes. The reservoirs have a usable storage capacity of 1.3 billion cubic meters of water;

they are located primarily in the plain and have an average life expectancy of about 30 years, after which the level of silt makes the reservoirs unusable. The main purpose of the reservoirs is to reduce the seasonal imbalance in the demand and supply of water. The peak demand for irrigation water is during the spring when 40 per cent of the annual requirement occurs; but this is a period of very low rainfall. Indeed, only 12 per cent of the yearly supply of water is available during the months of March–May; 64 per cent is available in the summer (June–August), 18 per cent in the autumn (September–November) and 6 per cent in the winter (December–February). The reservoirs thus are needed to store the water from the summer floods so that the crops can be irrigated in the following spring.

It is estimated by the prefecture authorities that there is a shortfall of 1.7 billion cubic metres of water. During the next few years, however, it is planned to build four new reservoirs, including a very large one in the Pamirs with a storage capacity of 0.8 billion cubic metres. In addition, there are plans to construct eight large drainage canals which should help to combat the problem of soil salinity. Total investment in the next five years in reservoirs, drainage and hydroelectricity is expected to be about 700 million yuan.

Meanwhile steps can be taken to use the existing water more efficiently. In general, the management of the irrigation system appears to be very good. Certainly there is no problem, common in other countries, of farmers located conveniently at the head of the system getting more than their share of water, or of the richer farmers obtaining extra supplies of water through bribery. The high degree of economic and social equality in the rural areas obviously helps to overcome problems such as these, as does the existence of well organised communal institutions.

Water is distributed throughout the system in proportion to land area, starting at the level of the prefecture and going down through the country and *xiang* until one reaches the village (or production team). At the village, particularly in the spring when water is very scarce, two persons are selected by the votes of all members of the village to oversee the distribution of water and the management of the irrigation system. Water, thus, remains under unified collective management – although crop cultivation is the responsibility of individual households – and irrigation water typically is allocated among households in terms of time (e.g. one hour of irrigation) and in proportion to the area farmed.

This system seems to work satisfactorily in regions where irrigation is entirely by canal and where there are no wells. Management problems become more complex, however, when private wells are combined with communally owned irrigation facilities. In Turpan, for instance, formerly the communes and later the townships were responsible for managing the irrigation system. Recently, however, about 100 wells have been dug by households and this has created a conflict of interest between the private and public sectors. Until now China has not needed a water law to regulate the private exploitation of groundwater, although groundwater is a public resource analogous to a common. Unfortunately, however, problems have emerged in Turpan which have brought this issue to the attention of the authorities. Quite often, apparently, privately owned wells either have been placed too close to publicly owned ones and have lowered the water table or they have been drilled too close to the *qanats*[9] and have had the same consequence. Ideally, wells should be at least 500 metres from a *qanat*, but cases are cited of private wells being as close as 100 metres and, in effect, stealing water from the underground tunnels. Regulations to prevent this do not at present exist and it is important to remedy this deficiency quickly before serious damage is done to the entire irrigation system.

In regions such as Kashgar, where private wells do not exist, the communal institutions still are able to mobilise resources for investment in public goods. For example, in 1985 the Kashgar prefecture spent 24 million yuan on small-scale investment projects such as farmland construction, small reservoirs and anti-salination works. This sum covered the cost of steel, cement and timber needed for the projects. The actual work, however, was organised and partially financed at the local level. These local-level contributions came from three sources: the collective accumulation fund of the village, direct contributions of labour by the intended beneficiaries in the village and voluntary contributions of cash by households. In fact, voluntary contributions in cash amounted to 4 million yuan in the first six months of 1985.

These voluntary contributions are a new phenomenon, having appeared only since the introduction of the household responsibility system in the prefecture in 1982. Already, however, they are more important in financial terms than the sums available from collective accumulation funds. It is impossible to know at this stage just how widespread and how large these voluntary cash contributions are, but it is certainly possible that the fear once expressed by this author and others, that the responsibility system would lead to a reduction in savings and in investment in public works, was misplaced.[10]

Technically, the most obvious way to improve efficiency in the use of existing irrigation water is to reduce the amount of water lost by seepage from the canals. At present only 30–37 per cent of the water in the canal system ultimately is used for irrigation; the rest disappears through evaporation and seepage. The main problem is that most of the canals are unlined earth ditches, and in these canals up to 90 per cent of the water is lost through seepage. In stone- or pebble-lined canals the seepage rate falls to 60 per cent and in the new plastic-lined canals the seepage rate is only 20 per cent. The immediate objective of the authorities is to raise the water use rate to 45 per cent, primarily by lining the general and main irrigation canals with thin sheets of plastic.

One ton of plastic lining is needed for each kilometre of canal and the cost is 3500 yuan per ton. This is only 20 per cent of the cost of cement or stone lining. Prior to 1983, very few canals were lined, but in the following two years the programme developed rapidly and by the summer of 1985 approximately 800 km of canals were lined with plastic. This is still only a tiny proportion of the canal system, and there is a long way to go, but policy is clearly pointing in the right direction. The new policy of promoting plastic lining supplements, but does not supersede, traditional techniques for controlling seepage, namely, planting grass, willow trees and poplars along the banks of the canals. In fact, the canals are lined with plastic only halfway to the top of the bank. In this way seepage is greatly reduced in the spring when the water in the canals is low, whereas in the summer, when water is relatively abundant, some seepage is allowed in order to irrigate the trees and grass planted alongside the canals.

An economic instrument also exists that can be used to encourage an efficient use of water, viz. water charges. At present, water is rationed and water charges are of little significance. Indeed, water charges in Xinjiang are the lowest in China and Kashgar's charges are the lowest in Xinjiang. There is thus a paradoxical situation where the greater the scarcity of water, the lower the charge for using it! There is almost no financial incentive in Kashgar for farmers to economise on their most precious resource, irrigation water, and this clearly ought to be changed by raising water fees substantially.

The water fee today is equivalent to about 1.5 per cent of the value of the gross agricultural output produced in the irrigated areas. This fee generated a total revenue of 6.1 million yuan in 1984, a sum that covered only 81 per cent of the running costs of the prefecture's irrigation service;[11] no contribution was made toward the amortisation of capital.

A similar situation exists elsewhere in Xinjiang. For example, in the Shihezi region on the edge of the Junggar basin, the Da Quan Gou reservoir supplies irrigation water for 2.9 million mu, mostly to state farms. Prior to the reform of the state farms in 1984, the water fee was exceedingly low, viz. 0.0045 yuan per cubic metre. The charge has recently been raised by more than three-quarters, to 0.008 yuan, but even so, it still is well below the cost incurred by the irrigation authority. In fact, running costs, excluding capital depreciation, are reckoned to be 0.015 yuan per cubic metre and hence water fees cover little more than half operating costs.

In Turpan, too, the driest place in China, water charges are very low. The scale of fees depends on the source of water, which varies from no charge for water obtained from wells; to 0.0015 yuan per cubic metre for water from *qanats*; to 0.003 yuan for river water and 0.004 yuan for water from a reservoir. The quota of water per mu is 1200 m^3 and, hence, assuming a farmer uses the full quota of water and obtains it from the most expensive source (a reservoir), the cost of irrigation per mu is a maximum of 4.8 yuan. This can be compared with a gross output value per mu which varies from 100 yuan for grain to 500 yuan for grapes. That is, the maximum amount that a farmer would pay for irrigation water is less than 5 per cent of the value of his output and most farmers must be paying only about 1 per cent. Clearly there is considerable scope for raising water fees.

Indeed, peasants were accustomed to paying much higher charges in the past. Before Liberation, Turpan was dominated by water lords, who often would own 8–10 *qanats* and who demanded payment in kind for the use of water. Peasants on the best land were charged 50 jin of cotton per mu for irrigation, or roughly 100 yuan in today's terms. Those on second-class land had to pay 200 jin of wheat per mu, or 40–60 yuan, while those on the worst land paid 100 jin of wheat, or 20–30 yuan. In other words, before 1949 the cost of irrigation was at least 4 to 20 times higher than it is today. It is not suggested that water fees should be raised to pre-Liberation levels, but it is evident that present charges are too low to discourage farmers from wasting water and they consequently should be increased.

CONTROL OF THE DESERT

One quarter of Xinjiang is true desert and much of the rest is arid. A precondition for rural development therefore is control of the desert. Alas, for many years the desert appeared to be out of control in Xinjiang. True, the amount of arable land increased from 15 million mu in 1949 to 48 million in 1985, but a third of the land suffered from salination and the problem seemed to be getting worse. In addition, 8 million mu became hard-baked or heavily eroded. Finally, the forest cover contracted steadily and today it accounts for only 1.1 per cent of the land area or 26.8 million mu. Xinjiang's problems, in other words, were not very different from those of arid and semi-arid regions in other parts of the world.

The basic cause of desertification was, of course, the neglect of forestry. In the early years after Liberation few trees were planted, perhaps only 10 000 mu per annum, and by 1982 the problem of deforestation was very serious. It was then that a massive tree planting programme was launched. By 1984 the programme was in full stride and 600 000 mu of forest was planted. This is the rhythm the region plans to maintain for at least the next 15 years, and most officials are confident that in practice the target will be exceeded. Assuming the target is achieved, and there is no reason to doubt that it will be, then by the end of this century Xinjiang will have 36.5 million mu of forest accounting for 1.5 per cent of the total area of the region.

In the past, tree planting was the responsibility either of the state farms or of the production brigades of a commune. Today, however, most of the trees are planted and cared for by individual households. In 1984, for example, 20 per cent of the trees were planted by the state farms, 20 per cent by production brigades and 60 per cent by households. The overall plan is drawn up by the Forestry Bureau of the regional government and this is then sent to the county governments, which are responsible for information and propaganda. Disaggregation occurs further at the township level and actual implementation at the level of the village or production team. Within the village each member of the labour force is expected to plant 3–5 trees a year voluntarily. Households supply their own saplings or seedlings, although in the case of very poor households these are supplied free of charge by the state. In most instances, however, the cost to individual families is negligible, since most plantings consist of cuttings from local poplars and these can be obtained for practically nothing. The death rate among new trees is quite low: only about 20 per cent die within a year of planting.

The most successful tree planting programme in Xinjiang is in the Kashgar prefecture. Indeed, between a quarter and a third of all the trees planted in the region are planted in this prefecture. In 1985, for instance, more than a million mu of trees were planted in Xinjiang (compared to the target of 600 000 mu), and of these, 266 000 mu were planted in Kashgar. Considering the entire period since Liberation in 1949, about 1.4 million mu of natural forest have been destroyed, but 3 million mu of artificial forest have been planted, giving a net gain in the prefecture of about 1.6 million mu.

The total forest area of Kashgar is 5 million mu. This can be divided into several categories as follows:

natural forest	2.0 million mu
windbreaks	0.7
fuel forests	1.0
orchards	0.6
anti-erosion forests	0.6
timber forests	0.1

This division, however, is a little artificial since many forests serve multiple purposes. Windbreaks, for example, also are used as a (regulated) source of fuel and provide some fodder for animals. The timber forests also help to control erosion, etc. Despite this ambiguity, it is clear from the data that the tree planting programme recognises explicitly the need of the rural population for wood as fuel and it also recognises the connection between the provision of fuel and the control of the desert.

The success in Kashgar in mobilising 'voluntary' labour for tree planting on such a massive scale rests, in this author's judgement, on three pillars. First, communal institutions exist and are strong enough to organise the workforce at the local level. Communes as such no longer function, but the 'village' does and it is able to undertake large and important educational and organisational tasks.

Second, the prefecture's Forestry Department provides technical assistance and, when necessary, the seedlings. Most important, it makes a modest cash payment to households for 'volunteering' their labour. In other words, there is a small monetary incentive to plant trees. The rate of pay is 5.5 yuan per mu. This is put in perspective

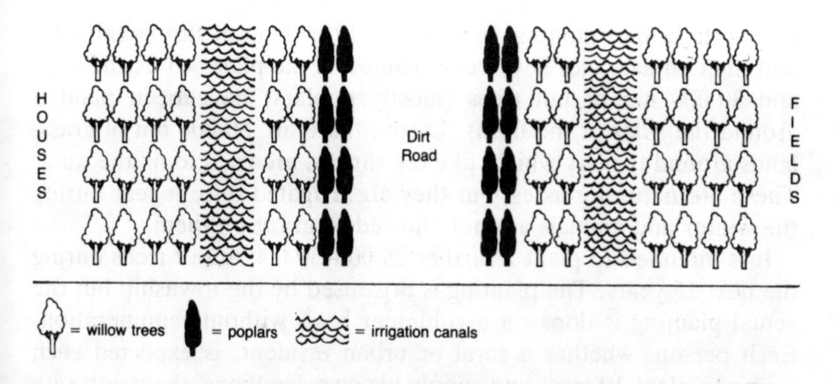

Figure 6.1 Tree planting along rural roads.

when one considers that in a fuel forest it takes two and a half days for one person to plant a mu with 200 trees.[12] That is, the daily rate of pay is equivalent to 2.2 yuan or £0.56. This may not seem a lot, but it probably is not too far below the opportunity cost of labour in rural areas and it is quite likely that the incentive of an immediate cash wage helps to account for the remarkable achievements in Kashgar.

Third, those who plant trees derive long-run benefits from their labour. Under the responsibility system once the trees are planted their care is entrusted to individual households; these households then have the right to use the trees on an agreed basis, whether as a source of fuel, or timber, or fruit or foraging by livestock. Thus there is a direct link between effort and reward – not just a temporary link between tree planting and the wage payment, but a permanent link between the care and protection of trees and the resulting continuous flow of benefits from the artificial forest created by the local population.

The extent of tree planting in Kashgar must be seen to be believed. In Shulu county, for instance, most of the roads are lined with Xinjiang poplars and willow trees. Most fields of maize, cotton, sunflower, Hami melon or watermelon are completely protected on all four sides by trees, although the paddy fields adjacent to the river sometimes were not fully protected. A typical planting pattern along a rural road is depicted in Figure 6.1.

The oasis city of Turpan, with a population of 190 000 persons, also is well protected from the desert. There is an immense belt of trees, 5 km long and 40 trees thick, designed to protect the city from the strong north-westerly winds and sand storms that blow upon it during the winter months. In addition, 12 000 mu of shrubs (about 5 feet high on average) have been planted in the plains to fix the sand and 30 000 mu of tall trees (mostly poplars) have been planted around the sides of the farms. Lastly, there are 80 000 mu of grasslands around the city which, like the shrubs, are used to fix the sand. These are natural grasses, but they are irrigated once a year during the winter and animals are not allowed to graze on them.

It is intended to plant a further 28 000–30 000 mu of trees during the next 15 years. The planting is organised by the township but the actual planting is done on a volunteer basis without remuneration. Each person, whether a rural or urban resident, is expected each spring to plant 10 trees and supply his own seedlings; the death rate of newly planted trees is about 30 per cent. An interesting aspect of the work in Turpan is that each 'unit' is assigned a specific piece of land for planting, i.e. each village, each hospital, school, institute, factory, etc. The Forest Department of the city merely checks each year that the work is properly done and then assembles the leaders of each unit to discuss, analyse and criticise the programme and plan for the following year's campaign.

Once the trees are planted their care is ensured in a variety of ways. In some cases specialised teams or households are created whose main task is to look after the trees and whose livelihood then comes to depend on fee income earned from managing collectively owned forests. In other cases, a household enters into a contract to look after collectively owned trees. The contract would specify the number of trees (e.g. 10 000) and the year when they could be felled for timber or fuel (usually 3–5 years after planting). At the time of felling the household would pay one yuan per tree to Turpan city, who supplied the tree at that cost, and then divide the remaining sales receipts between the collective and itself in the ratio 40:60. Thus, if a mature tree sells for 15 yuan, the division of sales revenue would be Turpan city, 1 yuan, the collective, 5.60 yuan and the household, 8.40 yuan. As part of the contract the household would be required to replant the forest and the cycle would then start all over again. In yet another variant, the collective (or state) instead of receiving 40 per cent of the net proceeds, receives a fixed sum to be paid at the time of felling. The household, in effect, enters into a loan agreement with the collective rather than a profit-sharing agreement.

The city authorities carefully supervise those entrusted with protecting the forest. Permission must be obtained before trees can be felled and replanting is mandatory. The timing of replanting, the

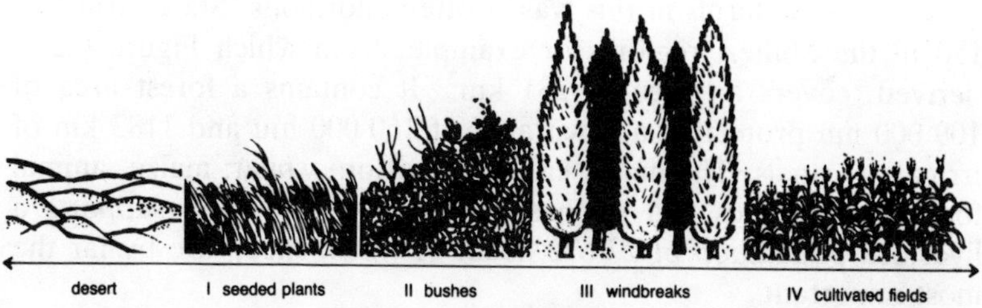

Figure 6.2 Transition zones from desert to cultivated fields

varieties planted and the frequency of watering are all controlled by the local government. Unauthorised destruction of trees is severely punished by fines: 5 yuan or three new trees for every young tree destroyed, 30 yuan for mature trees and 100 yuan for 10-year-old trees. In addition, those guilty of such vandalism are subjected to public criticism and humiliation. Life in Turpan depends on its forests and anything which puts life at risk is a serious matter.

Quite apart from the oases, the state farms, particularly those located on the edge of the Tien Shan, have played an important role in reclaiming land from the desert and increasing the area under cultivation. A number of techniques have been developed since the work of reclamation began in the 1950s, but the most successful seem to entail constructing a wide zone of transition separating the desert proper from the cultivated fields. This zone of transition can itself be divided into several sub-zones, as illustrated in Figure 6.2.

On the far left of the diagram is the desert of the Junggar basin, consisting of pebbles, sand and a few low sand dunes. The first sub-zone contains a belt of drought-resistant plants. These have been deliberately seeded but the plants are not watered; no one is allowed to gather fuel in this sub-zone nor are animals allowed to graze here. Next comes a belt of bushes, often tamarisk, which is planted to stabilise the sand. The vegetation in this sub-zone is irrigated once a year, usually in the winter. Behind this sub-zone of bushes and stabilised sand is a thick belt of trees, mostly poplars, which acts as a massive windbreak and protects the land that is actually cultivated. The trees in this sub-zone are irrigated four times a year.

The cultivated fields on the far right of the figure have, of course, been levelled and are served by a dense network of irrigation canals. Small windbreaks normally are interspersed among the fields and planted alongside the roads and canals. The area reclaimed from the desert by state farms in this way is often enormous. State farm No. 150 in the Shihezi region, for example, from which Figure 6.2 is derived, covers an area of 231 km^2. It contains a forest area of 109 000 mu protecting a sown area of 160 000 mu and 1183 km of irrigation canals. The major crops are cotton, wheat, maize, animal fodder, vegetables and melons; in addition, the farm supports a livestock population of 27 672 head, of which sheep are by far the most important.

In some parts of Xinjiang, attempts to reclaim the desert and expand the area under grain cultivation were carried too far, with the result that soil erosion, salination and desertification actually increased. This error is now recognised and efforts are being made to rectify the situation by converting some marginal grain land into grasslands or forests. In Kashgar prefecture, for instance, 60 000 mu of land formerly used to grow wheat was converted in 1985 into forests and orchards; another 60 000 mu of wheat is planned to be converted during the next four years. In this way, gradually, some of the excesses of previous policy will be corrected and measures to control the desert improved.

REFORMS ON THE STATE FARMS

There are more than twice as many state farms in Xinjiang, viz. 320, than in any other region of China, although the area cultivated (1.05 million ha or 15.8 million mu) is only 54 per cent as large as the area in Heilongjiang. The farms were started in the 1950s with the purpose, not only of reclaiming the desert and expanding the area under cultivation, but also of increasing population density in the sparsely settled regions along China's sensitive borders with the Soviet Union. The farms were organised by the army along military lines – with companies, divisions, etc. – and the workers were paid cash wages like any other employee of a state enterprise.

The workers, however, were far from privileged. Indeed, living conditions in the first few years were harsh and uncomfortable, with workers living in tents or in pits dug in the ground, in remote, isolated areas with few services or amenities. In the 1950s many of the workers were ex-soldiers who settled in Xinjiang; then during the period of the Cultural Revolution, many youths from the large metropolitan areas of eastern China were sent to work on the state farms; more important than both these groups, however, were peasants from other poor but densely settled regions of China. Looking back over the last 30 years, about a million peasants were moved to state farms in Xinjiang, 200 000 ex-soldiers settled on state farms, approximately 120 000 criminals served sentences on state farms and remained there after rehabilitation and less than 100 000 youths became workers on state farms.

The organisation of the state farms remained more or less unchanged until about 1979, when reforms in the commune system throughout China began to affect thinking in the state farm sector. In the Shihezi region, for example, contracts with individual companies, platoons or sections were introduced in 1979. Three years later, in 1982, the sections were sub-divided into groups and the state farm entered into contracts with them. Most workers, however, still received a fixed wage equivalent to 80–90 per cent of their total income and only the residual 10–20 per cent depended on the output performance of the group. In 1983 the system was refined further and wages were linked entirely to output. A production quota was set, usually based on the average of the last three years' output, and the group retained all above-quota output for its members (and assumed full responsibility for losses).

The reforms were carried a major step forward in 1984 when, throughout China, the state farms were broken up into group or household farms and agricultural wage workers were transformed into peasant cultivators and herdsmen. The nature of the contract varied slightly from one farm to another and from one economic activity to another, but the broad general outlines are clear.[13]

In the settled agricultural areas, contracts may be (i) with a single household for a minimum of 50–100 mu per worker, (ii) with a small group of three or four workers for 500 mu of arable land, or (iii) with a large group of, say, 10 workers for anything between 1500 and 20 000 mu depending on the nature of the land. The output quota typically is 90 per cent of the average of 1981–3 and is expected to be adjusted every five years. All output above the quota is kept by the household or group farm and once the quota is fulfilled the farmers are free to grow any other crop they want. Security of tenure is guaranteed for 15 years. Finally, in addition to the contracted land, each household is allocated 2 or 3 mu for a private plot and house space.

In the livestock sector the arrangements are slightly different. The state farms usually do not sell the livestock to herders but simply entrust them to their care. That is, the state farm continues to own the livestock, but the herdsmen are responsible under contract for meeting a quota of wool, skins, meat, etc. The households or groups are assigned a specific area of pasture in the hope that they will then have an incentive to improve their pasture by planting grass or trees and, where possible, irrigating the land with seasonally surplus water. In the good pasture areas the contract is drawn up in such a way that the state farm receives about 40 per cent of the output and the herdsmen 60 per cent. In very poor areas, however, the state farm may take nothing, the herdsmen being allowed to keep everything they produce.

Some households, mostly ethnic minorities, specialise completely in raising animals for the state farms. The majority of households, however, particularly the Han, who are a farming people, prefer to concentrate on cultivating crops and regard livestock as a secondary activity. Such households often join together with similarly minded households to form a group to assume joint responsibility for a flock. Each member of the group contributes some labour to the livestock sector, but most of their time is allocated to agriculture. In state farm No. 151, for instance, 26 000 sheep divided into 65 flocks are managed under contract. Ten of the flocks are under contract to individual households of minority nationalities. The remaining 55 flocks are under contract to groups of Han households who combine livestock with farming.

Finally, there are the contracts in areas being reclaimed from the desert. In these areas the state provides the roads, irrigation facilities and electric power and the individual household provides everything else. All output from newly cultivated land is kept by the household for the first three years. Thereafter the state receives a portion, the exact amount depending on the condition of the land. In good areas, for example, the quota might be 90 per cent of the average output of the first three years combined with guaranteed tenure for 15 years.

Specific details of contracts differ from one state farm to another. The directors of farms do have considerable discretion as to how best to implement the reforms and this leads to variation in the degree of control exercised by the centre. For example, most land is distributed on an equal-per-labour-force basis, but some farms (e.g. state farm No. 150) allocate land on an equal-per-capita basis. Similarly, most directors encourage households to form groups or cooperatives in order to permit greater diversification of output and to spread risks, but some directors are more sympathetic to small family farms. Again, most contracts now are fairly simple, concentrating on the output quota, but in a few cases (e.g. state farm No. 121) the contract is very detailed, specifying not only the output quota, but also the type of seed to be used, the area of land to be cultivated, the amount of fertiliser and irrigation water and even the use of machinery. These detailed contracts are necessary, it is argued, because many of the workers on state farms were highly specialised and lacked general farming knowledge and hence required careful guidance during the early years of the reform. Lastly, the control of farm machinery varies. Some state farms continue to own and operate the major pieces of equipment, others have formed a specialised machine team or group which manages the equipment for the state under contract; while still others have sold machines to individual households or groups of households working as a cooperative. In all cases, however, the state farm is responsible for planning production of the major crops, setting output quotas, providing technical assistance, transport and marketing services and managing the irrigation system. What it no longer does, and this is fundamental, is engage in direct cultivation. In this sense, state farms no longer exist; they have been replaced by family farms and small cooperatives.

It is too early to reach a definitive judgement on the effects of the reforms, but a few initial impressions may be of interest. First, it appears that the reforms have contributed to a rapid rate of growth of agricultural output. The 18 state farms in the Shihezi region, for example, grew by 11.1 per cent in 1984, the year after the reforms were completed, as compared to 8.0 per cent per annum in the period 1978–83. One year does not, of course, prove very much, but at least the outcome was encouraging. Similarly, average per capita income on the 160 state farms mentioned in note 13 rose from 460 yuan in 1983 to 570 yuan in 1984, in constant price terms, or by 23.9 per cent. Again, this is an encouraging outcome.

The effects on the distribution of income are even less certain. The indications, however, are that inequality on the state farms has increased. First, the people on the state farms were workers not peasants and most workers had little if any experience in farm management. The specialised workers in particular sometimes found it difficult to adapt to their new role as all-round farmers and required special assistance. This, to be sure, is likely to be a problem during the transition only, and it should disappear in the long run, but meanwhile some households will experience a fall in their real income. Second, given that land usually was distributed on an equal-per-worker basis, rather than on an equal-per-head basis as in most communes,[14] existing inequalities would tend to be consolidated rather than reduced. Third, there are frequent reports that while 80 per cent of the people on state farms have experienced a substantial increase in income, about 20 per cent have suffered an absolute fall in their standard of living. Given that average incomes have risen, this almost certainly implies a less equal distribution around the average.[15]

Even so, the distribution of income within a state farm tends to be very equal. Moreover, where inequality is thought to be a problem, directors sometimes attempt to control inequality by adjusting a household's quota, as on state farm No. 121, or by adjusting the quotas of groups of households, as on state farm No. 151. Differences among state farms also appear to be relatively modest. The 18 state farms in District No. 8 of the Shihezi region, for instance, tend to cluster within a fairly narrow range of incomes, as can be seen in Table 6.4.

The table contains data on average income per worker on 18 state farms with a total population of 350 000. As can be seen, the weighted average income from contracts, i.e. collective income, is 784.70 yuan. The distribution around this average, as measured by the coefficient of variation, is relatively even, viz. 0.28, and the richest state farm is 4.97 times more prosperous than the poorest. The figure for the range of incomes, furthermore, gives a slightly misleading picture of overall inequality because it is strongly influenced by the extraordinarily low contract income on state farm No. 148. If one removed this farm from the sample, the range declines sharply to 2.4.

Workers supplement their contract income with private income. The table indicates that average private income is 232.76 yuan and accounts for 22.9 per cent of total income. The range of private incomes, however, is enormous and this component of total income is distributed very unevenly, as indicated by the high coefficient of variation. Unevenness in the distribution of private income, however, appears not to be reflected in unevenness in the distribution of total income. On the contrary, the range of total income is slightly smaller than the range of contract income and hence there is a faint hint in the data that in the Chinese institutional framework the existence of income-earning opportunities outside the collective sector may help to reduce inequality in the overall distribution of income.[16] If state farm No. 148 is removed from the sample, how-

Table 6.4 Income per Member of the Labour Force, Shihezi Division No. 8, 1984 (yuan)

State farm number	*Contract income*	*Private income*	*Total income*
121*	932	19.41	951.41
122	1140	129.91	1269.91
132	780	83.30	863.30
133	602	62.14	664.14
134	841	404.60	1245.60
135	875	25.19	900.19
136	579.80	170.69	750.49
141	783	434.78	1217.78
142	706	73.62	779.62
143	859	302.39	1161.39
144	973	370.58	1343.58
145/6	925	341.09	1266.09
147	928	994.25	1912.25
148	261	190.11	451.11
149	539	286.86	825.86
150*	681	147.47	826.47
151*	969	480.87	1449.87
152	1296	444.92	1737.92
Unweighted average	814.99	275.51	1089.94
Weighted average+	784.70	232.76	1017.49
Range	4.97	51.22	4.24
Coefficient of variation	0.28	0.83	0.34

Notes: *Farms visited by the author.
+Figures weighted by size of the labour force.

Source: Data kindly supplied by Mr Liu Cheng Zhi of the Policy Research Centre, Shihezi.

ever, the range of total income exceeds that of contract income and even with farm No. 148 retained, the coefficient of variation of total income is larger than the coefficient of variation of contract income. Thus at the moment the impact of private activities on overall inequality is unclear – the data are too limited to permit firm conclusions – but there is no doubt that the degree of inequality on the state farms is remarkably low so far.

THE PASTORAL ECONOMY

The pastoral economy of Xinjiang revolves around sheep, which account for two thirds of all livestock. Next in importance comes goats, followed by cattle and then horses and donkeys. In 1984 there were nearly 30 million animals in the region divided as follows:

	millions
sheep	20.00
goats	4.00
cattle	2.80
horses	1.00
donkeys	1.00
camels	0.16
pigs	0.70

Most of these animals, excluding the pigs of course, graze on natural pastures, of which there are 700 million mu suitable for grazing.

The pastoral economy is semi-nomadic. That is, the household often has a permanent base where the women and children live, but the menfolk and older boys move with the herds in well established seasonal patterns. These patterns usually contain three grazing areas: one pasture used in the spring and again in the autumn, a winter pasture and a summer pasture.

Sometimes the distances travelled are relatively modest. For example, one group of Kazak herdsmen visited in the Nan Shan region near Urumqi had summer pastures only 30 km from their winter pasture and spring/autumn pastures 40 km from their winter pasture. In other areas, in contrast, the distances covered can be vast. In Fu Yun county in the Altai region, for instance, the herds are moved about 90 times in the course of a year and travel 800–1000 km.

The livestock economy is very extensive in its use of land and is fairly well adapted to the environment of Xinjiang. Productivity, however, is generally very low. One reason for this is an imbalance in the seasonal availability of pasture. Grass is abundant in summer – indeed, there is enough to support 60 million sheep – but is very scarce in winter and early spring. The scarcity is due partly to natural conditions and partly to policy mistakes which resulted in grasslands being converted into wheat fields. As one authority has forcefully put it, 'In recent years, many fertile rangelands were blindly reclaimed for planting, and as a consequence the shortage of winter–spring seasonal pastures became acute.'[17]

Possible solutions to the problems of the livestock sector include (i) permanent settlement of herdsmen in towns, (ii) reconversion of marginal grain land into pastures and (iii) increased output from the existing resources employed in the sector.

Permanent settlement of the nomadic population may be a long-term solution, but for the time being it is unrealistic. An attempt forcibly to settle, say, half a million pastoralists would almost certainly lead to a decline in output in the sector and a fall in income of the pastoralists. True, it would be easier to provide the nomadic people with educational and health services, but it is unlikely that they would regard this as just compensation for their loss of livelihood. As other sectors of Xinjiang's economy continue to expand, however, it should be possible to absorb gradually part of the nomadic population and offer them a higher standard of living, better public services and a less arduous life.

Conversion of marginal grain land back to grazing land certainly is feasible and in fact is agreed policy. So far, however, reconversion has been on a relatively small scale and it probably would be sensible to expand the programme considerably. Moreover, the surplus in the region makes this a propitious time to reduce the area devoted to grains and to increase the amount of pasture. It must be accepted, however, that even a large reconversion programme would not markedly alter the prospects for the livestock economy. A major improvement depends upon changes within the sector itself, and it is these changes which the economic reforms hope to encourage.

The keystone of the economic reform of the pastoral economy is the transfer through sale of livestock from collective to private ownership. Beginning in 1978, the collective units have distributed their animals to individual households on the basis of publicly agreed criteria. In most cases animals have been allocated among households in accordance with the size of household, on an equal-per-capita basis. In a few cases, however, allocation has been according to the size of the labour force in the household. Occasionally, too, a commune has adopted a combination of the two criteria, i.e. part of the herd being allocated on an equal-per-capita basis and part on an equal-per-worker basis. These reforms were virtually completed in 1984.

It is noteworthy that the allocation criteria almost certainly imply a reduction in inequality among the pastoral population. The reason for this is that prior to the reforms a household's collective income was derived from work points earned by its able-bodied workers. Households with many workers and a low dependency ratio enjoyed relatively large incomes per head, while households with few workers and numerous dependents (either the very young or the very old) had relatively small incomes per head. Today, however, to the extent that livestock are allocated on a per capita basis, a household's income from grazing is a function of its total size rather than the size of its labour force. Of course, households with few workers may have to pay members of other households to look after their animals, and hence strict equality in the distribution of animals will not result in strict equality in the distribution of income derived from livestock, but it will result in less inequality than would otherwise prevail. In this sense the reforms have an egalitarian bias that runs counter to the anti-egalitarian pronouncements that are so common in official circles.

The price at which livestock are sold to households is higher than the price at which the communes could sell animals to the state but lower than the price at which households can purchase animals in the free market. In Kashgar in 1984, for example, the state purchase price of sheep was 0.7 yuan per kg liveweight. The free market price was roughly twice that price, viz. 1.5 yuan, whereas the price at which collectively owned sheep were sold to members of the commune was 1 yuan per kg liveweight. On the surface, compared to the free market price, it appears that households acquired their herds at a substantial discount, perhaps as much as 33 per cent. This is very misleading, however, because if all the collectively owned sheep had been sold on the free market, the free market price would have fallen substantially and no one would in fact have had to pay 1.5 yuan per kg. Indeed until recently, in the whole of Xinjiang, only 2–3 per cent of the animals in the region were sold each year on the free market. Given this, it seems unlikely that the purchase of livestock by households from the commune was heavily subsidised, although it is impossible to demonstrate this empirically.

The average size of herd received by households varied enormously from one part of Xinjiang to another. The average per household is about 100 head, but the maximum is more than 500 head. At the other extreme some households received as few as 4 animals per person, especially when the household also engaged in farming and regarded livestock as a minor activity. Predominantly pastoral households seldom have fewer than 50 animals. Of course, once the initial distribution of collective livestock was completed, households were free to buy and sell animals as they wished.

The grasslands remain under collective ownership. Each household, however, is allocated several pieces of pasture land – one in each seasonal location – for which it is responsible under contract. The amount of land received by each household depends of course on the size of its herd. That is, there is an equal allocation of land per head of livestock. The location of each household's pieces of land – an important consideration in a semi-nomadic society – is decided by the collective in public discussion. Often groups of households pool their land and manage their herds as small cooperatives and in this way they are able to take advantage of economies of scale in grassland management and improvement schemes.

The reformed livestock sector thus has three levels of organisation and ownership. The animals are privately owned by households. The pastures, although allocated to individual households, in practice frequently are managed by cooperatives, while the land itself continues to be collectively owned.

The contract between a household and its collective has two parts. First, the household must pay to the collective 1 or 2 yuan a year for each sheep or other animal it owns. This is intended to cover the collective's tax liability and its management costs and to sustain the collective accumulation and welfare funds. Second, the household is required to sell to the state 7–8 per cent of its animals each year at the state purchase price. The state marketing rate is not fixed but is determined periodically after discussion between state organs (at region, county and township levels) and, ultimately, households. The state purchase price is not uniform throughout the whole of Xinjiang but varies slightly from one area to another. The average price of sheep per kg liveweight was 0.6 yuan until the spring of 1985, at which time it was doubled to 1.2 yuan. (The average free market price in 1985 was, say, 2.5 yuan per kg.)

The reforms undoubtedly have improved incentives. Households have planted grass and increased winter forage. Herdsmen have taken better care of their animals and, for example, have reduced the death rate of animals in winter. Statistically, the gains have been impressive. The number of animals has increased from 24 million in 1978 to 30 million in 1984, an increase of 25 per cent in six years. The average weight of a sheep during the same period rose from 13 kg of dressed meat to 15 kg, a rise of 15 per cent. The marketing rate increased by nearly a third, from 9.9 per cent in 1978 to 13 per cent in 1984, and the marketing rate of livestock sold on the free market (where prices are much higher) rose from 2–3 per cent to 5–6 per cent, i.e. it probably doubled. Finally, gross value in the livestock sector (in constant prices of 1980) rose from 499 million yuan in 1980 to 830 million yuan in 1984, an increase of two thirds in four years. As a result of these changes, living standards among the pastoral population have increased considerably and the acute poverty that once afflicted the nomadic people is rapidly disappearing.

CONCLUSIONS

Xinjiang demonstrates that arid regions are not necessarily condemned to poverty and backwardness. Indeed rural development in the autonomous region has proceeded very rapidly in recent years and faster than in China as a whole. The tendency of the desert to spread has been checked and there are encouraging signs for the future. The pattern of land use has improved, the forest area is growing rapidly, some marginal grain fields are being reconverted into pasture and a beginning has been made in reducing salination. Much of course remains to be done, but it is realistic to hope that the desert will soon begin slowly to diminish, provided present policies continue without interruption.

The experience of Xinjiang shows yet again that deserts are partly man-made. Poor economic policies, neglect and abuse of the natural environment, can lead quite quickly to erosion, degradation of the soil, destruction of the forest cover and even micro-climatic change. Happily, however, the experience of Xinjiang also shows that these processes can be reversed. It requires enormous effort and progress inevitably is slow, but the desert can be reclaimed and a viable and prosperous economy created.

The success in Xinjiang is due in part to support from the central government, and particularly to the generous provision of resources necessary to sustain high rates of investment in mining, transport, power and irrigation. The region could not on its own have amassed the finance required for these major projects; support from the centre was vital. This support, moreover, was sufficiently large and sufficiently well used to enable Xinjiang to raise the living standards of its people to a level approaching the average for the nation as a whole. Government policy thereby contributed to a reduction in inter-regional inequality in China.

The institutional arrangements that have evolved in recent years appear to have been successful. Households now are responsible for farming throughout most of the region, particularly in the former production teams of the communes but also on a number of state farms. Furthermore, households now own almost all the livestock, except on the state farms where they are collectively owned but managed under contract by individual households or small groups of households. Communal institutions still exist and seem to function reasonably well. They are particularly important in managing irrigation systems and ensuring an equitable distribution of water and, as voluntary cooperatives, in managing collectively owned pasture land.

Collective investment and the mobilisation of local labour for public works projects continue, rightly, to play prominent roles. The massive tree planting programme – the key to controlling the desert – illustrates the importance of local institutions that are capable of organising locally available resources for projects of general benefit to the locality. Similarly, massive investment in small-scale irrigation works – the key to crop production in the region – would not have been possible in the absence of strong collective institutions.

The economic reforms in Xinjiang thus appear to be working satisfactorily. They have improved individual incentives and thereby contributed to greater output. They have led to a fuller utilisation of resources and to a more efficient allocation of land and labour. The household responsibility system has made a difference. Yet communal institutions have been kept in place and this has enabled economies of scale to be exploited where they exist and labour to be mobilised on public investment projects. Clearly, from the point of view of efficiency and growth, the current economic policies are superior to those, say, of the mid-1970s. Growth, however, is not the only consideration, although it obviously is an important one. We are interested, too, in poverty and inequality.

If the distribution of income in rural areas remained unchanged, the incomes of the poor would rise at about the same rate as average incomes in the countryside. On this assumption poverty in Xinjiang must have declined dramatically in the last decade. On the other hand, if rapid growth was accompanied by greater inequality, the reduction in poverty might conceivably have been rather modest. Much therefore depends on what has happened to the distribution of income in rural areas.

In China as a whole, we know that in the period 1978 to 1984, the real income of peasants rose very much faster than the real income of workers, viz. 15.0 per cent per annum as compared to 8.2 per cent. As a result, rural–urban inequalities diminished sharply.[18] Even so, the overall distribution of household income became less equal,

Table 6.5 Distribution of Income Among Households (Gini coefficients)

	1978	*1984*
Peasants	0.250	0.288
Workers	0.185	0.169
All households	0.237	0.264

Source: Li Chengrui, 'Réforme du système économique et amélioration du niveau de vie', *Beijing Information*, vol. 23, no. 29, 22 July 1985.

although the degree of equality in China remains very great compared to most other Third World countries. Official data indicate, for example, that the Gini coefficient for household income rose from 0.237 in 1978 to 0.264 in 1984.[19] (See Table 6.5.)

Within the urban areas the wage reforms seem actually to have reduced inequality among households of workers. Moreover, both in 1978 and 1984 the distribution of income among workers was more equal than the distribution among peasants. Finally, inequality among peasant households increased during the six year period[20] and it is this that accounts for the rise in the overall Gini coefficient.

Unfortunately it is not possible to be as precise about trends in the rural areas of Xinjiang. The best one can do at present is speculate about the forces at work in each of the three sub-sectors of the rural economy. As indicated above, it is likely that in the pastoral economy the economic reforms have contributed to a reduction in inequality. The main reason for this is that most livestock were distributed among households on an equal-per-capita basis rather than on an equal-per-labour-force basis.

On the state farms, in contrast, inequality has probably increased. Land usually was distributed among the former wage workers on an equal-per-worker basis and hence the resulting initial distribution of landed assets approximated to the previous distribution of wage income. Everything else being equal, this would have left the distribution of income essentially unchanged. Not every state farm worker, however, has proved to be a good peasant farmer and consequently the income of some households has fallen considerably. The result, inevitably, has been a greater variation of incomes around a higher average level of income.

The situation in the oases is even more complex. Collectively owned land was distributed among members of communes largely on a per capita basis and hence the initial impact of the reforms was strongly egalitarian. Recently, however, the rules governing employment of labour by households and private accumulation of the means of production have been relaxed and this has created opportunities for enterprising households to establish large and sometimes very profitable businesses.

For example, one household visited in Turpan established a grape canning factory in July 1985. The initial investment in buildings and machinery was 400 000 yuan and at the time of our visit in September 1985 there were 80 employees, with an additional 20 employees expected to be hired in the near future. The design capacity of the factory was 100 000 jars of grapes a day and the planned profit was 300 000 yuan a year. This, obviously, was an unusual and perhaps even unique case. It is significant, however, in that large private factories are now allowed, whereas previously factories of such a size would have been organised as a cooperative.

High private profits from factories owned by households will of course result in a few very high incomes at the top end of the distribution. The profits mentioned above are truly exceptional, but rich peasant households – the so-called 10 000 yuan households – are not uncommon, and their presence is a clear signal that greater average prosperity has been accompanied by greater inequality.

One must be careful, however, not to exaggerate the changes that have occurred in the distribution of income. Dramatic gains by a tiny minority of very prosperous households are highly visible, whereas improvements at the bottom end of the distribution can easily be overlooked. The community still assumes responsibility for meeting the basic needs of all families and the five-guarantee programme still operates. Moreover, the level of support to poor households has been increased broadly in line with the rise in average incomes. For example, in An Ning Qui township, a prosperous township 20 km north of Urumqi, per capita income rose from 255.24 yuan in 1983 to 354 yuan in 1984, an increase of 39 per cent. During the same time the incomes received by five-guarantee households rose from 180 to 240 yuan, a rise of 33 per cent.

A distinctive feature of Chinese policies to combat poverty is the emphasis placed on increasing the production potential of households; relatively less emphasis is placed on transfer payments designed to maintain the level of consumption. Consider, for instance, the case of Turpan city.

The population of the city is 190 000, of which 130 000 are classified as agricultural. This agricultural population is divided into 25 049 households. Just under 6 per cent of the population, or 1470 households, have a per capita income of 100 yuan or less. These poor households are known as 'difficult households' and are singled out to receive special support. The type of support offered can be divided into two categories: assistance intended to enable poor households to increase production and thereby raise their income levels; and assistance designed to maintain an adequate level of consumption (see Table 6.6).

As can be seen, assistance given to 'difficult households' to increase production took several forms: grants of seed, fertiliser and implements; gifts to 100 households of four sheep each; gifts to 900 households of one donkey cart each to enable them to enter the transportation business; and interest-free loans, repayable over 3–8 years, to help households set up independent businesses. Finally, not listed in the table, from August 1985 the city decided to give members of 'difficult households' priority in employment in state enterprises and, additionally, to help 'difficult households' to transform themselves into 'specialised households'. The objective of the city is to solve the problem of poor households within two years.

Meanwhile, assistance also was provided to help poor households maintain a decent standard of living. Most important was the distribution of foodgrains. This was distributed on a topping-up basis on the assumption that each person needs 400 jin a year. The total amount allocated was thus sufficient to feed 750 persons for an entire year. In addition, cash grants were made to enable poor households to buy cloth which could be made into clothing. Assuming a metre of cotton cloth cost 1.80 yuan, the total grant allocations of 60 000 yuan was equivalent to 33 333 metres, or nearly 23 metres of cotton cloth per 'difficult household'. Lastly, poor households were not required to pay for medical attention, to pay the agricultural tax or to contribute to public accumulation and welfare funds. The significance of these concessions was relatively minor, since medical charges and tax rates are low, but even so, the concessions have been of some benefit to those who are forced to survive on very small budgets.

The final impression, thus, is that in Xinjiang the economic reforms have been accompanied by some increase in inequality in the rural areas, particularly on the state farms (where the problem, perhaps, is largely transitional) and in the oases. The incidence of poverty, however, has clearly declined. This is due in part to a fuller and better utilisation of resources and in part to high levels of

Table 6.6 Measures to Reduce Poverty in Turpan

Type of assistance	*Amount of assistance*	*Number of beneficiary households*
To increase production:		
(i) Cotton and wheat seeds	110 000 jin	900
(ii) Fertiliser	70 tonnes	370
(iii) Small agricultural implements	n.a.	300
(iv) Sheep	400 head	100
(v) Donkey carts	900 carts	900
(vi) Interest-free loans	300 000 yuan	n.a.
To maintain consumption:		
(i) Foodgrains	300 000 jin	Enough to support fully 750 persons
(ii) Cloth	60 000 yuan	n.a.
(iii) Free medicines and medical care	n.a.	1 470
(iv) Excused payment of agricultural tax and contribution to collective accumulation and welfare funds	n.a.	1 470

investment which have led to rapid growth. The poor have gained more from the rise in average incomes than they have lost from increased variation in incomes. Moreover, government has not hesitated to intervene to help the poor and to prevent inequality from becoming unacceptably great. Intervention has taken a variety of forms, but the thrust of policy has been to reduce poverty and inequality by assisting poor households to increase production, as opposed to providing transfer payments to subsidise consumption.

Compared to other arid regions in the world, above all, of course, to the arid regions of Africa, Xinjiang has done exceptionally well. Where many countries have experienced agricultural stagnation, declining incomes of the peasantry and mass famine, Xinjiang has enjoyed rapid rural development and a sharp fall in the incidence of poverty. Success has owed little to the generosity of nature. Indeed, in few places on earth is the natural environment less promising or the achievements more impressive. Xinjiang shows that a prosperous countryside can be created under unfavourable circumstances and this demonstration can be a shining example to many millions of people everywhere.

Notes

1. The national minorities of Xinjiang include the Uygurs, Kazaks, Kirgiz, Tajiks, Ozbeks, Tatars, Dongxiang, Daur, Xibe, Russians, Mongolians and Hui. Strictly speaking, the Hui are not an ethnic minority; they are of Han descent and speak Chinese and differ from other Han primarily in their adherence to Islam.
2. Between 1964 and 1982 the Han population of China increased by 2.0 per cent a year; the Uygur by 2.3 per cent and the Kazak by 3.5 per cent.
3. At the national level, too, there is some positive discrimination in education in favour of members of minority nationalities. Oddly, there also is positive wage discrimination in favour of government officials who are members of ethnic minorities, although the degree of discrimination is slight.
4. The rates of exchange in the summer of 1985, when the research for this study was conducted, were US$1=2.96 yuan and £1=3.93 yuan.
5. 1 kg = 2 jin.
6. 15 mu = 1 hectare.
7. Over the long period 1950–84, agricultural output value in Xinjiang grew by 5.63 per cent a year in constant prices.
8. In the whole of Xinjiang there are only 800 km of railway and 23 000 km of roads. Transportation clearly merits the high priority it has been given in the most recent economic plan.
9. *Qanats* (also called *kanats*, *karjin* or *karez*) are underground tunnels

which carry irrigation water from the Tien Shan to the Turpan depression. There are 3500 km of *qanats* in Turpan, with an average length of tunnel of 3 km. They are the single most important source of water in the region and date back hundreds (perhaps a thousand) years. *Qanats* are also found at Hami and Yanqi in Xinjiang, but half of China's *qanats* are in Turpan. Iran, of course, is famous for its *qanats* and it is possible that this system of irrigation was imported into China from Iran.

10. Cf. Keith Griffin (ed.), *Institutional Reform and Economic Development in the Chinese Countryside*, London: Macmillan, 1984, Ch. 9.
11. The prefecture's current expenditure in 1984 was as follows:

	million yuan
Wages and salaries	4.7
Fuel and materials	0.8
Repairs and maintenance	2.0
Total	7.5

12. Forests which are intended to be used jointly for fuel and feeding livestock have a planting density of 60 trees per mu. These forests often consist of plantations of Chinese 'date' trees. Sheep and goats are allowed to graze on the grass growing beneath the trees and on the leaves and 'dates' which fall on the ground in the autumn. Wood from the trees is used for cooking. Such a forest would be irrigated three times a year, mostly in the winter, with water surplus to requirements for crop cultivation.
13. The information in the text is based on practices followed by the Agriculture, Industry and Commerce Federation General Corporation of China, an umbrella organisation responsible for 160 state farms in Xinjiang.
14. See Griffin (ed.), *Institutional Reform*.
15. Most of the losers, however, were specialised workers and if they were paid more than the average worker, a fall in their income could conceivably be associated with a reduction in inequality. This seems to be rather improbable considering the narrow wage differentials one finds in China.
16. This hypothesis was first advanced when analysing the distribution of income in the commune sector. See Griffin (ed.), *Institutional Reform*.
17. Shen Chang-jiang, *Pastoral Systems in Arid and Semi-Arid Zones of China*, Pastoral Network Paper 13b, Overseas Development Institute, January 1982, p. 11.
18. Li Chengrui, 'Réforme du système économique et amélioration du niveau de vie', *Beijing Information*, vol. 23, no. 29, 22 July 1985, pp. 18–24.
19. Note, however, that the coefficients refer to total household income not income per head. If households with large incomes also tend to be households with a relatively large number of members, as seems likely, the coefficients in the text exaggerate the degree of inequality among persons. It is less likely, however, that changes in the coefficients are misleading as to trends in inequality.

20. Chengrui, 'Réforme du système économique', does not contain Gini coefficients for peasant households. We have therefore inferred the values using the formula:

    $$G_t = 0.2G_w + 0.8G_p,$$

    where G = Gini coefficient and the subscripts t, w and p refer to total, worker households and peasant households, respectively. (Note that in 1982, 20.8 per cent of the population lived in urban areas.)

7 The Economic Crisis in Ethiopia

On the eve of the revolution of 1974 the economy of Ethiopia was perhaps the most backward in the world. Life was short; indeed a life expectancy at birth of 37.5 years for males and 40.6 for females was the lowest in the world. This short life expectancy was accompanied by a high infant mortality rate (178 per 1000 live births) and a high maternal death rate (20 per 1000 births). Ethiopia had the least favourable ratio of doctors to population (one physician per 75 320 people) and the lowest rate of calorie consumption per capita (1754) of any country on earth.

About 85 per cent of the population lived in rural areas, yet 90 per cent of the rural people lived in shelters which offered minimal protection against the weather, were shared with domestic animals and posed many safety and health hazards, especially for children. In the country as a whole, only 6 per cent of the population had access to safe water and most people had to work and live without the assistance of mechanical or electrical power. (Energy consumption per capita was only about 20 kg of coal equivalent.) The economy had to rely largely on man- and woman-power, supplemented by animal-power, and in consequence the productivity of labour was very low.

The population as a whole was both ignorant and extremely poor. Prior to the revolution, about 52 per cent of the urban population were illiterate and in rural areas the rate of illiteracy was 91.5 per cent. Only one or two countries suffered from a comparable degree of lack of education. Similarly, income per head, at roughly US$115, was about as low as could be found anywhere.[1]

This is the inheritance of underdevelopment. It would, of course, be unrealistic to expect that the poverty of centuries could be eradicated in a few years, but it would be reasonable to hope that a decade after the revolution some progress would have been made in increasing the appallingly low standard of living of the mass of the population. Alas, it was not to be.

The economy of Ethiopia has been in crisis for a long time. In particular the value of agricultural output per head has been falling at least since 1960, and given that the overwhelming majority of the people live in rural areas, this implies that living standards of most people have been declining for a quarter of a century. The decline has not been steady: living standards have tended to fluctuate with the harvests, which in turn are strongly influenced by the timing and amount of rainfall, but the trend has been clearly downwards. As a result of the negative trend the likelihood of a famine increases with each downswing of the cycle, and each famine now tends to be worse than its immediate predecessor. Thus the current famines are worse than those of 1972–4,[2] which resulted in the overthrow of Emperor Haile Selassie,[3] and those in turn were worse than the famine of 1965–6.

An alarming feature of Ethiopia's economy is that the rate of deterioration has accelerated since 1970 and the economy today teeters on the verge of collapse. For example, between 1960 and 1970 the value of agricultural output per head declined by 0.2 per cent a year on average, but between 1970 and 1982 the rate of decline accelerated to 1.1 per cent a year. Similarly, investment per head actually increased by 3.3 per cent a year during the first period and then declined by 1.3 per cent a year during the second (see Table 7.1). Although the dividing line between the two periods does not coincide with the date of the downfall of the Emperor, it seems clear that economic performance under the revolutionary regime has been even worse than under the *ancien régime*.

The most obvious immediate cause of the acute suffering currently being endured by the people of Ethiopia is the drought. The rains were particularly bad in 1984/5 and the 1984 harvests are estimated to have been between 25 and 40 per cent below normal.[4] A second cause is the depressed world economy and the poor trading environment that now confronts the country. This is reflected in a plummeting fall in the country's terms of trade, a decline in exports per head, a contraction of the country's capacity to import and a pronounced decline in imports per head, as shown in Table 7.1.

Third, there are the civil wars. The separatist movement in Eritrea goes back to 1961, but the violence of the conflict intensified greatly after 1975 when the Dergue (the Provisional Military Administrative Council) decided not to compromise but to seek a military solution to the problem.[5] In addition, there have been rebellions by several other non-Amhara groups, including the Somalis in the south, the Tigreans in the north and the Oromos, largely from Wellega in the west. In each case the Dergue has chosen to respond to these nationalist movements by using force rather than persuasion and

Table 7.1 Ethiopia: Indicators of Crisis, 1960–82
(annual percentage rates of growth)

	1960–70	*1970–82*
Population*	2.4	2.0
Value of agricultural output per head	–0.2	–1.1
Volume of agricultural output per head	0.6	–0.5
Volume of food output per head	0.5	–0.3
Exports per head	1.3	–0.7
Imports per head	3.8	–1.8
External terms of trade	n.a.	–4.9
Gross domestic investment per head	3.3	–1.3

Note: *The projected rate of population growth between 1980 and 2000 is 3.1 per cent per annum.

Source: IBRD, *Toward Sustained Development in Sub-Saharan Africa*, Washington, DC: 1984, Statistical Annex.

negotiation.[6] The cost, in terms of resources and human life, has been high.

Finally, the economic policies of the government must bear much blame for what has happened. Investment has been stagnant; national savings have been allowed to decline; foreign aid has increased substantially since 1974 but most of it has been used for military purposes. As a result, national product per head is lower today than at the time of the revolution. What little investment there has been has been concentrated on large-scale, capital-intensive industry in the three largest cities. Peasant agriculture has been utterly ignored; only the state farms have received significant resources and these have been wasted on huge, highly mechanised and inefficient operations. Ironically, a government which came to power because of the incompetence of the previous regime in coping with famine was itself unprepared when famine struck. The army, civil servants and the population in the larger urban centres had access to rationed food, but the majority of people did not, and hence when food became scarce and prices rose dramatically in 1984, millions of inhabitants in the rural areas were suddenly threatened with starvation.[7]

THE SOCIAL REVOLUTION OF 1974

Unlike other countries in Africa where radical change has occurred, the Ethiopian revolution of 1974 was directed not against a colonial power[8] but against an indigenous ruling class and imperial dynasty that had existed since the middle of the nineteenth century. The revolution was led from above by a bureaucratic and military elite. Indeed it can be regarded as a revolution from within the state itself, but its underlying cause was a prolonged agrarian crisis that drove an increasing proportion of the peasantry into destitution and, ultimately, mass starvation.

I Destruction of the feudal order

The revolution was directed against an order that can best be described as feudal. Land ownership and claims to land based on political office were highly concentrated; the overwhelming majority of peasant households were subjected to an onerous extraction of rent, to compulsory labour and to tribute in the form of cattle and honey. The main beneficiaries of this system were the Amhara monarchy, the nobility, the Coptic church and those whose services to the imperial regime were rewarded by grants of land, particularly in the conquered region of the Oromo people to the south of Shoa.

Ethiopia before the revolution was a true empire. The country was highly stratified along linguistic, religious and ethnic lines. At the top was an Amharic speaking, Christian elite from the central highlands. Below them were Muslim and other religious groups and numerous ethnic and tribal nationalities speaking more than eighty languages. Stratification was accompanied by fragmentation. The difficult mountainous terrain in the central highlands and the semi-deserts surrounding them led to regional heterogeneity while the exiguous communications system led to the acute isolation of most of the population.

The destruction of this feudal and imperial order was the first achievement of the revolution of 1974. The creation of a new order, however, has been painful and, so far, unsuccessful. Despite the fact that military expenditure accounted in 1982 for over half of total government expenditure and more than 6 per cent of gross domestic product, civil disturbances, armed conflict and separatist movements have continued and have possibly gained in force.

II Redistribution in favour of the peasantry

A second achievement of the revolution was a redistribution of income in favour of the peasantry. The chief instrument for achieving this redistribution was the land reform of 1975. Under the reform tenancy was abolished, the titles and rights of the former landlords were extinguished and the land was nationalised. Peasant associations were formed and given responsibility for redistributing land to households, establishing service cooperatives, collecting agricultural taxes, introducing improved technology and generally mobilising the rural population for development.

It is not possible to calculate accurately the extent to which the reform improved the standard of living of the mass of the rural people, but it is evident that the improvement must have been considerable. Indeed it is possible that incomes of the beneficiaries increased by as much as a half within a year. Given that the incomes of the peasantry had been falling prior to the revolution, this constituted a dramatic, once-and-for-all reversal of their fortunes. Unfortunately, however, the rate of growth of agricultural output remained alarmingly low and in fact, during the five years after the revolution, and long before the current drought began, agricultural output per head continued to fall by approximately 0.8 per cent per annum.

III Mass literacy campaign

The third achievement of the revolution was the National Literacy Campaign. Launched in July 1979 with the objective of reducing the rate of illiteracy from roughly 87 per cent of those aged 10 or older to zero within eight years, the campaign was able to mobilise thousands of students, teachers and educated youths, first to increase literacy in the urban areas and then to do the same in rural areas. By the end of 1982 the literacy rate in the nation as a whole was thought to have risen to about 45 per cent.

A STRATEGY FOR ECONOMIC PROGRESS

These, then, were the achievements of the revolution by 1982, when the author was invited by the government to advise on economic policy. The economic problems of the country were still extremely serious and the government faced a formidable challenge.

Table 7.2 Expenditure and Savings Ratios (percentages of GDP at market prices)

	1974/5	*1980/1*
Private consumption	79.99	79.66
Public consumption	12.75	15.64
Fixed investment	10.13	10.40
Foreign resource balance	-2.87	-5.60
Domestic savings	7.26	4.80

Source: Government of Ethiopia, Central Statistical Office.

Unemployment in the urban areas was about 20 per cent and rising, and among young school leavers it was higher still and rising faster. Real incomes of wage earners had fallen by about a third since 1975 and those of salaried workers by even more. A person receiving the minimum wage could no longer provide a family with its minimum food requirements even if the whole of his income was spent on food. In the rural areas living standards were even lower. Real incomes were falling and the gains of the land reform were fast eroding. Sadly, a majority of the people in Ethiopia were poorer in 1982 than they had been in 1974.

Gross domestic product per capita had risen only fractionally, if at all. The economy had been on a war footing for most of the previous six years and a rising proportion of a stagnant income had been allocated to military expenditure. Government administration and other items of public consumption also had increased their share of the domestic product. In contrast, the gross fixed investment ratio remained low and constant while the share of private consumption in domestic product remained high at around 80 per cent. Food production per head had declined by about 5 per cent.

Some of the essential facts about the economy are contained in Table 7.2. It can be seen from the table that private and public consumption in 1980/1 accounted for just over 95 per cent of gross domestic product. Domestic savings, consequently, accounted for just under 5 per cent. This was an extraordinarily low figure and underlined a serious problem of domestic resource mobilisation. The data also show that Ethiopia had become increasingly dependent on foreign aid: the negative foreign resource balance rose from 2.87 per cent of GDP in 1974/5 to 5.6 per cent in 1980/1. Despite the greater abundance of foreign capital, average incomes, as we have seen, failed to rise.

The reasons are not hard to find. Between 1974 and 1981, the six year period we are examining, the share of foreign aid in GDP rose by 2.73 percentage points. At the same time the domestic savings ratio fell by a very similar amount, namely, 2.46 percentage points, and the proportion of public consumption (including military expenditure) in GDP rose by 2.89 percentage points. These changes not only are of equal magnitude, they are intimately related. That is, we can say that the inflow of foreign resources went directly into increased public consumption. Alternatively, we can say that domestic resources were diverted from savings to public consumption and that foreign resources made up for the shortfall in domestic savings so that investment could remain unchanged. This is merely two ways of saying the same thing. Either way, the key point is that the mobilisation of domestic resources for investment and growth was seriously neglected and in consequence a catastrophe was inevitable. Only the timing of the catastrophe was uncertain.

An alternative vision of economic development within a socialist framework evidently was urgently required and this is what we attempted to supply in a report prepared for the Ethiopian government.[9] The report argued for attention to labour-intensive grassroots development that would be quite compatible with the ruling elite's socialist commitments.

I Accumulation and cooperation

The point of departure was agriculture, the foundation of the economy, the largest sector of production and the source of livelihood for the great majority of the population. Unfortunately, agriculture was by far the weakest sector of the economy and major efforts were required to reverse the decline. Incomes and the productivity of labour in the countryside were extremely low and hence both the marketable surplus and the internal rate of savings in agriculture were insufficient to finance either its own expansion or the development of the rest of the economy.

The main resource available was the seasonally surplus labour force. Our strategy for rural development was based on mobilising this force for a series of capital construction projects that would (i) bring more land under cultivation; (ii) raise yields on existing land, e.g. through land improvement projects; (iii) increase the cropping ratio, e.g. through small-scale irrigation works; (iv) increase the productivity of labour, e.g. by improving the quantity and quality of farm implements; (v) lead to the development of a local construction industry based on locally available materials; and (vi) encourage the establishment of small workshops and factories to process agricultural products, produce simple consumer goods used locally and provide inputs for further agricultural development. The initial investments would be financed not by lower consumption of the peasantry but by greater work and less seasonally idle time. Once output per head began to rise, part of it could be siphoned off as savings to finance further investment.

This process of labour-investment followed by savings-investment would have to be carefully organised. It is here that cooperation could play a vital role. Any form of viable cooperation should be encouraged, be it service cooperatives or producers' cooperatives. The thrust of the cooperative movement, however, should not be collective production, as the government envisaged, but collective accumulation. That is, the cooperatives should be regarded as institutions to promote investment, first, by organising labour for capital construction projects and, second, by amassing accumulation funds out of the revenue surpluses of cooperatively owned undertakings. Collective agricultural production should at best be a secondary objective of cooperatives and one which was subordinate to the imperative of accelerated accumulation.

Great care would have to be taken to ensure that cooperation was in the material interest of the peasantry. It was important that two dangers in particular should be avoided. First, force should never be used to establish cooperatives as it would only lead to resistance; not to accumulation. Second, the incomes generated by cooperatives should not be appropriated by the state in the form of high taxes or compulsory deliveries of grain at fixed low prices. Despite warnings, however, the government has committed both errors[10] and thereby nullified the purpose of the policy which was to encourage local initiative, local effort and local savings for investment in projects of direct benefit to the people making the sacrifices. The whole thrust of the strategy was to promote grass-roots development, building on the Peasant Associations.

II Infrastructure and the social services

The report advised the government to concentrate whatever resources it could devote to rural development on two things: providing economic and social infrastructure and improving the performance of the state farms.

Ethiopia has for a long time systematically underinvested in rural infrastructure – roads, power, irrigation, storage and processing facilities – and in the health, education and training of the rural population. One consequence of this is that the return on investment in other activities – in agriculture, industry and commerce – is low because their efficiency is greatly hampered by the lack of complementary services and facilities and skills. Investment in rural infrastructure, primary education, basic health services, potable water supplies and training are not only necessary in themselves, they also are a precondition for profitable investment in agriculture, rural industry and urban manufacturing. Unless the fragmentation and disarticulation of the economy can be overcome, the national market will forever remain small and the return on capital will remain low. Hence the importance of state investment in infrastructure.

Aside from physical infrastructure, the state also will have to provide basic social services. A good start was made immediately following the 1974 revolution, particularly with the literacy campaign and the provision of primary education, but progress was interrupted by famine and civil war. When conditions permit the approach developed in these two cases could be extended to other fields as well. The Peasant Associations and urban *kebeles* exist and they have demonstrated their ability to organise and run campaigns in their localities. They should be encouraged to expand their activities to include health, nutrition, family planning and the care of children.

There are two great advantages to a mass approach to the provision of basic social services. First, such an approach is essential in providing a floor to poverty and preventing large numbers of people from suffering economic catastrophe every time there is a fluctuation in the harvest. The central government cannot be solely responsible for the eradication of illiteracy, for universal primary education, for widespread preventive health measures, maternal and child care, etc. Yet these are the services every community must have if poverty is to be contained and every family is to enjoy minimum economic security.

Second, local involvement in administering the social services can lead to local involvement in financing them. This would relieve the central government of part of the financial burden and at the same time provide an incentive to the mass organisations to mobilise local resources for their continuation and expansion. Just as cooperation can lead to capital accumulation in the rural areas, so too can mass organisation play an important role in limiting economic hardship and guaranteeing minimum standards of public welfare.

III Food rationing

The most important piece of social infrastructure needed in Ethiopia is an efficient food rationing system. Given the precarious nature of food supplies, the government cannot escape the responsibility of ensuring that the entire population receives a guaranteed minimum amount of grain at prices the poor can afford.

Ethiopia in 1982 was in the fortunate position of having in place most of the instruments necessary to operate an effective rationing system. It would not have been difficult to cover the entire country, as was recommended, by distributing rationed food supplies through the *kebeles* in urban areas (as already happened in the larger towns) and through the Peasant Associations in rural areas. The tragedy of mass starvation could and should have been avoided.

Rationed supplies of grain could have been obtained from a number of sources: directly from the state farms, through open market purchases by the Agricultural Marketing Corporation and by making agricultural taxes payable in grain. Some help might have been forthcoming from the United Nations World Food Programme and the European Community, particularly in building up the stocks necessary to launch a nationwide programme.

The principles to be applied in distributing rationed goods should be considered carefully. First, the entire population should be entitled to purchase a specified quantity through the mass organisations to which they belong. In this way a minimum would be guaranteed to everyone. However, second, the rationing system should in practice discriminate in favour of the poor by choosing the kinds of goods and, more important, the quality of goods that normally are purchased predominantly by low-income groups. In Ethiopia this implies a concentration on inferior cereals such as sorghum, maize and black teff.

Third, the number of goods to be rationed should be as few as possible consistent with the government's ultimate objectives and with its actual ability to ensure that the rationed quantities are in fact delivered to the outlets and are available when people come to purchase them. Fourth, price controls should be applied to the rationed supplies, but the prices of unrationed supplies should be allowed to rise on the open market to soak up excess demand. The controlled prices of grains should be set in such a way that a person employed on a minimum wage could cover a household's minimum needs for food.

IV State farms

From the perspective of the central government, one of the disadvantages of a grass-roots strategy of development is that local resources will be mobilised and retained locally and not be made available to urban areas. An obvious worry is that the supply of food in urban areas will not be sufficient to feed the urban population. In principle, and in the long run, this should not be a problem in Ethiopia since less than one person in five lives in the cities. If agricultural output can be raised significantly the huge rural population should be able to feed the small urban population with ease. At a time when food production per head is low and falling, however, the government is right to be concerned about the size of the marketable surplus of food.

It is in this context that state farms assume importance. In Ethiopia state farms are few in number and account for less than 5 per cent of the land area and agricultural output. The average size of farm, however, is very large, often several thousand hectares. Moreover, the state farms absorb about 90 per cent of all investment in agriculture. They have been treated by the government as an insurance policy against severe food shortages in the cities and virtually the whole of the output from state grain-producing farms is available to the Agricultural Marketing Corporation to supply the army, government institutions such as hospitals and the public food distribution system in the larger urban centres.

Unfortunately, the insurance policy has proved to be very expensive. The state farms are both technically and economically inefficient and consequently the great majority operate at a loss. That is, they make a negative contribution to the resources available for accumulation and growth. Given that the absence of growth is the cause of the country's economic crisis, this is a pity.

The farms suffer from a great many difficulties, including (i) very high overhead costs, (ii) an excessive degree of mechanisation, (iii) poor capital equipment, high machine-operating costs, inadequate maintenance and consequently low capacity utilisation, (iv) shortages of labour, (v) undesirable labour recruitment practices and wage payment systems, (vi) poor choice of location partly resulting from excessively rapid expansion, (vii) an overcentralised management structure and (viii) an apparent disregard of financial considerations when making decisions. Until these difficulties are overcome and the state farms are reorganised and made profitable, further expansion of their activities can only aggravate the country's problems. The best that can be said of them so far is that they have supplied some food to the urban areas and thereby made a small but costly contribution to the government's programme of industrialisation.

V Industrialisation

The future of industrial development in Ethiopia should be profoundly affected by the structural changes that have occurred and hopefully will continue to occur in the agricultural sector. There has been a radical change in the distribution of landed assets and this has led to a more equal distribution of income in rural areas. This, in turn, can be expected to lead to a change in the pattern of demand and potentially to the creation of a much larger national market for manufactured goods consumed by the rural population. Only 'potentially' because whether these opportunities in fact materialise depends on whether agricultural incomes begin to grow and on whether an integrated national market can be created through government investment in infrastructure.

Assuming the necessary conditions are fulfilled, growth and structural change in agriculture have enormous implications for the composition of industrial output, the location of industrial activities and the choice of technology. Indeed, industrial and agricultural development should be seen as closely linked, the one supporting the other. Specifically, industry should serve agriculture by (i) processing agricultural commodities such as coffee, meat and leather products, vegetables and fruit; (ii) producing improved agricultural implements and modern inputs such as fertiliser for accelerated rural development; (iii) supplying the rural sector with simple consumer goods at affordable prices; and (iv) by developing a large, widely dispersed and efficient construction goods industry that can provide the physical foundation for rapid capital accumulation.

This last point is especially important. Regardless of the development strategy one follows, a major part of total investment, usually well over half, will be expenditure on construction. Therefore, a country that has a large, well-organised and efficient construction industry has the physical capacity to undertake a large investment programme based on domestic resources alone. Foreign resources then become unnecessary for sustained accumulation, although they may be welcomed on other grounds. In Ethiopia the construction industry should be dispersed throughout the country, partly to overcome the fragmentation of the economy, referred to earlier, and partly to support the grass-roots strategy of development that is being advocated.

An industrialisation strategy based on agro-industries and rural development creates many opportunities to reduce the regional concentration of manufacturing activities. New undertakings can be located near their sources of supply of raw materials or near the rural markets they will serve. The advantages are that transport costs (which are high in Ethiopia) can be minimised, industrial capital can be widely spread in efficient small-scale units, and regional inequalities in the distribution of income and industrial employment can be reduced.

This approach to industrialisation, however, is based on choosing labour-intensive technologies and spreading capital thinly. Present practice in Ethiopia is the opposite. The technology selected tends to be capital intensive, the scale of operation tends to be large, and the factories tend to be located in or near the three existing centres of manufacturing activity. The disadvantages of present practice are, first, that industrialisation increases the country's dependence on foreign exchange and foreign aid rather than reduces it; second, that industrialisation does little to reduce unemployment in the cities or increase incomes in the countryside; and third, that industrialisation exacerbates regional income differentials and thereby aggravates regional conflicts and resentments.

THE HORRENDOUS CONSEQUENCES OF WRONG PRIORITIES

This vision for Ethiopia of grass-roots development within a socialist framework has failed to materialise. The most charitable explanation is that famine struck before the government had time to reorient its policies. A more uncharitable one is that the government's priorities were unforgivably bad and greatly aggravated the effects of drought. At the top of the list of bad priorities was the decision to allocate a high proportion of the country's resources to the armed forces. Ethiopia now has the largest army in Black Africa. This army absorbs manpower and finance that are desperately needed for development. Next was the decision to spend approximately £200 million in September 1984 on celebrations connected with the tenth anniversary of the revolution. The desire of the government to consolidate its power evidently was regarded as a more important use of funds than purchases abroad of grain for starving peasants.

Then there was the decision, again taken in 1984, to concentrate administrative talent not in combating the famine but in organising the Workers' Party, the single political party allowed in the country. The task of organising the new party not only diverted attention away from the economic emergency, it actually made the work of famine relief more difficult. As one reporter put it, where once Ethiopian officials of the government's Relief and Rehabilitation Commission 'made immediate and on the whole pragmatic decisions, there is now the local party official to be considered. Often it seems that no decision is taken for fear of it being, in the party's eyes, the wrong one. Political priorities have come to supersede humanitarian ones.'[11]

Finally, there was the decision to seek a military solution to the country's political problems and to prosecute the civil wars with utter ruthlessness. The result has been to disrupt production in the northern parts of the country and to make the effects of the drought worse than they might otherwise have been. The government repeatedly rejected offers of a cease fire to enable the starving in Eritrea and Tigrai to be given relief. They also rejected proposals that vehicles carrying emergency supplies to areas controlled by guerrillas be given safe conduct passes. And they rejected two offers from the Assistant Secretary-General of the United Nations in charge of famine relief operations in Ethiopia for food to be distributed independently by the Red Cross and the UN in areas outside government control.[12]

The government claimed that its relief programme could reach the hungry wherever in the country they might be found, that the guerrillas did not occupy permanently any territory but were little more than roving bandits and, hence, that special measures to feed the starving in Eritrea and Tigrai were unnecessary. It subsequently became known, however, that the Relief and Rehabilitation Commission, in an internal report, estimated that only 22 per cent of the population of Tigrai was receiving famine relief.[13] These people were concentrated around the provincial capital of Mekele and were supplied by air; the remaining 78 per cent of the province's population was ignored. A similar situation probably prevails in Eritrea.

The circumstantial evidence thus suggests that famine in Ethiopia is being used as an instrument of war. A large number of people in the country, perhaps the majority by now, oppose Amhara domination in general and the present regime in particular. The country, undoubtedly, is in danger of falling apart and if this happens the claims of the Dergue to national leadership will vanish. The government uncompromisingly has responded to these threats by attempting to starve its opponents into submission. Indeed there are reports of 'a systematic attempt to deprive of food the region most severely affected by the present famine', viz. Wollo.[14]

Whether deliberate or not, the extent of starvation is horrific. Approximately 500 000 are believed to have died in the first part of 1985 and the United Nations estimates that another 8.5 million people in Ethiopia are at risk from starvation.[15] In addition, well over a million Ethiopians have fled the civil wars and the drought and have sought refuge in neighbouring countries. Accurate figures are difficult to obtain but it seems there are between 500 000 and 700 000 Ethiopian refugees in the Sudan; 700 000 in Somalia; and 15 000 in Djibouti.[16] In total, between a quarter and a third of the entire population has been forced to take desperate measures to avoid dying because of insufficient food.

The options open to starving people and to the authorities are limited. First, people can stay in their villages, live off their reserves as long as possible and when the reserves are exhausted hope that emergency supplies (or cash grants) will be brought to the village. This is by far the best way to handle relief. It avoids dislocation of the population and enables agricultural activities to commence again as soon as the rains return.[17] If part of the relief is distributed as food-for-work, or cash-for-work, the population can be mobilised to undertake small-scale investment projects which should raise average incomes in future.

Second, the hungry can leave their villages and move to feeding centres in the provincial capitals and other large towns. Because of the poor transport facilities and poor security in much of the affected countryside, this appears to be the way most relief is provided in Ethiopia. The disadvantages of doing it this way are obvious, however. Not only must food be provided, but also housing and sanitation facilities. While people are in the feeding centres, they are unemployed and bored and are likely to become demoralised because of having to live on charity. In any case, being away from their farms, they are unable to resume cultivation even when climatic conditions improve. As a result, the relief operation is likely to last longer and be more costly than under the first option.

Third, if relief is not available in one's own province, and on terms that are tolerable, one can emigrate to a neighbouring country and become a refugee. As we have seen, mass distress migrations from

Ethiopia have become common and the burden that has fallen on the Sudan and Somalia is enormous; indeed, it is practically unendurable. From the point of view of the migrant, too, the cost of emigration is high. All of the disadvantages associated with migration to internal feeding centres apply here also, and in addition there are the problems that arise from moving to a strange land and living among people who speak a different language and who probably do not welcome large numbers of foreigners competing for limited resources. If one must suffer and starve it is better to do so at home than as an alien abroad.

Lastly, the government can organise resettlement programmes in other parts of the country where land is thought to be more abundant, more fertile or less subject to drought. The Ethiopian government does in fact have an ambitious scheme to move 1.5 million people from the northern provinces of Tigrai, Wollo and Gondar to the south-western provinces of Keffa, Illubabor and Wellega, and already about 70 000 people have been moved.[18] Such programmes inevitably are very costly. Transportation must be provided not only to move food to the hungry but also to move the hungry to the areas of settlement, and if transport vehicles are in short supply, as they are in Ethiopia, this means that the feeding centres in the north will be inadequately supplied.

Once the settlers have been moved, they will have to be supported, often for several years, until they are able to produce enough for subsistence. The land will have to be cleared, houses constructed, sources of safe water identified, road communications established, a commercial and trading network created, etc. It is most unlikely that Ethiopia has the resources to undertake a resettlement programme of the size envisaged. Indeed the government seems to have realised this, but instead of abandoning the programme it has abandoned the settlers. Each settler household is allocated two hectares. Thereafter, 'the assistance provided is minimal . . . Essentially, it is the same relief assistance that is being provided presently at relief shelters.'[19] Unlike the relief centres in the north, however, resettlement in the south is intended to be permanent. The settlers in effect are being dumped. They are being transferred from the highlands to the lowlands, where they are expected to learn a new type of farming, to cope with new diseases, to build new communities and, presumably, to learn the language and customs of the surrounding peoples, all with minimal assistance.

The government claims the resettlement programme is voluntary, but there is much evidence that suggests the contrary. There are reports, for example, that in the north the government withholds grain from relief centres for weeks on end but provides two cooked meals a day at resettlement transit camps half a mile away; that the government deliberately withholds trucks to move grain in order to starve those in relief centres into volunteering for resettlement; and when these tactics fail, families are split up and the men are ordered at gunpoint into trucks and airplanes for the journey south.[20] The economic justification for the resettlement programme is slight and there is no moral justification whatever for the tactics employed by the government. The explanation must be essentially political, namely, an attempt by the government to use the famine as an opportunity to weaken and scatter those in the north who oppose the regime and support the opposition.

What lessons does this sorry tale hold for people in the West? First, famines often are not short-term economic phenomena but the outcome of long-term political factors. Starvation in Ethiopia was foreseen long before the drought struck and the government was given more than adequate warning, but almost nothing was done because those who suffer most acutely during famines, namely, the very poor, have little influence and satisfying their basic needs is low on the list of government priorities. Second, a political solution in Ethiopia must take into account the claims of Eritrea and Tigrai in the north, the Oromos in the west and the Somalis in the Ogaden. Experience throughout the world has shown that repression cannot work indefinitely. Military measures cannot bring about a permanent solution to conflicts of the type which afflict Ethiopia. Ultimately a negotiated compromise will be necessary and the sooner this is recognised, the better for all concerned. Third, the involvement of the superpowers and the peninsular Arabs in the Horn of Africa has exacerbated conflict and made it more difficult to reach a political settlement.[21] Ethiopia's internal political difficulties are exceptionally complicated and outside interventions have added to the complexity by internationalising what are essentially domestic problems. In the process Ethiopia has become a battleground in the 'cold war' between East and West and as a result the level of violence and the degree of suffering inflicted on ordinary men and women are much greater than would otherwise have been the case.

Fourth, it has become clear that the response of the United States,

Britain and the European Community to the famine in Ethiopia was tragically slow,[22] presumably for political reasons, and that humanitarian aid commensurate with requirements did not begin to flow until the compassion of the general public was roused by the sight on its television screens of mass death by starvation. We have also learned, fifth, that even emergency food aid cannot be politically neutral in a country wracked by civil wars, that aid inevitably strengthens the recipient government relative to its opponents, and that in a world of sovereign nation states the international community has few effective means of feeding people if they are in open rebellion against their government.

Finally, perhaps the most painful lesson of all, it has become clear that unless one is careful the long-term effect of emergency aid can be to perpetuate the very conditions that made aid necessary. This is not an argument for being less than generous in times of crisis, but it is a warning that, in trying to do good, some harm is done as well. With luck and skill and perseverance we can hope the gains will exceed the losses. As T. S. Eliot said so well:

> There is only the fight to recover what has been lost
> And found and lost again and again: and now, under conditions
> That seem unpropitious. But perhaps neither gain nor loss.
> For us, there is only the trying.

Notes

1. Data on Ethiopia should be treated with caution. Agricultural statistics in particular are not very accurate and since agriculture accounts for about half the GDP, the figures for national income and output are subject to considerable error. Ethiopia was the only country in the world that had never had a population census. The first census was conducted in 1982 but the results have not been released. Thus neither the size of the population nor its rate of growth are known with certainty, but it is assumed there were 33 million people in 1982 increasing at a rate of 2.5–3.3 per cent a year. The level and rate of growth of output per head evidently is little more than a guesstimate, given our ignorance of both the numerator and the denominator.
2. For an analysis of the famines of the 1970s see Amartya Sen, *Poverty and Famines: An Essay on Entitlement and Deprivation*, Oxford University Press, 1981, Ch. 7.
3. For a description of the Emperor and his court in their final days see Ryszard Kapuscinski, *The Emperor: Downfall of an Autocrat*, London: Quartet Books, 1983.

4. The FAO estimates the 1984 harvests were 25–30 per cent below normal and the government of Ethiopia 40 per cent. See Relief and Rehabilitation Commission, *Early Warning System Meher (Main) Crop Season Synoptic Report 1984 Crop Season (April–December)*, Addis Ababa: January 1985.
5. For a concise statement of both sides of the Eritrean issue see Minority Rights Group, *Eritrea and Tigray*, Report No. 5, London: 1983.
6. The best book on the recent political history of Ethiopia is Fred Halliday and Maxine Molyneux, *The Ethiopian Revolution*, London: Verso, 1981.
7. The United Nations Food and Agriculture Organisation, in a report to the Relief and Rehabilitation Commission of October 1984, has made provisional estimates of gross production of carbohydrate food items, i.e. grains, pulses, enset, root crops, etc., as follows (in thousand metric tonnes):

1980/1	7113
1981/2	6610
1982/3	8249
1983/4	6667
1984/5	5280–5610
1985/6	7410

The projection for 1985/6 is based on an assumption of 'normal' rains in that year.
8. Ethiopia was colonised by the Italians only briefly. On 3 October 1935 Italy invaded the country and captured Addis Ababa on 5 May 1936, but the Italians in turn were driven out by the British in 1941. See Anthony Mockler, *Haile Selassie's War*, Oxford University Press, 1984.
9. The report to the Ethiopian government containing the alternative vision, alas never published, is entitled *Socialism From the Grass Roots: Accumulation, Employment and Equity in Ethiopia*, Addis Ababa: ILO (JASPA), September 1982.
10. See, for example, Paul Vallely's report 'How Mengistu hammers the peasants', in *The Times* (London), 1 March 1985.
11. Paul Vallely, 'Fear, Ethiopia's new disease', *The Times* (London), 16 February 1985.
12. *The Times* (London), 27 February 1985.
13. *The Times* (London), 25 February 1985.
14. *The Times* (London), 14 August 1985.
15. In December 1984 the Ethiopian government estimated that 7.75 million people required emergency relief, but since then independent observers have revised this estimate upwards, see Relief and Rehabilitation Commission, *Review of the Current Drought Situation in Ethiopia*, Addis Ababa: December 1984. The Ethiopian government itself, in January 1985, raised the estimate to 7.9 million people, see Relief and Rehabilitation Commission, *Early Warning System*.
16. The estimate of 700 000 Ethiopian refugees in the Sudan comes from *The Guardian*, 25 February 1985. All other estimates were supplied to

me by Rights and Justice, London. Curiously, there are between 15 000 and 120 000 Sudanese refugees in Ethiopia who have fled from the civil war in the southern Sudan.

17. The United Nations estimates that even if 'normal' rainfall occurs, production would be 10 per cent below 'normal' because of the dislocation of the population and the death of many ploughing oxen.
18. Relief and Rehabilitation Commission, *Review of the Current Drought Situation*, p. 24.
19. Ibid.
20. See, for example, the reports in *The Times* (London) on 20 February and 1 March 1985.
21. The United States supported the Ethiopia of Haile Selassie but switched its support to Somalia after the 1974 revolution. The Soviet Union, which formerly supported Somalia, then began to support Ethiopia. The conservative Arab states have supported the Eritreans, despite the socialist orientation of the separatists. The Sudan, presumably with the backing of the United States, has provided at least indirect support to the Tigreans and Eritreans. In retaliation it is alleged that Ethiopia provides some support to the rebels in the southern Sudan, and this may have been one of the factors which led to the overthrow of President Nimeiry of the Sudan in April 1985.
22. The Relief and Rehabilitation Commission first requested aid in December 1982. The response to this and subsequent appeals was negligible until after the RRC launched a final appeal on 7 August 1984, by which time it was evident that the 1984 harvest would be poor and starvation inevitable and massive.

8 Problems of Agricultural Development in Socialist Ethiopia

with Roger Hay

Agriculture is the base of Ethiopia's economy. It provides employment for 85 per cent of the labour force and accounts for nearly 50 per cent of the GDP. Agricultural exports (mainly coffee, hides and skins, pulses, oil seeds and cotton) provide 90 per cent of Ethiopia's foreign exchange, and taxes on coffee are the largest single source of government revenue. Most importantly, agriculture provides food for Ethiopia's large and expanding population.

The Revolutionary Government recognised the impossibility of constructing an egalitarian socialist society based on the rural structures it inherited and its first priority was to alter radically the production relationships between the land and the tiller. It now attaches great importance to consolidating these gains and to introducing increasingly progressive forms of collective agriculture. However, while the reform of production relationships may fulfil necessary conditions for agricultural growth and the distribution of its benefits, it clearly does not create sufficient conditions for a buoyant sector. Agriculture's growth record is less than satisfactory and levels of living in the countryside remain low.

In this chapter we review the gains made to the end of 1982 and show that the rural economy is not achieving its potential for growth and is characterised by regional concentration and economic fragmentation. The main theme of this chapter, that an adjustment in the role of the smallholder and collective sectors could provide the engine for increased rates of growth, is based on a comparative analysis of the modes of production to be found in Ethiopia.

The increase in agricultural growth required by the growth in demand for food and industrial crops and the need to increase agricultural exports will require substantial investment in rural areas. This, we suggest, will be achieved in a way best suited to growth with equity by allowing rural institutions to play a more prominent role in accumulating savings and investment in the countryside. The struc-

Table 8.1 The Contribution of Agriculture to the Gross Domestic Product (million birr)

	1977/8	*1978/9*	*1979/80*	*1980/1**
Total agriculture	1922.2	1968.4	2062.2	2112.7
Agriculture	1808.1	1852.3	1943.0	1990.6
Forestry	109.2	111.2	114.3	117.2
Hunting	1.3	1.3	1.3	1.3
Fishing	3.6	3.6	3.6	3.6
Total GDP	4009.3	4221.7	4454.2	4600.4

Note: *Preliminary estimate .

Source: Central Planning Supreme Council, August 1982.

tural conditions for these innovations have now been fulfilled, but technical and economic issues require attention. Agriculture in Ethiopia is characterised by four conditions: a slow rate of growth, concentration of output in about a third of the land area, economic fragmentation, and instability due to climatic variations. We will examine each of these in turn in order to build up a picture of the magnitude of the problems which agricultural planners face.

RECENT AGRICULTURAL ACTIVITIES

Table 8.1 shows the contribution of agriculture to the gross domestic product between 1977/8 and 1980/1. According to official estimates during those four years the trend value of the sector grew by 3.3 per cent per annum in real terms or at a compound rate of 2.4 per cent per annum using end values for the calculation. Over the same period the sector's contribution to GDP fell from 47.9 per cent to 45.9 per cent.

Table 8.2 provides more detailed information about the growth of arable agriculture between 1974/5 and 1979/80. In quantity terms the trend growth rate in food crop production was a disappointing 1.3 per cent per annum, and even this modest gain was achieved by area expansion rather than by a growth in crop yield. Land productivity in fact, appears to have declined during the period. Population is estimated to be growing at 2.6 to 2.8 per cent per annum. This suggests that food production per capita for the nation as a whole may be falling.

The exception is teff, a low-yielding fine-grain cereal. Its growth

Table 8.2 Recent Trends in Agricultural Growth 1974/5 to 1979/80 (per cent per annum)

Commodity	*Production*	*Area*	*Yield*
All food crops	1.3	2.6	–1.4
All cereals	1.2	1.9	–0.7
Teff	4.2	1.3	2.8
Barley	3.4	5.6	–2.2
Maize	2.0	4.9	–2.8
Wheat	–4.4	–3.5	–0.8
Sorghum	1.1	2.1	–1.0
Millet	–2.7	–0.2	–2.4
Pulses	1.4	5.4	–4.0
Cotton (state farms)	5.1	5.3	–0.2
Coffee	2.2	n.a.	n.a.

Note: Calculated as trend growth rates to take into account considerable year to year variations.

Source: Economic Memorandum on Ethiopia, Washington DC: World Bank, December 1981.

rate was on average 4.2 per cent per annum. While this reflects the preference Ethiopians have for teff, the amount of land devoted to its production appears to have expanded at the expense of other cereals which offer greater returns at least to land, if not to labour.

There are no reliable data available about trends in either rural or urban food consumption but the general impression is that, with the operation of state farms and government food marketing institutions favouring urban populations, the gains in food consumption in rural areas resulting from land reform are now being eroded. In any event, the overall picture is one of stagnation in food production and an increasing gap between trends in production and population growth.

Further evidence of the failure of the agricultural sector to meet food demand comes from import statistics. Between 1974/5 and 1979/80 the current value of imports of food and live animals rose from 18.7 million birr to 62.4 million birr, an average annual growth of 22.2 per cent. During the same period the food import share of the foreign exchange bill rose from 2.7 per cent to 4.2 per cent.

The growth of cash crop production appears to be more promising. The production of cotton grew in quantity terms by 5 per cent per annum between 1974–5 and 1979–80 although no gains were made in yield. During the same period coffee production grew at more than 2 per cent per annum but yields remain low and export growth has been achieved mainly by restricting domestic consumption.

The value of agricultural exports in current terms grew at a trend rate of 15.8 per cent per annum between 1974/5 and 1979/80. The export value of hides and skins grew most rapidly at 27.0 per cent per annum and this export is marked for increasing attention in the future.

Although the sector as a whole is not yet performing at the levels required of it, new rural institutions have been built and are being slowly transformed. Their introduction has a greater significance than to spur agricultural growth. However, in this chapter we concentrate on their potential role in the revitalisation of the agricultural sector and the effort to redress the regional inequalities which are another important characteristic of Ethiopia's rural economy.

REGIONAL CONCENTRATION AND ECONOMIC FRAGMENTATION

Before the revolution Ethiopia's economy was directed towards supporting the urban elite concentrated in the central highlands and, in particular, in Addis Ababa. This orientation determined the selection of the economic activities receiving central government support, directed the development of the road and transport systems, and allowed the unrestricted development of regional inequalities. The result was the concentration of rural production in a few favoured areas, an absence of inter-regional trade and a fragmented economic system. To a large extent these features still characterise Ethiopia's rural economy. Ethiopia's natural resources are poorly distributed and a conscious effort will be required to effect a reversal of regional inequalities in production patterns, the patterns of marketable surplus and the distribution of cash cropping in order to achieve the egalitarian society to which Ethiopia aspires.

There is very little information available about the way land quality is distributed but inferences can be drawn from indirect evidence. Table 8.3, for example, shows crop yields in 1979/80 for 12 administrative regions in the country. The differences are considerable, although, of course, these may arise from other reasons than variations in land quality.

Land is not scarce in Ethiopia in comparison say with South or South-east Asia and, on average, 11 per cent of all holdings lie fallow each year. However, there are significant regional differences in the access people have to farming land. As an admittedly imperfect

Table 8.3 Crop Yields 1979/80 (kg per ha)

Region	*Cereals*	*Pulses*
Bale	1280	860
Arssi	1240	910
Wollo	1070	950
Gondar	930	840
Shoa	890	840
Keffa	790	880
Sidamo	790	810
Illubabor	780	260
Gojjam	730	680
Harrarghe	710	730
Wellega	520	490
Gemu Goffa	490	250

Source: *Agricultural Sample Survey, 1979–80*, Vol. V, Addis Ababa: Central Statistical Office.

Table 8.4 Average Size of Holding by Region, 1979/80 (hectares)

Gemu Goffa	0.728
Sidamo	0.791
Harrarghe	0.856
Keffa	0.874
Wollo	0.939
Illubabor	1.163
Bale	1.180
Shoa	1.463
Wellega	1.528
Arssi	1.797
Gojjam	1.820
Gondar	2.048

Source: *Agricultural Sample Survey 1979–80*, Addis Ababa: Central Statistical Office.

indicator of land security, Table 8.4 shows the distribution of holding size in 12 administrative regions. As there has been comparatively little migration during the process of land redistribution, these data suggest that there was nearly three times as much land available in Gondar per peasant family at the time of land reform as there was in Gemu Goffa or Sidamo.

Table 8.5 Food Crop Production per Capita by Administrative Region, 1978/9 (kg per capita per annum)

Arssi	528
Bale	207
Gemu Goffa	44
Gojjam	183
Gondar	279
Harrarghe	55*
Illubabor	198
Keffa	179*
Sidamo	49
Wellega	127
Wollo	81

Note: *Population includes pastoralists.

Sources: Food crop production from *Crop Production Survey 1978–9*, Addis Ababa: Ministry of Agriculture, June 1979.
Population estimates from National Sample Survey, Second Round 1969–77, Central Statistical Office.

It is also worth noting that with one exception (Wollo Administrative Region) the five regions with the highest levels of land productivity are not those where land is most scarce, suggesting that in addition to enjoying the benefits of better quality of land, the farmers in these regions also enjoy better access to land. Regional inequalities in holding size thus tend to be reinforced by differences in land quality leading to even greater regional differences in output per holding.

These differences are summarised in Table 8.5 which contains information about regional differences in per capita food crop production.

It is evident that the results can be criticised on many grounds. The data on which the table is based do not include root crops, oil seeds and enset which are important food crops. Enset in particular, is a major staple food in southern Shoa, Arssi, Gemu Goffa, Illubabor and Keffa. The population estimates used to construct the table include both urban and pastoral populations on the grounds that both exert a demand on food crop production. However, it could be argued that because the pastoralists derive 50 per cent of their energy from milk and meat the data should have been weighted to take this into account.

Laying these objections aside for the moment, and assuming a national average energy intake of 1760 kcals per person per day and a constant share of energy derived from food crops of 80 per cent, a very rough notion of regional food production compared with a nutritional benchmark can be obtained. The cereal/pulse equivalent of an intake of 1400 kcals is about 0.43 kg which if consumed each day for a year would amount to an annual consumption of 157 kg. These calculations suggest that the regional concentration of food crop production is such that, first, Gemu Goffa, Harrarghe, Sidamo and Wollo do not produce enough food to feed their population at the national average and, second, that the main food surplus regions are Arssi, Bale, and Gondar. These results should not be interpreted to mean either that everyone in Ethiopia consumes at the national average or that the rural population exercises no demand at all on marketed surplus from other regions. Instead the results are intended to show the general distribution of food crop production with respect to the distribution of population and to emphasise the importance of redistributive mechanisms if the benefits of growth in food crop output are to be realised in terms of nutritional welfare.

As might be expected at a more aggregate level, agricultural production, at least as far as food crops are concerned, is concentrated in a few regions. Table 8.6 contains data on production in 1978/9. The main cereal-producing regions in order were Shoa, Arssi, and Gondar. Assuming 1978/9 was a typical year, the table suggests that these three provinces produce more than half the nation's cereals. Shoa alone produces 28 per cent of all cereals and 36 per cent of the country's maize. Arssi is notable for its dominant share of wheat production and Gojjam joins the important cereal-growing areas by virtue of its contribution of highly prized teff. It is no coincidence that each of these areas is linked to Addis Ababa by some of the country's better roads.

It is therefore not surprising that the pattern of purchases by the state marketing agency follows much the same pattern. Although private traders operate as well, the pattern of Agricultural Marketing Corporation (AMC) purchases shown in Table 8.7 is a reasonable indicator of the main sources of smallholder sales – that is production which is surplus to the producers' requirements for consumption.

The evidence presented here suggests then, that there is considerable variation in land availability and its quality, in per capita food production and in the share each region contributes to national

Table 8.6 Production of Cereals and Pulses by Region, 1978/9 (thousand tonnes)

Region	*Cereals*							*Pulses*
	Teff	*Barley*	*Wheat*	*Maize*	*Sorghum*	*Millet*	*Total*	
Arssi	32.8	178.8	203.3	65.1	37.6	0.0	517.7	55.5
Bale	5.3	104.9	70.8	4.7	1.0	0.5	157.3	14.1
Gemu Goffa	6.7	7.3	0.4	20.9	3.7	1.3	39.8	1.7
Gojjam	180.9	37.2	20.0	32.4	5.9	44.0	320.4	33.2
Gondar	205.9	91.0	11.1	18.6	60.2	59.7	446.5	95.0
Harrarghe	1.8	0.8	3.5	30.3	123.1	0.8	160.3	2.7
Illubabor	32.5	1.3	0.4	54.0	16.9	6.3	111.3	2.2
Keffa	91.4	18.3	8.6	145.2	20.3	3.5	287.2	15.3
Shoa	268.7	112.6	82.4	301.6	156.5	1.7	923.4	162.0
Sidamo	12.7	17.9	0.7	90.0	1.8	0.0	123.0	8.4
Wellega	83.0	7.3	1.2	72.7	48.3	22.9	235.4	6.5
Wollo	67.3	2.2	18.5	6.8	70.8	0.4	165.9	35.2
Total	988.6	579.6	390.9	842.3	546.1	114.1	3488.3	432.5

Source: *Crop Production Survey 1978–9*, Addis Ababa: Ministry of Agriculture, June 1979.

foodgrain production and to marketed supply. Futhermore, although there are exceptions, five administrative regions – Arssi, Gojjam, Gondar, Shoa and Wollo – figure prominently in having the better crop yields, the larger holdings, the larger share of national production and in making the greatest contribution (other than state farms) to national foodgrain supply. It is in these five regions that agriculture is concentrated.

Provided income is fairly well spread and an efficient marketing system is operating it does not matter much if food production is confined to one part of the country. Indeed many countries which have a low rate of malnutrition produce the bulk of their food in one region. However, the conditions for the effective distribution of food from surplus to deficit areas are not fulfilled in Ethiopia and the grain market remains extremely fragmented outside the area of the AMC's operations.

This is illustrated in Table 8.8, in which data on inter-regional price differences for six grains are given. The data refer to October 1981 and were obtained from 11 administrative regions. As can be seen, there is an enormous difference between maximum and minimum prices. The difference is never less than 100 per cent and in the case of sorghum it rises to 346 per cent. The coefficient of variation is also

Table 8.7 AMC Purchases of Agricultural Products by Region, 1981/2, from sources other than state farms (thousand tonnes with percentage share in brackets)

	Foodgrains	*Oil seeds*	*Total*
Gojjam	81.2	20.0	101.2
	(31.6)	(40.35)	(33.02)
Shoa	56.0	6.4	62.4
	(21.81)	(12.96)	(20.38)
Arssi	59.6	5.8	65.4
	(23.22)	(11.7)	(21.37)
Gondar	26.3	7.0	33.3
	(10.25)	(14.05)	(10.86)
Wollo	17.2	0.1	17.3
	(6.68)	(0.26)	(5.64)
Wellega	3.1	9.2	12.3
	(1.22)	(18.49)	(4.01)
Bale	8.7	1.0	9.7
	(3.38)	(1.99)	(3.16)
Keffa	3.6	0.1	3.7
	(1.39)	(0.13)	(1.19)
Sidamo	0.8	—	0.8
	(0.33)		(0.28)
Illubabor	0.3	—	0.3
	(0.12)		(0.09)
Total	256.8	49.6	306.4
	(100.00)	(100.00)	(100.00)

Notes: No purchases were made in the other regions.

Source: Agricultural Marketing Corporation, *Annual Report*, Addis Ababa: 1982.

high for all six crops and the variability is generally greater for the four inferior commodities on which poorest populations depend, namely, millets, sorghum, maize and barley.

If one examines individual provinces it is discovered that Gojjam enjoys the lowest variability in prices for most crops – the region supplying the greatest share of AMC purchases – while Bale, Gemu Goffa and Tigrai appear to be highly volatile. Moreover, the relative prices of the different crops alter frequently and the price structure varies remarkably even between contiguous, well connected districts of the same region. The evidence thus points to a highly fragmented market with very imperfect flows of grain and information.

The first attempts, after the revolution, at market control were

Table 8.8 Inter-regional Price Differences for Six Crops, 1981

Crop	*Max. price* (birr/quintal)	*Min. price* (birr/quintal)	*Average price* (birr/quintal)	*Coefficient of variation*
Teff	128.3	36.9	68.7	34.4
Wheat	91.0	38.2	62.0	24.9
Maize	69.7	20.0	37.2	37.5
Barley	49.6	22.5	38.0	21.1
Sorghum	101.7	22.8	48.2	49.3
Millets	100.0	22.6	49.7	71.6

Source: Early Warning and Planning Service, Relief and Rehabilitation Commission, *Food Supply System: Meher Synoptic Report 1981*, Addis Ababa: March 1982.

directed toward food prices. The government began to announce official producer and retail prices by proclamation. The effect was negligible. The strategy then moved towards controlling supply and after some time the capacity of the AMC and the Ethiopian Grain Agency (now absorbed within AMC) to purchase in surplus areas was expanded by the provision of capital, transport and staff. Gradually the government was able to increase its share of the market for basic food commodities and now handles about 560 000 tonnes of cereals annually. This is equivalent to 30 or 40 per cent of the cereals retailed in Addis Ababa, Dire Dawa and Asmara and about 59 per cent of estimated marketed surplus. The AMC is now able to buy at announced prices and the government has been able to institute effective legal controls on the domestic grain trade in the main surplus-producing provinces. Quotas are set for each region and are passed down through district administrative levels to producers' cooperatives and Peasants' Associations. Merchants are still free to operate but in Gojjam, Gondar, Arssi they are now obliged to sell all that they buy to AMC at announced wholesale prices. Merchants in these provinces thus act as AMC agents. In Shoa and Wollo they are obliged to sell 50 per cent of what they purchase to the AMC. Recently Shoa merchants have been asked to sell all they buy to the AMC, but the AMC fears that this will impose an impossible burden on the organisation and leave it wholly responsible for feeding Addis Ababa, so the rule is not being enforced.

However, although the AMC distributes through the Basic Commodities Service Corporation to urban *kebeles* in Addis Ababa, Dire Dawa and Asmara it has little effect on supply outside these urban centres. In food deficit regions it purchases and sells locally but does not contribute at all to flows of grain from food-surplus to food-deficit regions except in its supply to Asmara and Dire Dawa. Although it has agents in all provinces the pattern of its operation is quite simple. It buys in five provinces to supply three cities. This is precisely the same pattern of distribution which prevailed before the revolution. It is therefore fair to say that although the means of distribution has changed its pattern has not.

Outside the area of AMC's operation the market is fragmented and prices vary widely between seasons and from year to year.

The most obvious reason for the limited movement of grain is the nature of the roads and the limited access they provide to rural areas. Grain may have to be packed by mule for days to reach a market where merchants are buying. Furthermore the road system has been developed to serve Addis Ababa. Direct inter-regional links are non-existent. In addition, or at least as a further consequence of Ethiopia's pre-revolutionary pattern of development, incomes are concentrated in surplus-producing agricultural regions and this concentration is reinforced by the presence of industries clustered around the capital, Addis Ababa, and surrounding parts of Shoa Administrative Region.

If the AMC were to set up an effective national distribution system it would have to increase the scale of its operation many times. It will clearly take some time for this to be achieved effectively. Meantime, regional concentration in terms of production is reinforced by the pattern of income distribution. A combination of demand pattern, the political imperative to feed the urban population and poorly distributed transport infrastructure determines the pattern of grain flows, leaving much of the rural areas isolated and without access to the national market.

PRODUCTION VARIABILITY

Ethiopia is well known for its vulnerability to drought and famine. The catastrophic events of 1973–4 and 1982–3 are, however, only extreme examples of fluctuating climatic conditions which induce year-to-year instability in the production system.

Climatic conditions also vary unduly from one part of the country to another and determine what can be grown where. Annual rainfall varies from less than 400 mm per annum in the desert skirt around the Ethiopian highlands, to levels in excess of 2700 mm per annum in the South-west, where two climatic patterns coalesce and it rains for seven months of the year. Over most of the country there are two rainy seasons and therefore two cropping periods a year.

The most favourable conditions for rainfed agriculture exist, as might be expected, in the five administrative regions where agriculture is concentrated. However, extreme variations exist within regions and Wollo, for example, is notable for producing a surplus in its highland regions, being marginal for rainfed agriculture as altitude falls, and encompassing a large area of lowland desert where cropping is only possible with irrigation.

However, the overwhelmingly important attribute of the Ethiopian climate is its variability. Crop yields can be expected to vary from year to year about a trend line by 10–15 per cent as a result of changes in the onset or the intensity of rainy periods, or both. Climatic variability is also more marked in some regions than in others. The eastern escarpment areas, central Wollo and southern Gemu Goffa have become notorious for their variable climate and the frequency with which they are affected by drought.

This variability places an additional burden on the distribution system. Every year managers in the AMC operate in conditions of great uncertainty. Although a rudimentary 'early warning' system exists, reliable crop forecast data are not available. The Relief and Rehabilitation Commission was established to deal with the most violent fluctuations in food output but adjustments of price, stock management and logistical arrangements constitute unending processes.

The lack of market integration adds to the problem. Prices outside the controlled market fluctuate wildly from year to year and, when they are high, imperil the livelihood of poor households which are, as we have seen, concentrated in areas cut off from the national market. Often the market, such as it is, breaks down entirely and there is little or no trading in areas where production has been disrupted by drought.

These four features – sluggish growth, regional concentration, a fragmented market and production instability – characterise Ethiopia's agriculture and define the problems faced by the country's planners if their ambition to achieve sustained growth with equity is to be realised. The problems they face are clearly considerable. Yet their task is not impossible. In a technical sense at least there is a considerable potential for growth and although an equitable distribution of the benefits of growth is difficult, because of the spatial concentration of production and incomes, improvement is possible. The reversal of regional concentration, however, depends critically on the means by which an increased rate of growth is achieved. It is to these issues that we now turn.

THE POTENTIAL FOR INCREASING OUTPUT

The first priority must be to increase the rate of agricultural growth. In physical terms, growth in agricultural output may arise from an expansion in land area or a rise in land productivity or both.

Ethiopia is relatively land abundant and a considerable expansion of land under the plough should be possible. The possibilities for internal land expansion, that is, a more intensive use of existing agricultural land, are considerable but vary from region to region. A broad strip of land, amounting perhaps to 30 per cent of Ethiopia's arable area to the west and south of the central highlands (running from the southern border of Gojjam south through western Gondar, Illubabor, Keffa and then east through northern Gemu Goffa, mid-Sidamo, northern Bale and up into Arssi) is relatively under-utilised. In these areas the constraints to expanding the area under production are first labour and then capital. A rough approximation derived from crop survey data suggests that reducing the area designated as 'fallow' by 50 per cent in these areas would add 8–10 per cent to Ethiopia's stock of productive land. However, labour-saving inputs will be required in these labour-scarce areas. The sharing of oxen would help but more are required. Alternatively, small cultivators could be used when funds to invest in them become available.

In the central and northern highlands the problem is different. Here land is either scarce (Wollo and Gojjam rank first and third in proportion of area under crops) or the land left idle is eroded, swampy or exhausted. The chief constraint to land expansion in these and other regions further north is not labour but capital. Land conservation, drainage and irrigation are required urgently to prevent further degradation, to improve land capability and thus to expand productive area. The potential for collective action in land improvement projects cannot be overemphasised.

The expansion of the area under production outside existing holdings is another possibility. Without irrigation and without undue destruction of natural forest the greatest scope for bringing in new land is along Ethiopia's western border, from the Gambella swamps in Illubabor north through western Wellega into Gojjam. It is estimated that the cultivation of this 100 km wide strip would add a further 10–15 per cent to Ethiopia's productive land stock.

Thus, without tapping the resources of the southern rivers to irrigate semi-arid land, it would seem that there is another 18 to 25 per cent to be added to the existing cultivated area without radical changes in present technology. The Ten Year Perspective Plan for 1982–91 calls for a growth in area under cultivation of 2 per cent per annum which at the end of ten years would amount to an addition of 22 per cent to productive land stock. This accords with our estimate of what is available. In order to achieve this, additional inputs of labour, or labour-saving technology, will be required in labour-scarce areas, additional capital investment in the form of land improvement will be required in land-scarce areas and both labour and capital will be required to bring in new areas. This implies three distinct strategies each designed to remove the dominant constraint in particular regions.

Another source of new crop land becomes possible with irrigation. Extensive feasibility studies have already been carried out for large-scale irrigation projects along the Awash, Wabe Shebelle and Omo Rivers. These projects would not provide much employment and would absorb a great deal of foreign capital, but would undoubtedly produce a lot of food for the cities and raw materials for industry. We will argue in the next section, however, that these projects should have a second priority to improving the productivity of peasant lands and labour.

The second source of agricultural growth is improved land productivity. The Plan calls for an average growth in agricultural output of 4.5 per cent per annum over the next ten years. This clearly has to come both from area expansion and from an increase in land productivity. At the end of ten years agricultural output is planned to be 1.6 times its present level. Assuming an increase in area of 2 per cent per annum, this would require that yields grow at 2.4 per cent per annum and on average achieve levels 27 per cent higher than they are today. This is certainly possible technically but the type of incentives the government chooses to use to achieve the goals will have a profound effect on the outcome in terms of the distribution of income, consumption and nutritional welfare.

Generally, crop yields in Ethiopia are low. Table 8.9 compares the range of crop yields achieved in different parts of Ethiopia with yields

Table 8.9 Actual and Potential Yields for Some Major Crops (kg/ha)

	Estimated yields 1978–9		*Potential yields*	
	Low	*High*	*Low input*	*High input*
Coffee	250	600	400–700	1200–2200
Wheat	230	1210	500–1600	1600–2500
Teff	470	1320	400–1100	1200–1800
Maize	650	3910	1200–1800	2800–8000
Sorghum	560	1500	600–1600	1700–2800

Source: Agricultural Survey, 1978–79, and personal communication, Land Use Planning Unit, Ministry of Agriculture.

thought to be possible under Ethiopian conditions. It is clear that considerable scope exists for improving land productivity but more and more modern inputs will be required to maintain the momentum of growth.

Increases in crop yields are likely to come from a combination of four inputs – fertiliser, improved seed varieties, irrigation and better crop management. In regions where crop yields are high the general impression is that peasant farmers may be operating near the optimum, given current crop and input prices and levels of investment. In other regions considerable improvement may be possible. Take fertiliser for example. Almost half the fertiliser used in Ethiopia goes into state farms. The high price of teff and wheat makes it profitable to fertilise these crops and yields can be doubled as a result. The use of improved seed varieties and fertiliser together would improve returns to land and labour still more and would probably mean that it was profitable to fertilise maize as well. Generally natural fertiliser is only used where wood is available, otherwise animal dung is required for fuel. Many of these areas which have been denuded of natural vegetation are also leached and eroded so that the natural levels of soil nutrients are exceedingly low.

SYSTEMS OF AGRICULTURAL PRODUCTION

Following the land reforms of 1975 there are now four distinct modes of production in the rural areas of Ethiopia. First, and by far the most important, is the peasant farming sector. The farms in this sector are usually quite small, viz. about 2 ha on average, yet they account for over 90 per cent of the cultivated land in the country. Production technologies are simple: capital consists of rudimentary implements (a sickle, a wooden plough, or a machete); power is limited to that provided by an inadequate number of draught animals; seeds are broadcast and almost no fertiliser is used.

The peasants who farm this land are organised into 23 497 Peasant Associations with a total membership of 7 247 209 households. Each Peasant Association, in principle, occupies approximately 800 ha, although some occupy more land and many a much smaller area, reflecting regional differences which are an important feature of the rural economy. The role of the Peasant Association is to promote economic and social development in the broadest sense and to prepare the way for the establishment of genuinely collective institutions. At present the associations are responsible for running the literacy compaign and the local primary schools (where these exist), for resolving local disputes, for allocating land among members of the associations, for collecting agricultural land and income taxes and the like.

Peasant Associations also are encouraged to cooperate and form service cooperatives. Some 3679 such cooperatives have been created with a membership of 5 054 892 households (Table 8.10). Service cooperatives thus have a limited but important task to fulfil. Moreover, they have the potential to expand their sphere of activity from processing and exchange to production and accumulation. This, we will argue, could be the basis for rapid gains in rural productivity and income.

Alongside the Peasant Associations is a small sector of producers' cooperatives. This is the second system of production in rural areas. As few as three households may pool their resources to form a producers' cooperative. A 'first stage' cooperative consists of collectively cultivated land with implements and draught animals hired by the cooperative from its members. The members retain some land for individual cultivation and share the collectively generated income on the basis of their labour contribution. Those who have provided oxen and implements also receive rent. At the second stage, a greater proportion of the land and all implements are held in common and collective income is distributed according to a work point system. The government has decided that the future of Ethiopia's agriculture lies with cooperatives, but in quantitative terms they are as yet of little significance. In fact, there are only 837 producers' cooperatives in the entire country with a membership of 54 423 households. Even

Table 8.10 Peasant Associations, Service Cooperatives and Producers' Cooperatives, 1982

Region	*Peasant Associations*		*Service Cooperatives*			*Producers' Cooperatives*			
	No.	*Households*	*No.*	*Member PAs*	*Households*	*No.*	*Area cultivated*	*Registered*	*Households*
Arssi	1 119	290 000	145	1 070	262 289	85	8 137	6	3 553
Bale	686	170 000	116	592	65 882	82	8 689	4	4 695
Eritrea	281	60 750	5	12	1 620	3	20	0	88
Gemu Goffa	777	211 976	90	371	113 501	16	7 141	2	1 881
Gojjam	2 690	456 242	380	1 607	335 776	83	13 673	10	2 765
Gondar	1 749	427 209	244	651	136 572	43	3 359	6	1 963
Harrarghe	1 608	420 957	257	1 088	886 678	94	7 116	5	4 995
Illubabor	908	190 546	183	874	231 040	71	4 560	3	3 781
Keffa	1 663	535 474	235	1 126	319 978	50	11 445	3	2 269
Shoa	3 485	1 703 662	1 044	5 262	1 259 971	86	14 653	7	5 812
Sidamo	1 482	601 043	299	1 159	506 399	69	214 106	2	12 002
Tigrai	1 064	499 076	138	302	129 153	8	351	0	230
Wellega	2 210	449 792	389	1 761	454 066	76	24 686	7	5 188
Wollo	1 703	1 022 482	224	745	349 967	71	5 840	2	5 194
Total	23 497	7 247 209	3 679	16 680	5 054 892	837	313 688	57	54 423

Source: Ministry of Agriculture, Government of Socialist Ethiopia, June 1982.

these figures, small as they are, may be misleading since 652 are small, first-stage cooperatives and the remaining 185 are somewhat larger second-stage producers' cooperatives, of which only 57 are registered and thus enjoy full legal status.

The existing producers' cooperatives tend to be larger in terms of land per household than peasant farms and to use more advanced methods of production. For example, they use more fertiliser per hectare than peasant farms, they have much more draught animal power (30 421 pairs of oxen for their 313 688 ha) and they may even possess a tractor (there are 30 tractors distributed among the 837 producers' cooperatives). Even so, labour and land productivity are low, the marketable surplus is small, non-agricultural activities are poorly developed and the rate of accumulation is distressingly modest.

The third system of production is the state farm sector. This sector was created after the land nationalisation programme of 1975 from commercial holdings that were thought to be unsuitable for redistribution in the form of small peasant holdings. Since then the size of the sector has increased substantially, viz. by about 300 per cent in the last three years, although in national terms it is still very small, accounting for less than 5 per cent of the land area and of agricultural output. The sector covers approximately 245 000 ha, of which about 14 000 ha are in coffee and the rest in a variety of crops of which grains and cotton are the most important.

The size of a state farm is very large, often several thousand hectares. Indeed if they were in another country and in the private sector they would be called latifundia. Ethiopia's 'state latifundia', if we may call them that, are highly mechanised and consequently generate relatively little permanent employment. Table 8.11 shows data on 26 state farms covering 150 711 ha, or over half the entire sector. As can be seen at a glance, almost all the farms use very extensive methods of cultivation. The wheat farms in particular often have only one permanent worker for every 30 or 40 ha, but even after taking all the other farms into account the weighted average number of hectares per worker is a remarkably high 14.28.

The peasant farms and producers' cooperatives are more efficient than the state farms and their financial returns are better. Although this may have something to do with the recent rapid expansion of state farms it is worrying that the overwhelming majority of state farms operate at a substantial loss, with only a few of the cotton farms making a consistent profit. Wage rates on state farms are low; in fact

Table 8.11 The Employment Intensity of State Farms

Name of Farm	*Main crop*	*Area (ha)*	*No. of Permanent workers*	*Hectares per worker*
Dubti	Cotton	5 266	291	18.10
Dit Bahari	Cotton	5 347	406	13.17
Asaita	Cotton	1 917	103	18.61
Mille	Cotton	875	159	5.50
Melkasedi	Banana	700	992	0.71
Amibara Angele	Cotton	2 652	359	7.39
AIP	Cotton	1 805	165	10.94
Defan Belhame	Cotton	1 400	89	15.73
Gewane	Cotton	2 083	626	3.33
Adelle	Wheat	6 000	149	40.27
Ardaita	Wheat	7 200	196	36.73
Dikisis	Wheat	10 320	252	40.95
Garadella	Wheat	11 350	294	38.61
Gofer	Wheat	8 500	220	38.64
Lele Netalle	Wheat	2 444	91	26.86
Dinkite	Wheat	10 000	241	41.49
Herere	Wheat	9 500	301	31.56
Sheneka	Wheat	10 000	226	44.25
Sinana	Wheat	8 500	258	32.95
Sirufta	Wheat	6 000	191	31.41
Harewa	Wheat	12 000	140	85.71
Abaya Bilate	Cotton	2 816	1 069	2.63
Arba Minch	Cotton	2 320	1 367	1.70
Awassa	Maize	15 211	1 676	9.08
Wajife	Cotton	505	308	1.64
Mitto	Maize	6 000	382	15.71

Source: Ministry of State Farm Development, Government of Socialist Ethiopia, August 1982.

state farms are not allowed to pay more than the legal minimum wage of 1.92 birr per day. While it is true that state farm managers effectively raise wage rates to perhaps 3 birr per day by paying piece-rates for additional work above a daily norm, they cannot pay the going rates for seasonal labour which, at least in one area, appear to be about 5 birr per day. In consequence they often have trouble competing with the peasant farm sector and resort instead to coercive labour recruitment practices.

The reasons state farms require large subsidies to cover their losses evidently have nothing to do with high wages or excessive levels of employment, since they employ few people and pay them little. The problems lie elsewhere. First, the sector was organised hurriedly and expanded rapidly and this has given rise to managerial problems. Few of the farm managers have experience in running large agricultural enterprises and many are not properly trained. No doubt this can be remedied given time. Second, although the 'state latifundia' possess a great deal of capital equipment, much of the machinery is out of operation at any given moment. Hence the productivity of capital is very low. Third, the control structure is excessively centralised and even routine decisions must be referred by the farm manager to a higher authority, i.e. to the enterprise, corporation or ministry or perhaps even the Central Planning Supreme Council. If the state farms are ever to be a success, a great deal more responsibility will have to be delegated to the farm manager. At the same time, the heavy overhead costs of the sector will have to be reduced by eliminating the enterprise level within the ministry or by separating the state farms from ministries and grouping them together under a single, autonomous corporation.

Fourth, management and planning in the state farm sector appear to be conducted essentially in physical terms based on agronomic notions about what constitutes good 'scientific' farming. Farm managers appear not to be told, say, the cost of fertiliser, or to have the freedom to vary the cropping pattern in accordance with relative returns, or to vary the terms and conditions of employment of their labour force, or more generally to be required to think in financial terms. It is hardly surprising that under such circumstances the financial results are poor. It would be better in our opinion, if delegation of responsibility were accompanied by the setting of specific profit targets for each farm and success assessed largely by comparing the actual profit performance with the planned profit target.

A final reason why the state farms have made large losses is because the government has imposed low output prices upon them and kept these prices fixed despite the fact that prices in general have risen substantially. The motive of the government is clearly to maintain reasonable prices for essential commodities. The consequence for the state farms, however, has been to exaggerate their losses and to create a slightly misleading impression of inefficiency. In our opinion the state farms (and producers' cooperatives) should be paid the going price for their produce and the cost of subsidising the price of essential commodities should be borne directly by the central government budget. In this way the government will have a clearer picture of the economic viability of the state farm sector and of the true cost of price subsidies.

The fourth system of production, a semi-nomadic form of pastoralism, is only to be found in the semi-arid lowland areas which skirt Ethiopia's central highlands and in the Rift Valley. Reliable data about the number of pastoralists and their animals are difficult to come by and somewhat artificial in as much as the migratory pattern of pastoral clans is determined by the availability of grazing and water rather than international boundaries. A number of different groups exist, for example the Afar and Issa peoples to the east, the Ogaden Somalia in southern Harrarghe and Bale and the Dorena in southern Bale and Sidamo. Each has developed a particular set of social and institutional structures so that the following description is of necessity general.

Cattle are the chief form of wealth, the most important mark of status, and the main source of food. They not only provide food directly but are exchanged for grain in local markets. At 'normal' exchange rates one mature animal will provide enough grain to feed a family for a year. Generally speaking Ethiopian pastoralists derive half their food (in terms of energy) from milk, blood and meat, and half from grain. Camels are also important and extremely valuable. They are beasts of burden, provide milk and are sometimes killed for meat on special occasions. Goats abound and are used for their milk and skins.

The pastoral social structure is a tightly knit kinship system with strong inter-clan connections which determine grazing and watering rights. Each clan and sub-clan has its 'base ground' where crops are cultivated in years when rainfall is adequate – about three or four out of seven. Pastoral migratory patterns are complex but well regulated by custom and season. They vary from year to year according to grazing conditions and harsh-year grazing grounds are carefully conserved.

Animal carrying capacity varies with rainfall from year to year and probably follows cyclical climatic patterns. Herd size tends to increase during 'good' periods and to overshoot the theoretically optimum carrying capacity of the range. Pastoralists are then criticised for overgrazing but, in view of the crucial importance of its herd to any given pastoral family, the aggregate optimum is likely to be below the average desirable herd size in the individual case. The drought years of the middle 1970s caused great loss of life – both of animals and people – and a refugee problem which remains to this day.

Two variants are worth mentioning. The Rare Bare group cultivate ground beside the Wabe Shebelle River each year, using flood irrigation, and is relatively more sedentary than other Ogaden groups. Along the southern escarpments a mixed peasant pastoral mode of production exists. Herds graze on crop residues and on seasonal grazing grounds near farms for much of the year but migrate to lowland grazing grounds during the rainy seasons.

It is the government's intention that pastoralists should be settled and finally form producers' cooperatives. This poses great social and ecological problems and is the subject of intense study and debate. The rivers which cross the southern deserts have tremendous irrigation potential but their use would jeopardise the pastoral way of life.

Meantime the rangelands are the main source of oxen for highland farming draught power and contribute the bulk of the hides and skins for Ethiopia's most rapidly growing export. Four rangeland development projects have been implemented in different areas to improve marketing facilities, range management methods and surface water availability but the future of migratory pastoralism remains in doubt.

A final and transient system of production should be mentioned – settlement farms. They were set up by the Relief and Rehabilitation Commission after the droughts which affected northern Shoa, Wollo and Tigrai to provide new agricultural opportunities for families from overpopulated areas. Settlement farms are intended to be the main instrument for expanding the area under cultivation. Each settlement receives government assistance for the first three years of its existence, after which it is intended that it should form itself into a producers' cooperative. By and large settlement farms have not yet achieved the objectives set for them. They have often been poorly located. They are intensive in their use of capital, much of which is foreign, and while returns to land are only slightly less than in the peasant sector (1241 kg per ha compared with 1323 kg per ha) they make substantial losses and progress toward collectivisation has been painfully slow.

The three main systems of arable agricultural production – peasant farms, producers' cooperatives and state farms – coexist in Ethiopia today. As we have seen, they differ from one another in terms of size, technology and employment. The question is whether one system is unambiguously superior to the others or alternatively, whether they also differ from one another, either actually or potentially, in terms of their basic function.

ADVANTAGES OF ALTERNATIVE FARMING SYSTEMS

Unfortunately, data are not available with which to answer this question fully or to make accurate quantitative estimates of the differences between the three systems of production. There does exist, however, enough fragmentary information from published sources and from our own field observations to enable us to make qualitative judgements about differences in performance. For the time being this will have to suffice for the purposes of this analysis.

We shall use five criteria to compare the performance and functions of peasant farms, producers' cooperatives and state farms. The first three criteria are concerned with the way given resources are used in the process of production. They thus refer to static allocative efficiency. The fourth criterion is concerned with the capacity of a particular system of production to grow and develop and hence to provide an engine for agricultural growth and a rising standard of living for the rural population over time. The fifth criterion is concerned with the supply of commodities for sale on the market in order to feed the urban population or to earn foreign exchange through exporting. Efficiency, growth and the marketable surplus will thus be the standards by which we will judge the three systems of production. Table 8.12 summarises the results.

Table 8.12 Criteria for Ranking the Three Systems of Production

	Peasant farms	*Producers' cooperatives*	*State farms*
1. Capacity to absorb labour	1	2	3
2. Rate of profit on capital	1	2	3
3. Crop yields	1 or 2	3	1 or 2
4. Potential for accumulation	2	1	3
5. Marketable surplus	3	2	1

I Allocative efficiency

Let us begin with the capacity of each system to absorb labour and use it productively. Labour is generally scarce in Ethiopia relative to land, but it is very abundant relative to capital. Moreover, in most regions, there is pronounced seasonal unemployment. In the past this was alleviated to some extent by temporary migration to the coffee regions and to large farms in the north-west during the harvest season. This intra-rural migration continues today but is much diminished and therefore temporarily surplus labour may be even more common now.

There is no doubt which system of production performs most badly in terms of its ability to absorb labour – the state farms. Indeed we have commented at some length on the low labour intensity of production of the state farm sector. Next in ascending order come producers' cooperatives and best of all, by this criterion, are the small peasant farms. If the sole basis for judging an agricultural system is employment per unit of land or per unit of output, the peasant farming system wins easily. In one respect however, it is a hollow victory, for the cost of high employment intensity is low labour productivity and hence low incomes. The cost is worth paying if the alternative is unemployment, but the fact that there is a high cost should not be forgotten.

Consider, second, output per unit of capital or the rate of profit on capital. Given the acute scarcity of all forms of capital in the Ethiopian countryside, it is important that it be used in the most efficient way possible. Here again, the state farms perform badly by this criterion. Methods of production are intensive in the use of mechanical equipment and imported inputs such as fertilisers and petroleum, yet the returns to this capital are at present negative. The results could hardly be worse.

Producers' cooperatives, in contrast, manage to generate a small financial surplus and thus by this criterion perform better than the state farms, although the rate of profit on the cooperatives is much lower than in principle it could be. The peasant farms, as before, do well by this criterion. The peasant producers have almost no capital with which to work, but their output per unit of capital is very high. Strictly in allocative terms there should be a redistribution of capital from the state farms to the peasant sector and a redistribution of labour from the peasant sector to the state farms.

The third criterion, and the final one concerned with efficiency, covers crop yields or output per unit of land. In general, given what was said before about labour intensity and the return on capital, one would expect small peasant farms to have higher yields than either of the other two modes of production, and in fact, this is often the case. Consider the important coffee export sector as an example. Peasant farms and state farms compete side by side, yet peasant farms typically obtain about 400 kg per ha whereas state farms do well to obtain 260 kg, a difference of nearly 54 per cent in favour of the small peasants. Similarly, pulses are grown in all three systems, yet yields on producers' cooperatives appear to be only about 43 per cent as high as on peasant farms, and on state farms the yields are only 33 per cent as high. This is the ranking one would expect.

When it comes to cereals, however, the results are different. Yields on the producers' cooperatives are only two thirds as high as on peasant farms, but the yields on state farms are a third higher than on peasant farms. In this case the state farms are able to compensate for their low labour intensity and low return on capital by massive applications of fertiliser and other modern inputs. Given the great importance of cereals in the composition of agricultural output in Ethiopia, the overall picture as regards yields is ambiguous. There simply are not enough data to determine which system of production – peasant farms or state farms – in general enjoys the highest output per unit of land. Hence in Table 8.12 we have ranked them both 1 or 2.

Looking at the situation as a whole, however, it is evident that the peasant system of production uses resources most efficiently. Next probably comes the producers' cooperatives followed by the state farms. In this respect Ethiopia is similar to other countries.

II The potential for accumulation

The process of development, however, depends not only upon how efficiently existing resources are used but also upon how rapidly capital can be accumulated and slack resources brought into productive use. That is, in the long run, average standards of living depend more on the rate of growth than they do on allocative efficiency. Hence if one system of production is superior to all others in terms of its potential for sustained rapid growth, that system should have a strong claim to being the preferred one.

Unfortunately it is very difficult to generalise in the abstract about the potential for accumulation and growth of the three farming systems with which we are concerned. Much depends upon the particular circumstances which can, of course, change. Thus in making judgements about the potential for accumulation of peasant farms, producers' cooperatives and state farms we are implicitly making judgements about conditions in Ethiopia today and over, say, the next ten years.

At the moment it is evident that the state farms are making no contribution to capital accumulation and growth. On the contrary, their deficits represent negative savings and, far from generating a surplus, they are absorbing surpluses generated elsewhere. Various suggestions to remedy this unhappy situation were made in the previous section of this chapter and if the suggestions are implemented the situation should improve considerably. Even so, it is doubtful if the state farm sector can ever be a powerful engine for generating surpluses, fostering a rapid rate of investment or promoting accelerated growth in the agricultural sector. To believe otherwise requires a leap of faith we are not prepared to make.

It is more difficult to assess the potential for accumulation and growth in the peasant farm sector. In principle, of course, peasants can (and in many countries do) save a significant proportion of their income. They also accumulate capital through the direct application of their labour, thereby bringing additional land under cultivation or improving land already being cultivated. In Ethiopia, however, it would probably be unrealistic to expect that spontaneous accumulation by peasants would be sufficient to produce sustained rapid growth of production.

Indeed the peasant sector is likely to come under increasing pressure in the near future and it will do well to avoid entering a spiral of cumulative retrogression. The benefits of the land reform, in this context, represent merely a short breathing space in which to reverse the process of underdevelopment. The first source of pressure is the accelerating rate of population growth. On this, as on other important topics, accurate data are lacking but it is quite possible that the rate of demographic expansion in rural areas is rising from 2.2 to 2.4 per cent a year. Second, the rural labour force already is growing faster than before, thus making it increasingly difficult for young entrants into the labour force to obtain a livelihood comparable to that obtained by their parents at a similar age. As a consequence, third, the productivity of labour in the rural areas is falling. Finally, after the once-and-for-all gains from the abolition of land rents are exhausted, the above trends imply that the incomes of peasant households will begin to fall and indeed may already have begun to do so.

A peasantry under this sort of pressure, and living so close to the edge of starvation is unlikely to be able to set aside resources each year for capital accumulation. The most that one can expect is that economic pressures will force peasants to exert themselves to the utmost to cultivate their land more intensively and whenever possible to expand the area under cultivation. Our judgement is that even with such exertions per capita agricultural output will continue to fall.

This brings us to the cooperative system of production. Cooperation among peasant farmers is part of Ethiopia's agricultural tradition but the scope for expanding cooperative activities is enormous and the advantages of doing so are considerable. Indeed it is hard to imagine how anyone could seriously believe that a half-starved, impoverished peasant working on his own with almost no capital could be the vehicle for rapid development. By working together, however, peasants could use the slack season to undertake land improvement works (field levelling and terracing), to construct drainage and small-scale irrigation facilities, or to plant trees (fruit orchards, coffee for export, forests for fuel and for erosion control). In addition, peasants could work together to expand the area under cultivation (by clearing scrub trees, removing stones from natural pastures and using them to erect fences, diverting streams from marshy land, etc.). All of these activities would increase peasant incomes and yet require little more than their own organised labour power.

Once a functioning organisation is established further opportunities emerge. One of the striking things about Ethiopia is the scarcity of draught animals. Perhaps as many as 29 per cent of all rural households do not own an ox for ploughing, the majority own only one while some share the ownership of an ox with another household. Despite this it is debatable if some areas could import more oxen without accelerating land degradation. Yet more land could be brought under cultivation, and the land could be ploughed better and more quickly if each household had access to a pair of oxen. Cooperation would permit this.

III. The marketable surplus

The final criterion we are using to compare the three systems of production is the marketable surplus produced by each. Fortunately on this subject it is possible to be brief.

Peasant farms in Ethiopia, except in areas specialising in coffee, are largely subsistence holdings. Only a small proportion of output is sold on the market, most of it being retained to feed the members of the household. In the important case of grains, for example, less than one fifth of peasant production would normally be marketed. Given the small size and low yields in the peasant sector this is hardly surprising. The implication, however, is that by the criterion of the marketable surplus the peasant system of production performs least well.

One would expect producers' cooperatives to do slightly better. In general they have a more favourable land–man ratio and capital–labour ratio and consequently output per worker is higher, despite the fact that yields tend to be lower. Thus the margin of output over bare subsistence is larger and this should be reflected in a larger proportion of output sold on the market. Moreover, if the cooperatives do succeed in accelerating the rate of accumulation and hence growth, the marketable surplus should rise persistently over time and readily surpass that achieved on peasant farms. Even so, it is obvious that if all that matters is the marketable surplus, the state farms are superior to the other two systems of production. In this, if nothing else, the state farms come into their own. Indeed virtually 100 per cent of their output reaches the market and this is a proportion that cannot be approached by peasant farms or cooperatives.

Given that this is the case, one still must ask whether it is sensible to choose a system of production because it disposes of a large proportion of its output on the market. Presumably in Ethiopia one is concerned about the marketable surplus primarily because one is anxious to ensure that enough food will always be available to feed the urban population. Happily for Ethiopia, however, the urban population is small, i.e. only about 15 per cent of the total, and hence the supply problems should be quite manageable. Indeed, if the peasant or cooperative sectors are preferred on other grounds, they could almost certainly be induced to increase their marketable surpluses through more favourable terms of trade, particularly if other reinforcing measures lead to an expansion of production. Failing that, the state in effect could replace the vanquished landlords and compel a larger proportion of output to be marketed by imposing additional taxation on peasant farmers and cooperatives.

Having said all this, state farms do have a role to play in providing a marketable surplus and especially in providing some of the food that could be needed for a nationalised public food distribution system, at least until producer cooperatives come into their own. To play this role effectively, however, they must cease to operate at a loss. Otherwise it probably would be cheaper to close them down and import food instead. In any case it would be a useful experiment to convert a few state farms into a number of producers' cooperatives and to compare their performance. A research project might be organised to monitor the results and more generally to investigate the difficulties the state farm sector confronts.

In addition to providing a marketable surplus the state farms have the potential for certain specialised functions and it would probably be better to work towards improving the profitability of existing farms with the potential to become viable economic units and to give them a more specific role within the agricultural sector rather than to rely on state farm production to supply the bulk of the marketable surplus in the long run. Coffee and cotton state farms have a role in the drive to expand exports although the possibility of improving the spread of small-scale cash croping should not be overlooked. As far as state farms producing food crops are concerned, they have potential as seed multiplication units and as experimental farms – places where new crops, rotation systems, production methods and processing techniques are introduced. Parallel to this, they could form part of a comprehensive nationwide system of farm extension and technical assistance. Even if ultimately they do not become the dominant system of production in Ethiopia, by being in the vanguard of technology they can lead the way to more scientific farming.

GROWTH WITH EQUITY: COOPERATION AS A SOURCE OF CAPITAL ACCUMULATION

We have shown that the problems of Ethiopia's agriculture stem in part from a legacy of concentration and fragmentation inherited from the previous regime. Since the revolution of 1974 there has been an attempt to organise the peasantry into Peasant Associations, but so far these associations have not been able to take advantage of the relative efficiency of peasant farming and realise their productive potential. We have argued for the advantages of cooperation. It must be accepted, however, that Ethiopia's peasant farmers have yet to be persuaded of the virtues of formal producers' cooperatives as the government conceives of them. None the less, the development of cooperative organisations in some form or another is likely to be central to an effective strategy for rural development in Ethiopia.

We are not arguing here in a doctrinaire manner for a particular institutional structure. Indeed the form of rural institution which will realise the benefits of cooperation and become a permanent part of the transformation of agriculture is one of the great challenges facing rural societies in Ethiopia and other parts of Africa. Instead we wish to underline the potential that rural cooperative structures offer, not only as a source of increased productive efficiency, but also as a self-sustaining source of surplus for investment and therefore as a widely dispersed engine of enhanced economic growth.

Given the extreme scarcity of investment resources in Ethiopia, the only alternative to cooperation seems to be a reliance on central funds and foreign aid for investment in large-scale projects. Such an alternative seems to us to be less desirable partly because large-scale projects tend to be inefficient, and partly because they tend to make the spatial and personal distributions of income even worse. The option of cooperation is therefore offered as a feasible path to higher rates of growth and reduced regional inequality.

The development of cooperative organisations could follow a stylised sequence. Initially cooperation would take the form of mobilising under-employed labour in the slack season essentially for earth-moving projects and similar labour-intensive construction schemes. This would have the advantage that in the beginning accumulation could occur at no cost to the peasants in terms of current consumption and at no cost to the goverment's central funds. Part of the additional output generated by this investment, however, could be retained by the cooperative as surplus and used first to establish security stocks and then to finance further accumulation in a second stage. A small fund could be created to pay for such things as improved implements, fertiliser, a few bags of cement, an irrigation pump, tree seedlings, or oxen. Again, a part – indeed a larger part – of the extra output arising from these activities could be set aside in an accumulation fund.

As the size of the accumulation fund increases and the peasants acquire experience in managing their cooperative, more ambitious projects could be undertaken. Small cultivators or tractors could be purchased (possibly with the help of a loan from the bank) to expand the area that can be ploughed, to transport produce to markets, and to clear more land. Small processing plants and workshops for making and repairing tools and implements might be established; an electric generator could be installed. Furthermore, the elements of a construction industry could be created based on local needs: a small quarry, a brick kiln, a sawmill or a small cement plant. This, in turn, could lead to further investments in directly productive activities, economic infrastructure (roads, bridges), social overhead capital (schools, clinics) and improved housing. In these ways cooperation leads to cumulative development in the rural areas, not only in agriculture but in small-scale rural industry, construction and the social services.

There are several distinctive features of the approach we are recommending which should be noted. First, emphasis is placed on the superiority of the cooperative as an institution promoting rapid accumulation of capital in rural areas. That is, the accent is on investment and growth. Second, this approach does not envisage the main role of producers' cooperatives to be the organisation of collective agricultural production. Indeed, if for any reason the peasantry are hostile to the idea of collective cultivation of the land, the idea need not be pressed. Once cooperatives have been formed and are operating successfully, one can be confident that collective cultivation will occur if this is in the economic interests of the members. Meanwhile, third, cooperation can be built around anything peasants are willing to support and which can generate a surplus for further accumulation. Examples include the collective ownership of draught animals, collective management of small irrigation works, small processing facilities managed by service cooperatives (as in the coffee regions) or the collective production of improved farm implements. In many cases it may be easier to start with service cooperatives (which have been established successfully in most parts of the country) and to extend their activities until they can be transformed into producers' cooperatives rather than begin by promoting producers' cooperatives directly. The approach we are recommending is flexible enough to accommodate such cases and this is one of its advantages.

Fourth, the sequence of development outlined here is entirely self-financing by the local community. The initial cost to the members of the cooperative is extra work (not less current consumption) and thereafter consumption and living standards will rise. On the margin, however, an ever-increasing proportion of the net output of the cooperative will need to be allocated to the fund for accumulation until the rate of accumulation reaches, say, 30 per cent of collective income. Indeed the success of this approach depends entirely upon the willingness of the members to adopt a high marginal propensity to invest.

Finally, from the point of view of the government, this approach has the great advantage that it reduces considerably the cost to the public revenue of rural development. The government still will have to invest in main roads, power and communication facilities, and large factories producing fertiliser and other essential inputs, but almost everything else can be produced and financed by the cooperatives. The government's limited investible resources can then be used for major industrial and construction projects.

This is not an easy development strategy to implement. It requires political commitment and determination, a massive organisational and educational effort and, above all, confidence in the peasantry; confidence that, once organised, they can manage their own affairs with little outside help; that, once rules of accumulation are agreed, they can invest wisely in projects of their choice; and confidence, too, that the sector employing 85 per cent of the labour force and producing nearly half the national output can be revitalised within a decentralised socialist framework.

The fact that Peasant Associations now involve the vast majority of the rural population and service cooperatives have been formed covering about 70 per cent of the Peasant Associations is a step in the right direction and provides an institutional framework for a rapid increase in cooperative effort. It is our view that Peasant Associations have not achieved their potential as a framework for collective ingenuity and that the drive for cooperative activities need not wait for the extension of producers' cooperatives. It must be recognised, however, that peasant collaboration will require sustained political effort and encouragement and perhaps a national campaign. If this is forthcoming, cooperation can flourish in Ethiopia; and if cooperatives finally take hold and flourish, there is no doubt that of all the systems of production they have the greatest potential for accumulation and therefore for sustaining growth with the possibility of increasing equity.

9 Doubts about Aid

Liberal and progressive people have few doubts about foreign aid, or indeed about the beneficent role of foreign capital in general, of which, of course, aid is only one form.[1] Most of the doubts, or at least the most outspoken criticisms, seem to come from the far right of the political spectrum,[2] from people who question on philosophical grounds the case for an international redistribution of income and who argue on empirical grounds that aid in practice has strengthened the state relative to the private sector, has promoted central planning and weakened the market mechanism and, more often than not, has supported despotism rather than liberty.

It must be said straight away that this author does not share the philosophical objections of the political right to foreign aid. On the contrary, a more equitable distribution of world income is desirable and, in principle, there is no objection to using government taxation to bring about the desired redistribution of resources and purchasing power. Any doubts about aid arise not from predispositions derived from theory, but from observation of the actual practice of aid programmes in the Third World.

THE VOLUME OF AID

Whatever one's views on aid, however, it is important to keep it in perspective. A vast amount has been written on the subject, particularly in the West, and one could easily get the impression that the volume of aid is considerable and increasing. This would be quite wrong. Indeed, whether one sees aid through the eyes of a donor or of a recipient, the volume of foreign aid per head is small and, if anything, is lower today than it was two decades ago. This can readily be confirmed by glancing at the data in Table 9.1.

These data include only official aid and therefore do not take into account assistance provided by non-official agencies such as Oxfam or grants from private institutions such as the Ford and Rockefeller Foundations. Moreover, the data refer to the OECD countries only,[3] and therefore exclude aid provided by the socialist countries and by OPEC. Aid from the socialist countries and from non-official Western sources is of little quantitative significance and can safely be

Table 9.1 Official Development Assistance from the OECD Countries

	1960	*1970*	*1981*
Official development assistance as percentage of GNP	0.51	0.34	0.35
Official development assistance per head of Third World population (US$ at constant 1980 prices)	7.77	6.81	7.73
Bilateral flow to 'low-income countries' of official development assistance as percentage of donor GNP	0.18	0.13	0.07

Note: All figures in the table are net of repayments of capital and interest.

Source: IBRD, *World Development Report 1983*, New York: Oxford University Press, 1983, World Development Indicators, Tables 1, 18 and 19.

ignored. Aid from the OPEC countries, on the other hand, is more significant. Following the sharp increase in oil prices in 1973 and 1974, the major oil-exporting countries did become important aid donors. In 1980, for instance, aid from OPEC countries accounted for 1.74 per cent of their GNP or about 25 per cent of the total amount of foreign aid provided by the non-socialist countries. None the less, the ratio of aid to GNP in the OPEC countries has fallen rapidly since 1975 and even the nominal amount of their aid now appears to be on the decline. Thus, despite omissions, the data in Table 9.1 are unlikely to be misleading as regards general trends.

As can be seen in the first line of the table, official development assistance accounts for a very small fraction of the donor countries' GNP, namely, 0.35 per cent in 1981. Furthermore, the ratio of foreign aid to donor country GNP fell by 31.4 per cent between 1960 and 1981. This reflects the fact that the national income of the donor countries grew much faster in the period 1960–81 than the amount allocated to foreign aid programmes. Indeed, aid increased only 2.2 per cent a year on average whereas GDP increased about 4 per cent a year. In relative terms, the donor countries have become less generous.

The picture is even less flattering when one examines the countries most affected by the topics discussed in this book, namely, the 34 'low-income countries' with a per capita income of $400 or less, and when one takes into account the fact that most foreign aid consists not of grants but of loans which must be repaid with interest. The net flow of aid to the 'low-income countries', after deducting repayments of capital and interest, is very much smaller than the gross flow and has been falling. Between 1960 and 1981, as can be seen in the third line of the table, the flow of bilateral aid to such countries declined by more than half and at the end of the period the net flow to the poorest countries was only seven hundredths of 1 per cent of the donor countries' GNP!

The situation is no better when viewed from the Third World. Between 1960 and 1981 there was zero growth in the amount of foreign aid received per head. Happily, however, GNP per capita increased by more than 3 per cent a year in the Third World during this period and consequently the ratio of aid inflows to national product fell by nearly one half. As is evident from the second line of Table 9.1, the net amount of official development assistance per head was virtually the same at the beginning and end of the period under review and in a few underdeveloped countries the net flow of official foreign aid has become negligible.

FOREIGN CAPITAL AND THE INDUSTRIAL COUNTRIES

It is widely believed that, if left to its own devices, capital would naturally flow from the rich countries to the poor, from the advanced industrial economies to the underdeveloped economies. In a sense, according to this view, foreign aid is unnecessary since the profit-maximising behaviour of banks and of companies engaged in the production of goods and services would lead more or less automatically to a transfer of finance capital and of private direct investment to the Third World, where capital is in short supply and the rate of return on investment should be high.

The validity of this belief, however, depends on the assumptions that the same technology is available to all countries, that there are no significant economies of large-scale production and that there are no increasing returns to investment or learning-by-doing effects. If these assumptions are not valid, then it is perfectly possible that the rate of profit and the real rate of interest will be higher in the advanced industrial economies and consequently that private capital will tend to move from the poor countries to the rich and not the

Table 9.2 Net Foreign Capital Inflow of Nineteen Industrial Market Economy Countries (per cent of GDP)

	1960	*1981*
Ireland	5	14
Spain	–3	2
Italy	0	2
New Zealand	2	2
United Kingdom	2	–3
Japan	0	–1
Austria	0	0
Finland	1	1
Australia	3	3
Canada	2	0
Netherlands	–2	–3
Belgium	1	4
France	–2	4
United States	–1	1
Denmark	1	0
West Germany	–2	0
Norway	2	–8
Sweden	1	1
Switzerland	0	2

Note: In this and subsequent tables, and in the text, the 'resource balance' is used as a proxy measure of net foreign capital flows. Strictly speaking, this is inaccurate as the resource balance term includes not only capital movements but also remittances and 'errors and omissions'. Our broad conclusions, however, are unaffected by the use of this slightly wider concept as a proxy for capital flows.

Source: IBRD, *World Development Report 1983*, New York: Oxford University Press, 1983, World Development Indicators, Table 5.

other way round.[4] That is, if the usual neo-classical assumptions do not apply, one would not be surprised to find that the advanced economies were net importers of capital rather than net exporters.

In practice it does seem that most of the industrialised countries are net recipients of foreign capital rather than net suppliers, even after taking foreign aid into account. This is demonstrated in Table 9.2, where 19 industrial market economy countries are ranked in ascending order of GNP per capita. Two years are compared: 1960, when growth rates were rapid, and 1981, when real rates of interest were high.

In 1960 there were only five industrial countries which were net exporters of capital (Spain, Netherlands, France, the United States and West Germany); four others were in balance; and the remaining 10 were net importers of capital. That is, the majority of the industrialised economies enjoyed a net inflow of capital in that year. The picture is much the same in 1981: four countries (the UK, Japan, Netherlands and Norway) exported capital, four were in balance, and 11 imported capital from abroad. Only one country, the Netherlands, had a net capital outflow in both 1960 and 1981, whereas 15 were net recipients of foreign capital in at least one of the two years. Thus even a cursory inspection of the data is enough to dispel the notion that rich countries usually are large exporters of capital and that the poor countries are the beneficiaries of this tendency. In fact, in 1981 only the high-income oil-exporting countries of Libya, Saudi Arabia, Kuwait and the United Arab Emirates were major suppliers of capital to the rest of the world.

FOREIGN CAPITAL AND GROWTH

Let us set this problem to one side, however, and assume, as is in fact often the case, that the poor countries are net recepients of foreign resources, i.e. aid and private loans and private foreign investment. What are the consequences of this? The standard answer[5] is that foreign resources will supplement the country's domestic savings effort and thereby raise the rate of investment by the amount of the capital inflow. This, in turn, will result in a faster rate of growth of output and income and in a reduction in the incidence of poverty. If, as is thought likely, the marginal propensity to save exceeds the average, higher incomes and faster growth fuelled by foreign capital should result in a rising savings ratio over time, which would further accelerate the rate of growth and hasten the time at which capital imports would no longer be necessary. If, in addition, foreign capital brings with it superior technology and better management, the productivity of investment should rise, thereby providing yet another reason to expect growth to accelerate.

In summary, the standard view is that capital imports have three beneficial effects: (i) they raise the rate of investment directly; (ii) they indirectly raise the domestic savings rate and hence lead to a further rise in the rate of investment; and (iii) they raise the incremental output–capital ratio. The combination of these three effects implies that the rate of growth should 'explode' in countries where foreign capital inflows suddenly increase and the rate of growth should be high and rising in countries which enjoy sustained high levels of aid and foreign private investment. In both cases therefore the recipients should experience rapid growth of per capita output and a sharp fall in poverty. This obviously is an attractive prospect to donors and recipients alike. The question is whether the process described conforms to reality or is merely the product of wishful thinking.

To help answer this question twelve countries have been selected for scrutiny. These countries were not chosen randomly but were specially selected for particular characteristics. Thus the data are intended merely to illustrate an argument, not to provide a definitive proof of any particular proposition. Ten out of the twelve countries are very poor and are classified by the World Bank as 'low-income economies'. The two exceptions are Senegal and Israel. Eight out of the twelve are from Africa (the region experiencing the most serious development problems), the two largest are from Asia (the most populous underdeveloped region), and there is one country from the Caribbean and another from the Eastern Mediterranean. In terms of the number of countries, therefore, the sample is deliberately biased towards Africa, although in terms of population, Pakistan and Bangladesh are larger than all the others combined. In eight cases there was a very sharp rise in net capital inflows between 1960 and 1981 (our two reference years), and in the other four cases net capital inflows in both years were equivalent to at least 6 per cent of the country's GDP and remained fairly close to the initially high level. Thus the latter cases represent countries which have experienced sustained high levels of capital imports. Basic information about our sample countries is contained in Table 9.3.

All of the countries in our sample are by world standards major recipients of foreign aid and private foreign investment. Ethiopia had the smallest net capital inflow in 1981, namely, $7.26 per capita, yet even this virtually matched the average receipts of official development assistance and represented about 6 per cent of the country's GDP. The next country, Zaire, received about twice as much foreign capital per head as Ethiopia and was well above world averages. The richest country in our sample, Israel, hardly deserves to be classified by the World Bank as a 'middle-income' developing economy since its per capita income is similar to that of Ireland and Spain, two 'industrial market economy' countries. Indeed, in 1981 Israel's GNP per head was nearly 37 times larger than Ethiopia's, yet Israel received 90 times more foreign capital per head than Ethiopia! That

Table 9.3 Foreign Capital and Economic Growth in Twelve Selected Countries

Country	*GNP per head, 1981* (US$)	*Net foreign capital inflow per head, 1981* (US$)	*Growth of GDP per head (% p.a.)* *1960–70*	*1970–81*
1. Bangladesh	140	19.70	1.2	1.6
2. Ethiopia	140	7.26	2.0	0.2
3. Zaire	210	14.44	1.4	–3.2
4. Tanzania	280	31.88	3.3	1.7
5. Haiti	300	37.41	–1.4	1.7
6. Benin	320	87.36	0.0	0.6
7. Central African Republic	320	34.50	0.0	–0.7
8. Madagascar	330	25.69	0.7	–2.3
9. Pakistan	350	29.78	3.9	1.8
10. Sudan	380	47.13	–0.8	1.0
11. Senegal	430	86.88	0.2	–0.7
12. Israel	5160	654.00	4.6	1.4

Source: IBRD, *World Development Report 1983*, New York: Oxford University Press, 1983, World Development Indicators, Tables 1, 2, 3, 5 and 19.

is, Ethiopia, arguably the most backward economy in the world,[6] received only a pittance compared to the prosperous Israel. One can hardly imagine a more regressive distribution of foreign capital, official and private.

Indeed, it is a striking feature of Table 9.3 that foreign capital inflows are positively associated with per capita income. The higher a country's GNP per head, the more foreign capital it tends to receive. Yet orthodox theory, as we have seen, would lead one to expect the opposite, i.e. that capital would flow most strongly to the poor countries, where capital is scarce and the return on capital presumably is relatively high. That is, orthodox theory predicts an inverse relationship between income per head and capital imports. Alas, the predictions of the theory are countered by the data in the table.

Equity requires that foreign capital should flow disproportionately to the poor countries and if the market mechanism cannot ensure this, then it becomes particularly important that official aid should discriminate strongly in favour of the poorest countries. Unfortunately, however, this does not occur. Indeed it has been apparent for a long time that foreign aid accentuates international inequality among Third World countries rather than reduces it. That is, there is a positive correlation between per capita aid and per capita income, and this is as true of aid in general[7] as of multilateral and bitaleral[8] aid separately.

Let us next consider the growth performance of our sample countries. The first thing to note is that in four cases the rate of growth of GDP per head was actually negative during 1970–81. Incomes declined very rapidly in Zaire and Madagascar (by 3.2 and 2.3 per cent a year, respectively) and quite rapidly in Senegal and the Central African Republic (by 0.7 per cent a year in both countries). Despite above-average inflows of foreign capital – see Table 9.4 – in three of the four countries (Madagascar is a partial exception) it was not possible to prevent economic decline and a substantial increase in mass poverty. Second, in four other cases – Ethiopia, Tanzania, Pakistan and Israel – the rate of growth of per capita output was lower in 1970–81 than it had been in 1960–70. Yet in none of these countries was there a fall in foreign resource inflows. Indeed there was a sharp rise in Tanzania, a moderate rise in Pakistan, constancy and then a sharp rise at the end of the period in Ethiopia and a sharp rise followed by partial retrenchment in Israel.

Third, in only four countries, namely, Bangladesh,[9] Haiti, Benin and the Sudan, was the growth of per capita output faster in 1970–81 than in 1960–70, and in each case the increase in foreign capital imports was dramatic. Thus in Haiti the net foreign capital inflow rose from 2 per cent of GDP in 1960 to 12 per cent in 1981, or by 10 percentage points. In the Sudan, the rise was 12 percentage points, in Bangladesh, 16 percentage points and in Benin, 31 percentage points. Oddly, the increase in the rate of growth of GDP per head between 1960–70 and 1970–81 was inversely related to the rise in capital imports: in Bangladesh, per capita growth rose by 0.4 per cent; in Benin, by 0.6 per cent; in the Sudan, by 1.8 per cent and in Haiti by 3.1 per cent. The smaller was the increase in foreign capital, the larger was the increase in the rate of growth.

The picture would be slightly different if one substituted 1976 for 1981 in the comparison, but the general point stands: the connection between an increase in foreign capital and an increase in the rate of growth, even if it is positive as one would expect, is very weak. Indeed, in a surprisingly large number of cases the rate of growth of output per head fell when capital imports increased and in the four cases where growth accelerated, the extent of acceleration appears almost to have been inversely proportional to the increase in capital imports.

Finally, notwithstanding the fact that all twelve of our sample countries were relatively large recipients of foreign capital in 1970–81, not one managed to grow as fast as the average of the 'low-income economies' as a whole. Indeed, per capita growth in the 'low-income economies' accelerated during the 1970s whereas there was a marked slowing down of growth in our sample countries. The best performance in the 1970s in our sample was in Pakistan, where the rate of growth of GDP per head was 1.8 per cent per annum, as compared to the average for all 'low-income economies' of 2.6 per cent. That is, our best performer was 31 per cent below average. Even more disturbing, the unweighted average growth rate in our sample in 1970–81 was only 0.3 per cent per annum per head or less than one eighth as rapid as the weighted average for the low-income economies as a whole. Unless one believes that foreign capital is channelled deliberately and systematically by aid donors and overseas investors to slowly growing economies, and this is hardly plausible, one must doubt the beneficial effects enumerated above of foreign capital growth.

FOREIGN CAPITAL AND DOMESTIC SAVINGS

A key assumption of the orthodox analysis is that capital imports are complementary rather than competitive with domestic savings, both in the short run (when foreign capital supplements local savings) and in the longer run (when higher per capita incomes lead to a higher domestic savings ratio). The validity of this proposition seems doubtful, as it is very likely that an inflow of foreign resources in practice will result in some combination of increased expenditure on private consumption, armaments, other forms of public consumption and investment.[10] That is, once all general equilibrium effects are taken into account, one might expect that a large proportion of any injection of foreign capital ultimately will be used to finance additional consumption and only a small proportion will be used to finance additional investment.

If this view is correct it implies that, in general, the increase in investment will be much less than the increase in capital imports and consequently, as a logical corollary, the domestic savings ratio will decline. Foreign capital, far from being associated with a rise in domestic savings, is in practice associated with a fall. A further implication is that, everything else being equal, a given increase in capital imports relative to total investment will be associated with a less than proportional increase in the rate of growth. Admittedly, the growth rate should accelerate, but if the decline in the domestic savings rate is substantial, the acceleration is likely to be modest.

These, then, are readily testable propositions and it is instructive to see what the effects of capital imports have been in our twelve countries. The relevant data are presented in Table 9.4, where once again we compare 1960 with 1981, although data for 1976 also are included.

A number of interesting points arise from the table. First, in three cases (Bangladesh, Zaire and Tanzania) foreign capital imports were negative in 1960. In other words, these three countries were net suppliers of capital to the rest of the world rather than recipients. Bangladesh was at that time the province of East Pakistan and was forced by the central government of Pakistan to transfer resources for the industrial development of West Pakistan.[11] Zaire was in its first year of independence – it did not cease to be the Belgian Congo until 30 June 1960 – and no doubt the large capital outflow was one of the symptoms of the pain that accompanied the birth of the new nation, a pain which still is present. Tanzania was then the colony of Tanganyika and had one year to go before independence. In each case, therefore, there were special reasons for the capital outflow.[12]

Second, in all twelve cases capital imports as a percentage of GDP were higher in 1981 than in 1960 and in every case but one, they were higher in 1976 than in 1960. In many cases, as mentioned earlier, the rise was dramatic; in a few, the rise was relatively slight, e.g. the Central African Republic and Madagascar; but in no case did capital imports fall over the period as a whole. The countries in our sample are among the relatively small number where capital imports either were high initially or rose sharply or both. In this respect they can be considered to be rather privileged.

Third, in nine out of twelve cases the domestic savings ratio fell between 1960 and 1981. In these cases there was a clear inverse relationship between larger capital inflows and lower domestic savings. Moreover, fourth, in three cases the rate of domestic savings had become negative by 1981. That is, foreign capital not only financed all of the investment that took place in the country but some of the consumption as well. In another case the domestic savings rate had fallen to zero by 1981, implying that all of the investment in that

Table 9.4 Foreign Capital, Domestic Savings and Investment (per cent of GDP)

Country	*Net foreign capital inflow*			*Gross domestic savings*			*Gross investment*		
	1960	*1976*	*1981*	*1960*	*1976*	*1981*	*1960*	*1976*	*1981*
Bangladesh	−1	7	15	8	−1	2	7	6	17
Ethiopia	1	1	6	11	9	4	12	10	10
Zaire	−9	21	8	21	13	25	12	34	33
Tanzania	−5	2	14	19	19	8	14	21	22
Haiti	2	4	12	7	7	1	9	11	13
Benin	6	16	37	9	4	−2	15	20	35
Central African Republic	11	13	12	9	9	−3	20	22	9
Madagascar	6	−1	8	5	14	7	11	13	15
Pakistan	7	9	10	5	8	7	12	17	17
Sudan	0	10	12	12	8	0	12	18	13
Senegal	1	6	22	15	9	−5	16	15	17
Israel	13	34	15	14	−6	5	27	28	20

Source: IBRD, *World Development Report 1983*, New York: Oxford University Press, 1983, World Development Indicators, Table 5. The data for 1976 are from Table 5 of the 1978 *Report*.

year was financed with foreign resources. These four cases represent one third of our sample.

The negative savings in Benin and Senegal are associated with an exceptionally sharp rise in capital imports. Indeed the increased inflow of foreign capital was greater in these two countries than in any other country in our sample, viz. by 31 percentage points in Benin and 21 in Senegal. In the Sudan, too, the zero savings rate was associated with a substantial increase in foreign capital from nothing in 1960 to 12 per cent of GDP in 1981. In the Central African Republic the domestic savings rate declined from 9 per cent of GDP in 1960 to minus 3 per cent in 1981 although capital imports increased by only 1 percentage point of GDP to 12 per cent.

Fifth, quite apart from changes in savings rates and in the rate of foreign capital inflow, the data in Table 9.4 suggest that countries which receive large amounts of foreign capital are likely to save rather little and, conversely, countries which receive little foreign capital are likely to compensate for this with relatively high domestic savings. This can readily be seen in Figure 9.1, which shows, for each of the twelve countries for 1960, 1976 and 1981, the gross domestic savings against net foreign capital inflows (both expressed as a percentage of GDP). The inverse relationship is very clear[13] and is consistent with the results obtained in numerous other studies.[14]

It is a characteristic of the social sciences, however, that there are always counter-examples to any generalisation. Our sixth point consists of three exceptions to the rule that savings and capital inflows are inversely associated. In Zaire, Madagascar and Pakistan the savings rate was higher in 1981 than in 1960 and rose roughly in parallel with a rise in foreign capital inflows. Thus the inverse relationship we have identified is far from inevitable. There is, however, a sting in the tail: in all these three cases the rate of growth of output per head declined – despite higher savings, larger capital imports and greater investment! In Pakistan the growth rate fell by more than a half and in Zaire and Madagascar the growth rate became negative. Clearly aid, private foreign investment and a greater savings effort were unable to prevent a sharp deterioration in macro-economic performance.

FOREIGN CAPITAL AND INVESTMENT

Normally, of course, the outcome is not quite so disappointing. Our analysis indicates that capital imports should lead to a rise in total

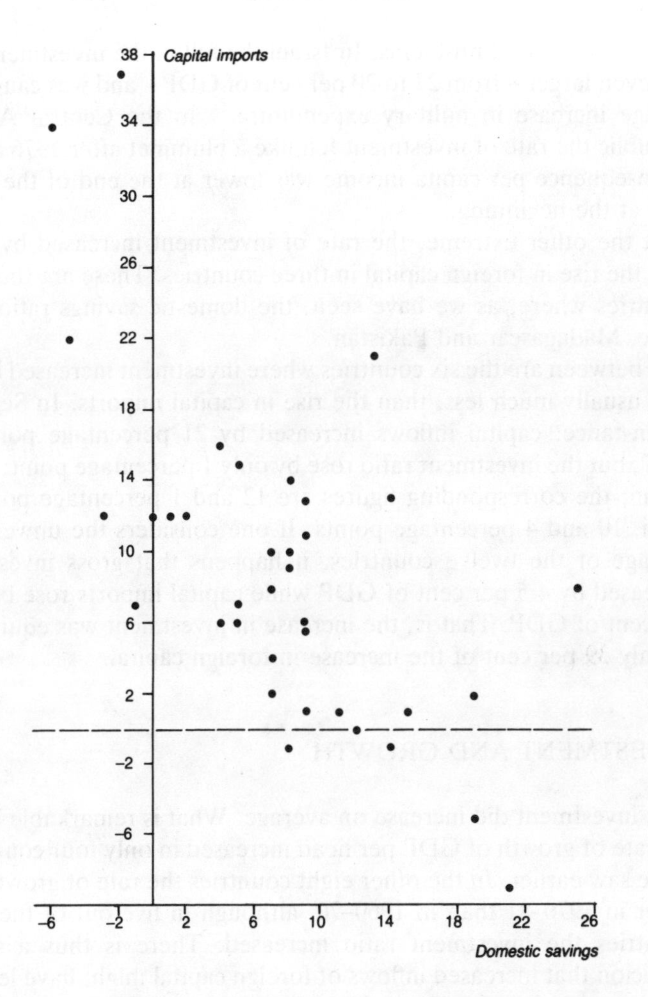

Figure 9.1 The Relationship Between Capital Imports and Domestic Savings

investment, but by less than the amount of foreign capital received. Higher investment, in turn, should result in faster growth, everything else being equal.

The data in Table 9.4 tend to support the hypothesis as regards investment. In nine countries gross investment as a percentage of GDP was higher in 1981 than in 1960. This is what one would expect. In three cases, however, the investment ratio fell. In Ethiopia the fall was from 12 per cent of GDP to 10 per cent and reflects a decision by the military government to seek a military solution to the country's political and social problems. In Israel the fall in the investment rate was even larger – from 27 to 20 per cent of GDP – and was caused by a huge increase in military expenditure.[15] In the Central African Republic the rate of investment fell like a plummet after 1976 and as a consequence per capita income was lower at the end of the 1970s than at the beginning.

At the other extreme, the rate of investment increased by more than the rise in foreign capital in three countries. These are the three countries where, as we have seen, the domestic savings ratio rose: Zaire, Madagascar and Pakistan.

In between are the six countries where investment increased but by less, usually much less, than the rise in capital imports. In Senegal, for instance, capital inflows increased by 21 percentage points of GDP, but the investment ratio rose by only 1 percentage point; in the Sudan, the corresponding figures are 12 and 1 percentage point; in Haiti, 10 and 4 percentage points. If one considers the unweighted average of the twelve countries, it happens that gross investment increased by 4.5 per cent of GDP while capital imports rose by 11.6 per cent of GDP. That is, the increase in investment was equivalent to only 39 per cent of the increase in foreign capital.

INVESTMENT AND GROWTH

Still, investment did increase on average. What is remarkable is that the rate of growth of GDP per head increased in only four countries, as we saw earlier. In the other eight countries the rate of growth was lower in 1970–81 than in 1960–70, although in five out of the eight countries the investment ratio increased. There is thus a strong suspicion that increased inflows of foreign capital might have led to a decline in the productivity of investment. Moreover, in some cases the decline in the productivity of investment might have been greater than the increase in the rate of investment with the result that the rate of growth of output fell.

There are reasons to believe that foreign aid in particular often distorts the pattern of investment in such a way that the productivity of investment falls. First, the major motives of aid donors are not to increase efficiency and growth. Bilateral donors have made it transparently clear that their primary motive is to promote the political, diplomatic, industrial and commercial interests of the country offering foreign assistance. Given that aid is not intended to accelerate growth, it is unlikely that efficiency and growth would increase except by chance. For example, the Economic Support Fund of the US Agency for International Development is explicitly intended to provide support to countries on the basis of US political and security interests, and about 40 per cent of all US bilaterial aid comes from this fund.[16]

Next, in order to maximise the political impact of their foreign assistance, donors often prefer large and prominent projects which can stand as monuments to their generosity. Such projects, although possibly successful in political terms, are unlikely to represent an efficient use of investment resources or to make a substantial contribution to growth. The bias in favour of large, monumental projects is not confined to bilateral donors. The EEC, for example, concentrates much of its assistance on large-scale industrial and infrastructural projects. All of us want to be seen to be generous. Moreover, donor agencies understandably wish to minimise their costs of administration, and this predisposes them to favour a small number of large projects rather than a large number of small projects. The problem, however, is that a strategy that minimises the cost of providing foreign aid is unlikely to coincide with a strategy designed to make the most effective use of investible resources. What is good for the donor may not be particularly good for the recipient.

Finally, there is the knotty problem of tied aid. Most aid is tied in at least one of three different ways, and much aid is tied in all three ways. First, aid is tied to specific projects. It is usually not available for general programme support. Moreover, it is tied to the capital component of a project and cannot be used to finance the recurrent expenditure items associated with that project. Second, aid is tied to the foreign exchange component of a project. Domestic currency costs, e.g. of a machine manufactured locally, are not eligible for aid assistance. Third, bilateral aid usually is tied to purchases from the donor country. For example, in the UK over 60 per cent of the foreign aid is bilateral and 80 per cent of this is tied to purchases from the donor country; in Canada, 80 per cent of CIDA's aid is tied to procurement in Canada.

Tied aid introduces a series of inefficiencies into Third World countries.[17] It biases investment towards highly capital-intensive projects. It biases investment in favour of schemes which are intensive in their use of foreign exchange. It artificially increases the capital costs of aid-financed projects, since goods obtained under tied aid will tend to be significantly more expensive than similar goods obtained at world prices. And it will also tend to increase the operating costs of aid-financed projects, since tied aid is likely to lead to a continuing flow of relatively expensive imports in the form of spare parts and ancillary equipment complementary to the aid-financed imports. The ultimate effect of all this is to reduce the competitiveness of recipient countries, to alter the pattern of investment and lower its productivity, and to reduce the rate of growth.

INEQUALITY, POVERTY AND POLITICAL REPRESSION

Perhaps growth would not matter very much if it could be shown that foreign capital, and especially foreign aid, helped to reduce inequality and poverty and to promote social justice and freedom. Unfortunately, however, it is impossible to demonstrate this. Indeed, one could go further: donor countries can, in principle, concentrate their aid on the poorest countries (although in practice they do not do so), but it is almost impossible for donor countries to ensure that their aid reaches the poorest people (even if they wished to do so).[18] The most a donor can do, probably, is to support governments whose domestic policies are designed to ensure that the benefits of economic activity accrue to the poor in full measure.

Alas, there is very little evidence that the governments in the countries in our sample have made much effort to reduce inequality in the distribution of income and wealth. Moreover, circumstantial evidence suggests that the concentration on industry and the neglect of rural development have led to greatly increased inequality in most countries. In fact, the problem is more serious than this. It is quite likely that the standard of living of many poor people, particularly those in the rural areas, has fallen substantially in the last 10 or 15 years. The neglect of the countryside has been so extreme that in most countries agricultural production has failed to keep pace with the expansion of the population. This is shown in Table 9.5.

In nine out of our twelve countries the agricultural labour force accounts for at least 72 per cent of the total. That is, in terms of the number of people involved, agriculture is by far the largest sector of the economy, and the fate of the poor depends primarily upon the performance of this sector. This statement is slightly less true in Benin and Pakistan (where the agricultural labour force accounts for 46 and 57 per cent of the total, respectively) and obviously does not apply to Israel; but in general if agriculture performs badly, poverty will increase.

Data on agricultural performance exist for ten of our countries. In only one of these ten, namely in Tanzania, has agricultural output per

Table 9.5 Size and Performance of the Agricultural Sector

	Growth of agricultural output per head, 1970–81 (% p.a.)	*Percentage of labour force in agriculture, 1980*
Bangladesh	−0.2	74
Ethiopia	−1.1	80
Zaire	−1.5	75
Tanzania	2.1	83
Haiti	−0.6	74
Benin	n.a.	46
Central African Republic	0.0	88
Madagascar	−2.3	87
Pakistan	−0.4	57
Sudan	−0.8	72
Senegal	−0.1	77
Israel	n.a.	7

Source: IBRD, *World Development Report 1983*, New York: Oxford University Press, 1983, World Development Indicators, Tables 2, 19 and 21.

head increased. In one other (the Central African Republic) there has been stagnation since 1970, and a precipitous decline in the ten years before that. In each of the remaining eight countries per capita agricultural output was lower in 1981 than in 1970. In two cases (Bangladesh and Senegal), the rate of deterioration was gentle, in three (Ethiopia, Zaire and Madagascar) it was extraordinarily rapid, and in the other three (Haiti, Pakistan and the Sudan) agricultural production per head declined by between 0.4 and 0.8 per cent a year. In all eight of these countries, therefore, and possibly in the Central African Republic too, there is a strong presumption that mass poverty has increased. And this has occurred despite a substantial inflow of foreign capital.

The poor have been neglected by their own governments. There can be no doubt about that. Indeed, in a great many cases the government is a dictatorship – usually a military dictatorship – and actively and violently suppresses the poor. The most obvious examples in our sample are Bangladesh and Pakistan in Asia; Ethiopia, Zaire and the Sudan in Africa; Haiti in the Caribbean. In practice foreign aid is doing little to promote growth in the Third World and even less to alleviate poverty. In the end it appears to be doing little more than sustaining corrupt and often vicious regimes in power, sometimes deliberately (Guatemala, El Salvador) and sometimes perhaps not. In either event, the time may have come to abandon the enterprise, to set ourselves the goal, not of increasing foreign aid, but of reducing it gradually over, say, the next five years to the minimum necessary to meet humanitarian calls for emergency assistance.[19] We may well do more to help the poor in future by being less paternalistic, by supporting those in the Third World who favour a policy of self-reliance[20] and by discontinuing long-term programmes of foreign assistance.

Notes

1. See, for example, two international reports which ably summarised the liberal opinion of the time: *Partners in Development*, the Report of the Commission on International Development chaired by Lester B. Pearson, London: Pall Mall Press, 1969; and *North–South: A Programme for Survival*, the Report of the Independent Commission on International Development Issues chaired by Willy Brandt, London: Pan Books, 1980.
2. P. T. Bauer, *Dissent on Development*, London: Weidenfeld and Nicolson, 1971, pp. 96–135.
3. The 24 countries that are present members of the OECD are Italy, New Zealand, the UK, Japan, Austria, Finland, Australia, Canada, Netherlands, Belgium, France, USA, Denmark, Federal Republic of Germany, Norway, Sweden, Switzerland, Spain, Greece, Ireland, Iceland, Luxembourg, Portugal and Turkey.
4. This possibility is discussed more formally in Keith Griffin, *International Inequality and National Poverty*, London: Macmillan, 1978, Introduction and Ch. 1.
5. See H. B. Chenery and A. M. Strout, 'Foreign Assistance and Economic Development', *American Economic Review*, vol. LV1, no. 4, September 1966.
6. ILO (JASPA), *Socialism From the Grass Roots: Accumulation, Employment and Equity in Ethiopia*, Vol. 1, an unpublished report, Addis Ababa: September 1982, Ch. 1.
7. Consider, for example, the net inflow per capita of 'public and publicly guaranteed medium- and long-term loans' in 1981. The 'upper middle-income economies' received nearly 22 times more per head than the 'low-income economies' and more than twice as much as the 'lower middle-income economies'.
8. For an early study of the British case see the *Report from the Select Committee on Overseas Development*, Session 1972–3, Minutes of Evidence with Appendices, Vol. II, 24 July 1973, Appendix 23 by Keith Griffin and Frances Stewart, pp. 320–4. Also see note 16 below. It should be added that the British record in this respect is not so bad as

that of most donors, because of the substantial amount of UK aid that is allocated to South Asia.

9. Bangladesh did not become an independent country until 1971. Prior to that it was, of course, East Pakistan.
10. The author's doubts were first expressed in Spanish twenty years ago in Keith Griffin and Ricardo Ffrench-Davis, 'El Capital Extranjero y el Desarrollo', *Revista de Economia* (Santiago, Chile), vol. XXII, nos 2 and 3, 1964. More refined versions have appeared at regular intervals, see, for example, Keith Griffin, *Underdevelopment in Spanish America*, London: Allen and Unwin, 1969, Ch. III; Keith Griffin and John Enos, 'Foreign Assistance: Objectives and Consequences', *Economic Development and Cultural Change*, vol. 18, April 1970; and Griffin, *International Inequality and National Poverty*, Ch. 3 and Appendix.
11. See Keith Griffin and Azizur Rahman Khan (eds), *Growth and Inequality in Pakistan*, London: Macmillan, 1972, Commentary to Part One.
12. This does not imply, however, that conditions in these three countries were unique. Several countries in our sample, for instance, achieved independence in 1960, viz. Benin, Central African Republic, Madagascar and Senegal.
13. The regression equation is:

$$S = 12.0 \quad \underset{(1.68)}{-\;0.48\,F}; \quad R^2 = 0.40$$

where S = gross domestic savings as a percentage of GDP,
F = net foreign capital inflow as a percentage of GDP
and the number in brackets is the t-ratio.

14. See, for example, Thomas Weisskopf, 'The Impact of Foreign Capital Inflow on Domestic Savings in Underdeveloped Countries', *Journal of International Economics*, vol. 2, no. 1, February 1972 and W. T. Newlyn, *The Financing of Economic Development*, Oxford: Clarendon Press, 1977, Ch. IV.
15. Between 1972 and 1980 military expenditure in Israel rose from 17.6 to 31.2 per cent of GNP.
16. Political, military and strategic interests dominate the US aid programme and account for the fact that in 1981–2 Israel and Egypt received 31.4 per cent of total US bilateral assistance. See OECD, *Development Cooperation*, Paris: 1984, p. 233.
17. See, for example, M. ul Haq, 'Tied Credits – a Quantitative Analysis', in J. H. Adler (ed.), *Capital Movements and Economic Development*, London: Macmillan, 1967; and J. Bhagwati, 'The Tying of Aid', UNCTAD, TD/7/Supp. 4, 1968. The evidence suggests that tieing raises the cost of purchases by 20–50 per cent. See J. White, *The Politics of Foreign Aid*, London: St Martin's, 1972, p. 151.
18. See Paul Mosley, 'Aid for the Poorest: Some Early Lessons of U.K. Experience', *Journal of Development Economics*, vol. 17, no. 2, January

1981 and two publications by the Independent Group on British Aid: *Real Aid: A Strategy for Britain* (1982) and *Aid Is Not Enough: Britain and the World's Poor* (1984), both available from Oxfam, 274 Banbury Road, Oxford.

19. For a similar proposal, see Dudley Seers, *The Political Economy of Nationalism*, Oxford University Press, 1983, pp. 181–2.
20. See, for example, Rehman Sobhan, *The Crisis of External Dependence: The Political Economy of Foreign Aid to Bangladesh*, Dhaka: University Press Limited, 1982. I cannot resist the temptation to point out that shortly after Bangladesh became independent I emphasised the danger for domestic resource mobilisation of relying on foreign aid. See, E. A. G. Robinson and Keith Griffin (eds), *The Economic Development of Bangladesh*, London: Macmillan, 1974, pp. 138–9.

10 The Debt Crisis and the Poor

The current economic crisis is global in nature and is not to be explained simply by mistakes made by borrowing countries or by lending institutions. That is not to say that some governments were not imprudent or that some banks did not make foolish loans, but the essence of the problem arises from the unsatisfactory performance of the world economy rather than from excessive international lending and borrowing. It is deplorable that part of the foreign debt has been used to finance a boom in imported consumer goods (as in Chile), or to pay armaments (as in Argentina) or to facilitate capital flight (as in Mexico), but borrowing for such purposes was not the cause of the crisis. The cause lies elsewhere. Indeed, had the commercial banks been incapable of lending the surpluses generated by the major oil-exporting countries and had other countries been unwilling to borrow abroad in order to maintain their capacity to import, there would have been a sharp decline in aggregate demand at the global level and the worldwide recession would have been even worse than it is.

This is especially true of the 1970s and the origins of the current massive imbalance of international payments. Since 1981, however, the OPEC countries as a group have been in balance of payments deficit. Moreover, there is a statistical discrepancy in global balance of payments figures so that the total for the world is not zero but a very large deficit.

None the less, it remains true that the massive borrowing by Third World countries in the last decade arose from the need of the international system as a whole to recycle the balance of payments surpluses of a small number of Arab petroleum-producing countries. The net transfer of savings from lenders to borrowers via the commercial banking system was mutually advantageous and is no cause for criticism. Indeed, by preventing further deflation, the recycling activities of the commercial banks were of general benefit, even to those countries which were neither lenders nor borrowers.

Again, it must be said that the above does not imply that the way the recycling was done was necessarily the best way to do it. It is a cause for regret that the structure, the resources and the policies of the IMF did not permit it to play a more constructive role, and in particular to lend more for longer periods on more generous terms. In retrospect it is a great pity that the liquidity of the international economy, as measured, say, by the ratio of liquid international reserves to the value of world trade, has been allowed to decline in recent decades. But given the reduced liquidity of the system as a whole, and given that there is no international lender-of-last-resort, recycling by the commercial banks has played a very positive role.

The so-called debt crisis is essentially the financial counterpart to the current prolonged recession. There is no financial crisis apart from the crisis in the real economy. That is, if the recession were to disappear, and sustained worldwide expansion were to be restored, the debt crisis would abate and perhaps disappear.

Whether one agrees with this view or not, the fact remains that a crisis exists and the burden of adjusting to the crisis has fallen disproportionately on the Third World. Different countries have been affected in different ways and in different degrees, but it may be helpful to list the most important ways in which Third World countries have been harmed.

THE EFFECTS ON POOR COUNTRIES

First, the slowing down of growth in the world economy has led to slower growth of the volume of exports of Third World countries. For example, between 1960–70 and 1970–81, the rate of growth of the volume of exports from the 'low-income economies' fell from 4.9 per cent a year to minus 0.7 per cent a year. This has been accompanied, second, by a decline in the price of exports. For example, in 1981, the worst year, the export price of sugar fell by nearly 40 per cent, lumber by nearly 17 per cent, natural rubber by 24.5 per cent, tin by nearly 15 per cent and copper by over 20 per cent. The combination of a more slowly growing volume of exports and lower prices has resulted, third, in a marked reduction in the rate of growth of the value of exports. In several cases, fourth, these unfavourable tendencies produced by market forces have been exacerbated by rising protectionism in the advanced economies as a result of the imposition of higher tariff and non-tariff barriers to trade.

The prices of goods imported by Third World countries have not in general fallen, and in the case of oil, prices were raised sharply in 1973–4 and again in 1980. The result has been, fifth, a deterioration in the net barter terms of trade. The deterioration affected all groups of countries except for the oil-exporting ones and was particularly severe during the period 1978–81. Brazil's terms of trade, for instance, declined by 48 per cent during that period and that of the 'low-income economies' by just over 20 per cent. Sixth, in a great many cases the income terms of trade (or the capacity of a country to pay for imports out of exports) also declined.

Our seventh effect has received a great deal of attention, namely, the dramatic increase in the real rate of interest paid by debtor countries. Nominal prime rates of interest charged by US commercial banks rose from an average of 8.1 per cent in 1970–9 to 14.95 per cent in 1980–3; real rates of interest increased from 1.33 to 7.9 per cent between the two periods. That is, real rates increased six-fold. Most Latin American governments, however, must pay a premium over prime rates of 0.5–2.0 per cent and thus the real rate paid by them probably approaches 10 per cent (or even more) today.

Moreover, Latin America's foreign debt is denominated in dollars and since 1981 the US dollar has appreciated against other currencies. This, our eighth effect, has made it even more difficult for the debtor countries to service their loans and has greatly increased the domestic resource cost of interest payments. That is, the borrowing countries have had inflicted upon them a nearly intolerable combination of a higher real rate of interest on dollar denominated debt and a higher price of the dollar.

Lastly, unable to import capital on acceptable terms, the Third World finds it increasingly difficult to export labour. Both in Europe and in North America the advanced economies are adopting more restrictive policies towards immigration in an attempt to reduce their own high rates of unemployment. The Third World thus is assailed from all directions: its trading environment has deteriorated; foreign borrowing has declined and become much more expensive, and the net movement of capital has in some cases become negative; and the possibility of the poor escaping economic hardship by emigration has become more difficult.

THE POLICIES OF RICH COUNTRIES

Viewed as a whole, the main problem of the world economy is that since 1974 the rate of growth of the seven major OECD countries (USA, Japan, Canada, France, Germany, Italy and the UK) has been very slow, although there was some acceleration in 1984. The weight of these economies in the world economy is so great that poor performance by these seven countries makes it very difficult indeed for the rest of the world to sustain an acceptable rate of growth.

Unfortunately, the seven major OECD countries have collectively deflated their economies since the mid-1970s and apart from 1978 the 'cyclically adjusted budget deficit' as a percentage of GNP has declined steadily. In fact since 1979 the rise in the budget deficit of the Group of Seven has been due entirely to the operation of automatic stabilisers, e.g. higher unemployment compensation and lower tax receipts because of a lower level of economic activity. That is, discretionary government policy has been strongly deflationary and the reduction in aggregate demand has plunged the world into a lengthy recession – the worst since the 1930s – which has created in its wake a nasty international debt crisis. The only positive outcome, possibly only temporary, has been a reduction in the international rates of inflation.

The balance of fiscal and monetary policy within the Group of Seven has varied from one country to another. Fiscal policy, i.e. tax and expenditure policy, has been restrictive in Japan and Europe, particularly in the United Kingdom. In the United States since 1982, however, a policy of high interest rates pursued by the autonomous Federal Reserve System has been combined with a cyclically adjusted budget deficit (largely caused by the decision of President Reagan to increase substantially expenditure on armaments). The United States is thus experiencing an armaments-led expansion of aggregate demand. This has re-ignited a worldwide arms race, but at the same time has provided a faint hope that the world recession may slowly be coming to an end.

The set of policies that ideally should be pursued by the Group of Seven are rather obvious. First the European nations should relax their fiscal policies, preferably by increasing public investment in labour-intensive construction activities. Second, the United States should relax its monetary policy (thereby lowering real rates of interest) while changing the balance of fiscal policy (switching from armaments to more productive activities). It is important, however, that the USA should not reduce interest rates through a large unilateral reduction in its budget deficit, for this would almost certainly lead to a contraction of aggregate demand which would threaten any hope there may be for an expansion of the world economy. Third, expansion would be more rapid and more certain if it were possible for the OECD countries, or any large sub-set of them, to coordinate their economic policies, but alas this seems to be politically impossible, at least for the time being.

The ultimate objective, however, should be an expansion of aggregate demand in Europe and a consequent balance of payments deficit there. This would permit an easing of monetary policy in the United States and lower real rates of interest combined with a slight reduction in the growth of aggregate demand, which probably is increasing at a pace which cannot be sustained much longer.

THE RESPONSE OF THE THIRD WORLD

The policy responses in the Third World to the problems that beset them have been: (i) devaluation, in an attempt to switch resources to exports and reduce the demand for imports; (ii) deflation of aggregate demand (higher taxes, tighter control over the money supply, lower levels of public investment and a reduction in welfare services) in an attempt to reduce domestic absorption and generate savings that can be transferred abroad to service the foreign debt; and (iii) renegotiation of the overseas commercial debt on an *ad hoc* basis in an attempt to ease the burden of adjustment while avoiding an outright default.

Narrowly viewed, the policies that have been adopted have enjoyed some success. Default has been avoided, domestic absorption has been reduced and Latin America as a whole has generated a large and rising trade surplus which has enabled at least part of the interest on the debts to be paid. Far from being a recipient of foreign capital, Latin America since 1982 has been a net exporter of capital, some of it in the form of capital flight. This raises three possible problems. First, Latin America's balance of trade surplus will have to be accommodated by the creditor countries in the form of a balance of payments deficit. This will create adjustment problems in the United States and Europe which may be difficult to overcome, particularly in the context of a depressed international economy. Indeed the rising protectionism to which we have already referred indicates that the problem may be a real one. Second, if the debtor countries deflate in an attempt to create larger export surpluses and the creditor countries pursue restrictive monetary and fiscal policies in order to avoid large trading deficits, there is a danger that the Third World's efforts to solve the debt crisis will give a further deflationary bias to the entire world economy. Finally, there is a danger that, in practice, the net transfer of resources from Latin America and other debtor countries may be too small to end the world banking crisis while being so large in relation to the debtor countries that their economies are severely damaged. Certainly the damage they have suffered so far has been considerable.

The consequences for the debtor countries of the current prolonged recession and the policies they have been forced to adopt have been the following:

(i) higher unemployment and disguised urban under-employment combined with an expansion of the low-productivity petty services sector;
(ii) a reduction in real wages and living standards, particularly of those employed or formerly employed on fixed wages in the organised urban sector;
(iii) a reduction in the rate of investment and in the growth of the potential productive capacity of the economy;
(iv) a reduction in the actual rate of growth of industrial output and domestic product;
(v) a fall in average income per head;
(vi) a rise in the tax burden or the ratio of taxes to GNP;
(vii) a sharp rise in political and social discontent which if continued could lead to grave instability in several countries.

Perhaps ironically, inequality in the distribution of income may not have increased and in some cases may have diminished. That is, it is possible that a smaller national income may be distributed more equally. The reason for this is that the effects of the economic contraction may have fallen most severely upon those who are relatively better off rather than upon the poor. The contraction in aggregate demand has been greater in the urban areas than in the rural, and greater in manufacturing and the public sector than in agriculture. In fact, agricultural exporters in some countries may have enjoyed absolute gains in income, and where peasant agriculture is important, the poor may have shared in the rise in income.

The largest losers are likely to include (i) urban entrepreneurs in construction and manufacturing; (ii) those in relatively highly paid urban wage employment, including civil servants; (iii) those receiving welfare payments and food subsidies, including members of the armed forces and the civil service; (iv) those forced to bear the burden of higher taxation, which could, of course, be the poor if the tax system on the margin is regressive; and (v) borrowers from the domestic banking system who have to pay higher real rates of interest. (Net savers with the commercial banking system would, of course, benefit from the present state of affairs.) Most of these losers are likely to have incomes above the median level and hence the decline in average incomes may well have been accompanied by an improvement in the distribution of income. I hasten to add that this is no consolation to those concerned with alleviating poverty, but it does suggest that political protest, where it occurs, will come not from the poorest members of society but from those who once were relatively prosperous.

POSSIBLE SOLUTIONS

A solution to the current problems of the world economy will require both financial and macro-economic measures. Let us begin with the financial measures.

It is possible that an *ad hoc*, case-by-case approach favoured by the governments of most creditor countries can be made to work, in the sense that the commercial banking system can avoid collapse. A 'cap' can be put on interest rates, repayments of interest can be 'postponed', the commercial banks can reduce the balance sheet value of some of their overseas 'assets', the banks can 'agree' to make further loans to the debtor countries to enable them to continue paying at least part of the interest owed, etc. All of these solutions are largely cosmetic, but they do entail a partial default and they might just provide a breathing space in which to design more fundamental policies.

The first thing that should be done is to strengthen international monetary institutions. The IMF should be enlarged substantially, preferably by the creation of SDRs, and should become an international lender-of-last-resort. That is, the Fund should be transformed into a world central bank. The Third World should have much greater representation on the executive board of the reformed IMF than it presently enjoys and the staffing arrangements within the Fund's bureaucracy should be overhauled. Further comments on the IMF are made below. Next, the global debt should be restructured or funded with a view to switching from variable interest rate loans to fixed interest rates, and from short-term commercial credit to long-term loans. This switch is likely to imply a reduction in private lending (particularly from the commercial banks) and an increase in public lending (not only from a greatly enlarged IMF, but also from the IBRD, IDB and other regional development banks). Finally, the governments of creditor countries should announce publicly that, should the need ever arise to protect the banking system as a whole, they stand prepared to bail out their own commercial banks on a case-by-case basis by acting as a domestic lender-of-last-resort.

These arrangements should ensure that the commercial banks are protected from the worst consequences of default, the debtor countries are given relief from a situation not of their own making and for which they are not responsible, and the international monetary system as a whole has a regulatory institution of a size and scope that is adequate for the tasks it confronts.

Even if all this is done, however, the problems of the world economy will persist unless there are changes in macro-economic policy. Real interest rates must be reduced, and this requires a change in US monetary policy. Effective demand must increase, and this requires a change in fiscal policy in Europe. World trade must be stimulated, and this requires lower protection in the Group of Seven. If dollar-denominated debts are to be repaid, the overvaluation of the US dollar must end, and this too requires changes in monetary, trade and fiscal policies in the United States. Finally, it would be advantageous to countries such as Mexico if the United States were to relax its restrictions on the immigration of labour from westerm hemisphere countries. The purpose of this set of policies thus is two-fold: to shift more of the burden of adjustment from debtor to creditor countries, from South to North; and to stimulate the overall growth of the world economy. It is possible, and perhaps even likely, that an expansion of aggregate demand at the global level would result in some increase in the rate of inflation, but this is a very small price to pay for a solution to problems that have seemed to be intractable for a decade or more.

What should the Third World do? To answer this question it is necessary to go back to the beginning, to the fundamental cause of the current crisis. There is no doubt that bankers, like any other businessman, can make mistakes or be less than prudent; equally, there is no doubt that borrowers can use the resources put at their disposal foolishly; but such actions do not account for the current recession, the worst recession in the world economy in the last half century.

The crisis – a crisis which now has lasted for a decade – was caused by governments in the advanced industrial capitalist economies deliberately reducing aggregate demand in an attempt to control domestic inflation. It may appear to be even-handed to share responsibility for the resulting disaster among the banks, the borrowers and the governments of the major OECD countries, but this is a curiously wrong-headed view of our problems. The responsibility lies entirely with the advanced economies including, of course, the UK.

In the 1930s world expansion was limited by beggar-thy-neighbour protectionism. Later we saw countries engage in competitive devaluation in an attempt to reduce imports. Today we live in an era of competitive deflationary policies. The 'first world' deflates by choice and the Third World has no choice but to do the same. Indeed, of the major OECD countries, only the United States is running a discretionary, cyclically adjusted budget deficit – and that is due entirely to very rapid expansion of expenditure on military equipment. Keynes must be turning in his grave.

The effects, as we all know, of the macro-economic mismanagement of the world economy have been horrific and even optimistic forecasts of future prospects leave no hope that there will be a substantial fall in unemployment, a reduction in mass poverty or a rise in living standards for many millions of ordinary working people, in the rich countries as well as in the poor.

It must be emphasised that the author attaches strategic importance to a complete overhaul of world financial institutions and, in the struggle to create a New International Economic Order, this surely deserves high priority. Our present arrangements, centred on the IMF, impart a strong deflationary bias to the world economy. This institutionalised policy stance must be changed. And this implies a transformation of the IMF into a lender-of-last-resort, a massive expansion of its resources and a change in its *modus operandi*, the replacement of the US dollar as a reserve currency by an international financial instrument, and much increased representation of the Third World on the governing board of the transformed institution.

Let us turn now to policies that can be adopted by Third World countries acting unilaterally or, preferably, in cooperation. Two countries – Brazil and Mexico – have such large commercial debts that they are a genuine threat to the banks. Hence their bargaining position potentially is very strong. On the other hand, both have been able to respond quickly to the crisis and now have a negative net transfer of resources to the rich countries. This may reduce their incentive to use their strong bargaining position. (In the old days a transfer of savings from the poor countries to the rich would have been regarded as exploitation; today, ironically, it is regarded as successful economic policy. This author, being an old-fashioned person, considers the former view was the right one.)

Be that as it may, several other countries – Argentina, Chile, Bolivia, Peru – are in a weaker bargaining position but have gained less from their involvement in the international banking system: growth has been slow, poverty has increased, costs of adjustment have been exceptionally high. The same has been true of a number of African countries. Thus these countries in Latin America and Africa have a greater incentive to exploit whatever bargaining power they have.

Ideally, the debtor countries should get together and form a cartel. Their differing situations and interests, however, suggest that formation of a formal cartel is, alas, unlikely. It might be possible, on the other hand, to form an informal cartel and for a member of the group – acting in a similar way to a 'price leader' in an oligopolistically organised industry – to take on the role of 'default leadership'.

It is taken for granted here, as obvious and unnecessary for debate, that default – disguised, partial but more than marginal, done in a polite, quiet and gentlemanly way, but default none the less – is the name of the game. It is bound to play a strategic role in future economic policy in many Third World countries unless there is a radical improvement in the performance of the world economy. If the politicians will not default on the debt, then surely the people will.

The purpose of a debtors' cartel, of 'default leadership' and of creeping or disguised renunciation of the debt is twofold. First, to buy time, to bring short-term relief to the major debtor countries so that more of their resources can be devoted to raising the living standards of their people. Second, to increase pressure on the major OECD countries to transform international institutions and international economic policy. In short, the purpose is to force them to the bargaining table.

It might be thought that the massive foreign debt of the United States will some day encourage that country to seek a global solution to the world's financial difficulties. Unfortunately, however, that would be wishful thinking. The difference between the American debt and that of the Third World lies in the fact that the US dollar is a reserve currency – indeed it is still the dominant reserve currency – and there is almost nowhere else for savers to place their capital, especially if they wish to place large amounts of capital. The dollar, like sterling in the first two decades after the Second World War, is grossly overvalued and it is virtually certain that at some stage it will be devalued sharply. When that happens, those who hold dollar assets will find in effect that part of their assets have been expropriated. The US 'debt problem' will be solved by a transfer of the real purchasing power of assets – a capital transfer – from the Arabs and other creditors to the US economy.

There are enormous advantages to a country in being at the centre of the world's trading and financial system. The point just made illustrates one aspect of this, namely, that US banks can earn very large incomes lending other people's money at usurious interest rates. At the same time, the USA as a whole can borrow heavily from the rest of the world, and if the debt becomes inconveniently large, it can reduce the real burden on the country merely by changing the exchange rate.

How nice it would be if other debtor countries – the debtor countries of the Third World – could solve their problems so easily! The alternative open to them to reduce the burden of their debt is a partial default and probably, in one way or another, default is essential and hence inevitable.

First Presentation of These Essays

Chapter 1

Presented to a conference on Food Security and the International Political Economy at Utah State University, Logan, Utah, 2–4 May 1985.

Chapter 2

Presented at a Regional Seminar on Monitoring Poverty and Anti-Poverty Policies in Rural Asia at the Bangladesh Institute of Development Studies, Dhaka, 7–9 April 1984 and published in Rizwanul Islam (ed.), *Strategies for Alleviating Poverty in Rural Asia*, Geneva: ILO (ARTEP), 1985.

Chapter 3

Written in 1983 and published in Sanjaya Lall and Frances Stewart (eds), *Theory and Reality in Development: Essays in Honour of Paul Streeten*, London: Macmillan, 1986.

Chapter 4

Forum Address at Brigham Young University, Provo, Utah, 7 May 1985.

Chapter 5

Unpublished.

Chapter 6

A shortened version was published in *Third World Quarterly*, vol. 6, no. 3, July 1986.

Chapter 7

Convocation Address at Utah State University, Logan, Utah, 2 May 1985.

Chapter 8

Written jointly with Roger Hay and published in *The Journal of Peasant Studies* , vol. 13, no. 1, October 1985.

Chapter 9

Presented to a seminar organised by Michael Lipton at All Souls College, Oxford in June 1984 and published in the IDS *Bulletin*, vol. 17, no. 2, April 1986.

Chapter 10

Presented to a Seminar on Planning in Times of Crisis in Mexico City, 26–28 July 1984.

Index